A Kodansha Comics Trade Paperback Original
Rent-A-Girlfriend 4 copyright © 2018 Reiji Miyajima
English translation copyright © 2020 Reiji Miyajima

All rights reserved.

Published in the United States by Kodansha Comics, an imprint of Kodansha USA Publishing, LLC, New York.

Publication rights for this English edition arranged through Kodansha Ltd., Tokyo.

First published in Japan in 2018 by Kodansha Ltd., Tokyo as *Kanojo, okarishimasu*, volume 4.

ISBN 978-1-64651-064-1

Original cover design by Kohei Nawata Design Office

Printed in the United States of America.

www.kodanshacomics.com

4th Printing
Translation: Kevin Gifford
Lettering: Paige Pumphrey
Kodansha Comics edition cover design by Phil Balsman

Publisher: Kiichiro Sugawara

Director of publishing services: Ben Applegate
Associate director of operations: Stephen Pakula
Publishing services managing editor: Noelle Webster
Assistant production manager: Emi Lotto, Angela Zurlo
Logo and character art ©Kodansha USA Publishing, LLC

One of CLAMP's biggest hits returns in this definitive, premium, hardcover 20th anniversary collector's edition!

"A wonderfully entertaining story that would be a great installment in anybody's manga collection."
— Anime News Network

"CLAMP is an all-female manga-creating team whose feminine touch shows in this entertaining, sci-fi soap opera."
— Publishers Weekly

Poor college student Hideki is down on his luck. All he wants is a good job, a girlfriend, and his very own "persocom"—the latest and greatest in humanoid computer technology. Hideki's luck changes one night when he finds Chi—a persocom thrown out in a pile of trash. But Hideki soon discovers that there's much more to his cute new persocom than meets the eye.

KC
KODANSHA
COMICS

PERFECT WORLD

Rie Aruga

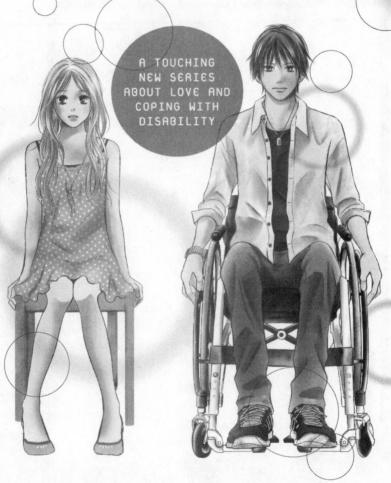

A TOUCHING
NEW SERIES
ABOUT LOVE AND
COPING WITH
DISABILITY

An office party reunites Tsugumi with her high school crush Itsuki. He's realized his dream of becoming an architect, but along the way, he experienced a spinal injury that put him in a wheelchair. Now Tsugumi's rekindled feelings will butt up against prejudices she never considered — and Itsuki will have to decide if he's ready to let someone into his heart...

"Depicts with great delicacy and courage the difficulties some with disabilities experience getting involved in romantic relationships... Rie Aruga refuses to romanticize, pushing her heroine to face the reality of disability. She invites her readers to the same tasks of empathy, knowledge and recognition."
—Slate.fr

"An important entry [in manga romance]... The emotional core of both plot and characters indicates thoughtfulness... [Aruga's] research is readily apparent in the text and artwork, making this feel like a real story."
—Anime News Network

KC KODANSHA COMICS

A SMART, NEW ROMANTIC COMEDY FOR FANS OF *SHORTCAKE CAKE* AND *TERRACE HOUSE*!

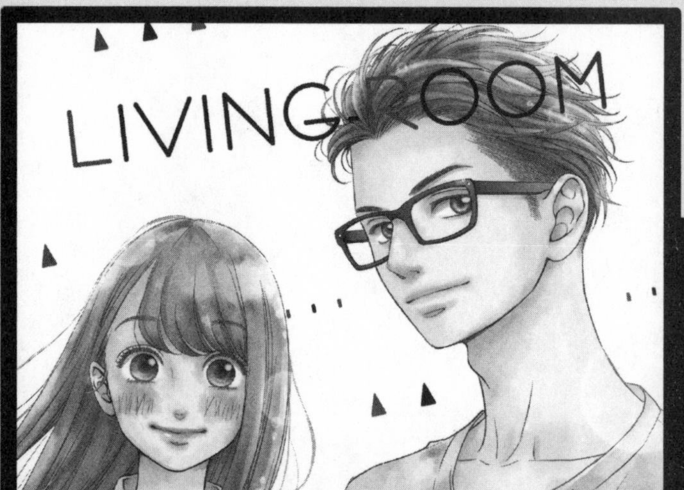
LIVING-ROOM
MATSUNAGA-SAN
Keiko Iwashita
1

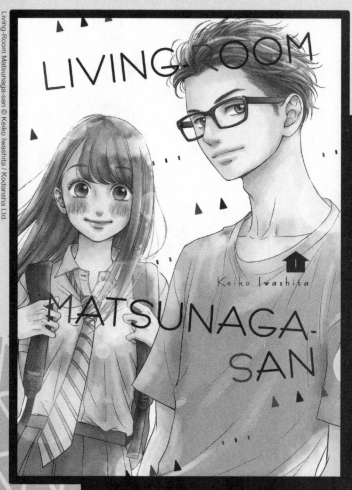

A romance manga starring high school girl Meeko, who learns to live on her own in a boarding house whose living room is home to the odd (but handsome) Matsunaga-san. She begins to adjust to her new life away from her parents, but Meeko soon learns that no matter how far away from home she is, she's still a young girl at heart — especially when she finds herself falling for Matsunaga-san.

THE SWEET SCENT OF LOVE IS IN THE AIR! FOR FANS OF OFFBEAT ROMANCES LIKE *WOTAKOI*

Sweat and Soap © Kintetsu Yamada / Kodansha Ltd.

In an office romance, there's a fine line between sexy and awkward... and that line is where Asako — a woman who sweats copiously — meets Koutarou — a perfume developer who can't get enough of Asako's, er, scent. Don't miss a romcom manga like no other!

RENT-A-GIRLFRIEND STAFF: A, IROHKI, TEMAENO, KUSUMI, MITSUKI

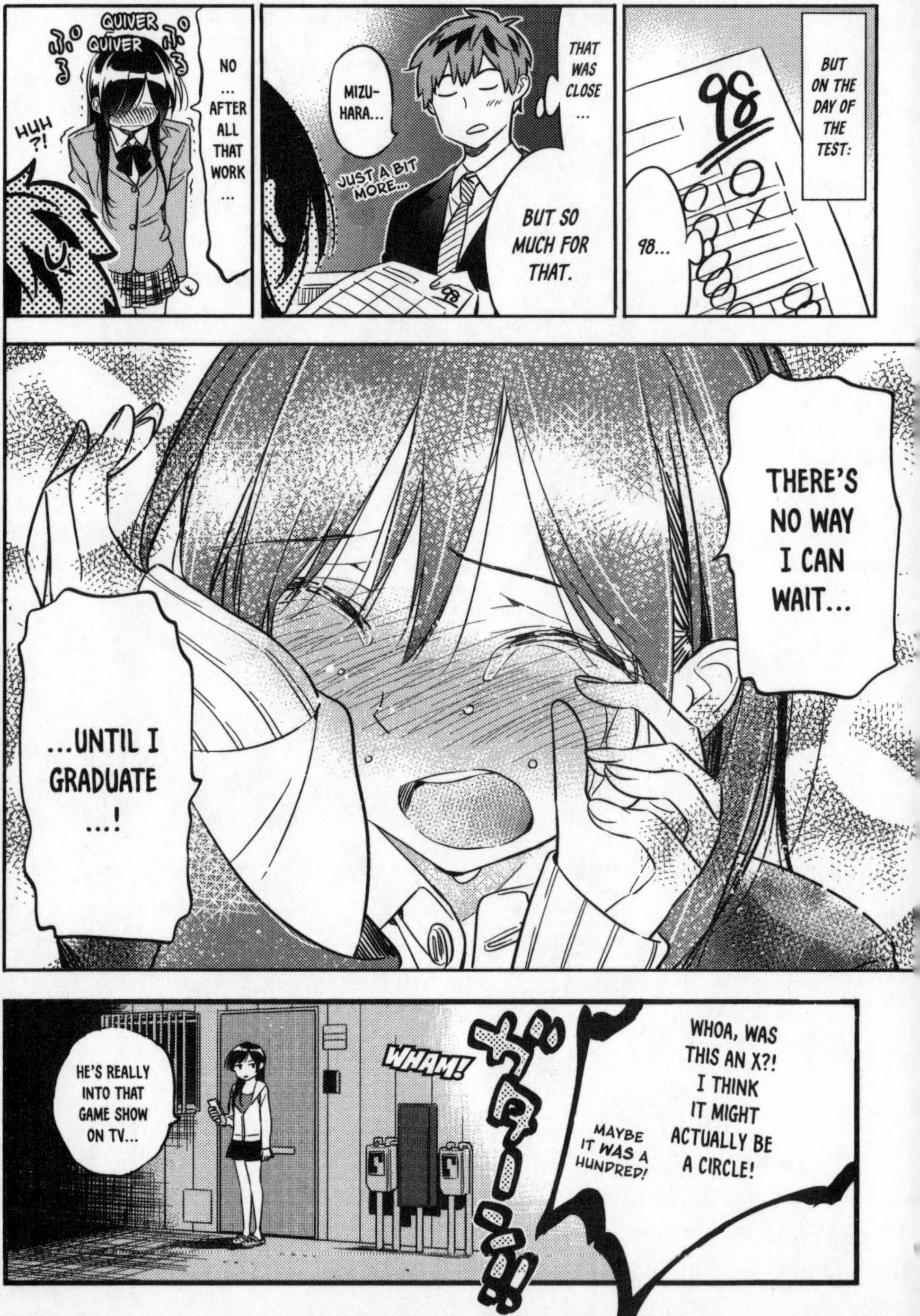
BUT ON THE DAY OF THE TEST:
98...
THAT WAS CLOSE ...
MIZU-HARA...
JUST A BIT MORE...
BUT SO MUCH FOR THAT.
NO ... AFTER ALL THAT WORK ...
QUIVER QUIVER
HUH ?!
THERE'S NO WAY I CAN WAIT...
...UNTIL I GRADUATE ...!
WHOA, WAS THIS AN X?! I THINK IT MIGHT ACTUALLY BE A CIRCLE!
MAYBE IT WAS A HUNDRED!
WHAM!
HE'S REALLY INTO THAT GAME SHOW ON TV...

EDITORS: HIRAOKA-SAN, HIRATSUKA-SAN, CHOKAI-SAN THANKS TO EVERYONE ELSE WHO PICKED THIS UP!

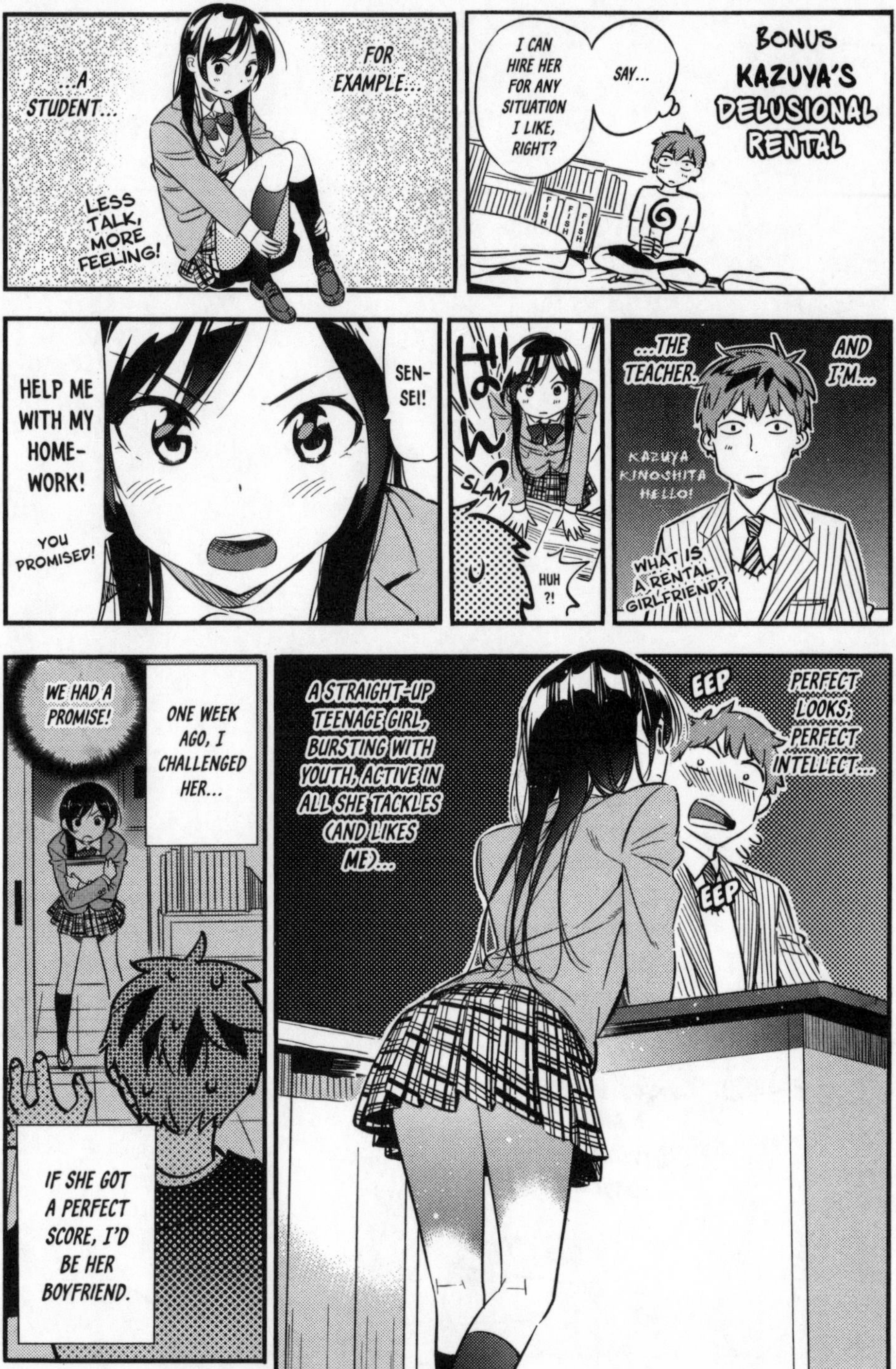
BONUS
KAZUYA'S DELUSIONAL RENTAL
I CAN HIRE HER FOR ANY SITUATION I LIKE, RIGHT?
SAY...
FISH
FISH
FISH
FOR EXAMPLE...
...A STUDENT...
LESS TALK, MORE FEELING!
AND I'M...
...THE TEACHER.
KAZUYA KINOSHITA HELLO!
WHAT IS A RENTAL GIRLFRIEND?
ばんっ
SLAM
HUH ?!
SEN-SEI!
HELP ME WITH MY HOME-WORK!
YOU PROMISED!
PERFECT LOOKS; PERFECT INTELLECT...
EEP
A STRAIGHT-UP TEENAGE GIRL, BURSTING WITH YOUTH, ACTIVE IN ALL SHE TACKLES (AND LIKES ME)...
EEP
WE HAD A PROMISE!
ONE WEEK AGO, I CHALLENGED HER...
IF SHE GOT A PERFECT SCORE, I'D BE HER BOYFRIEND.

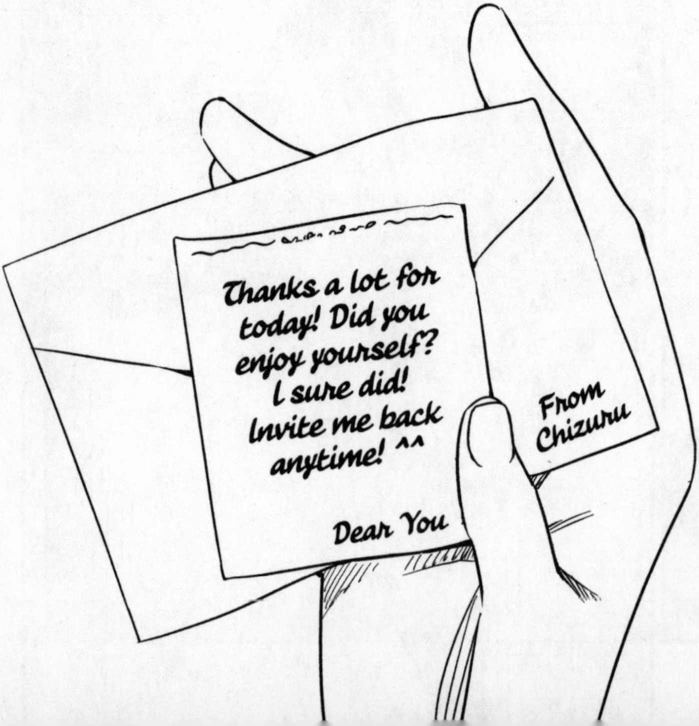
Thanks a lot for today! Did you enjoy yourself? I sure did! Invite me back anytime! ^^
Dear You
From Chizuru

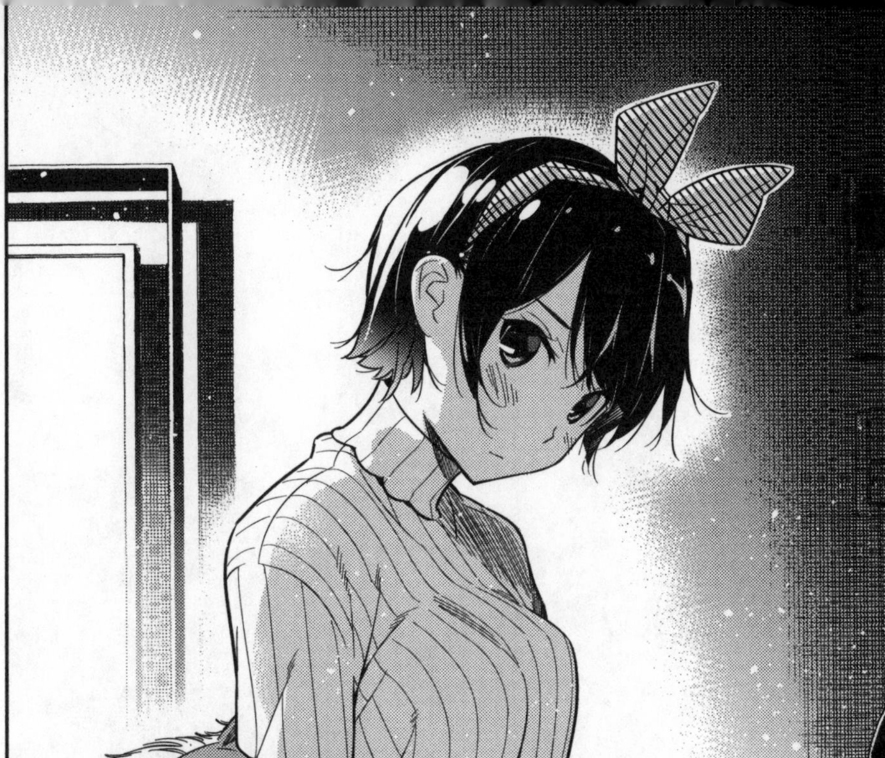
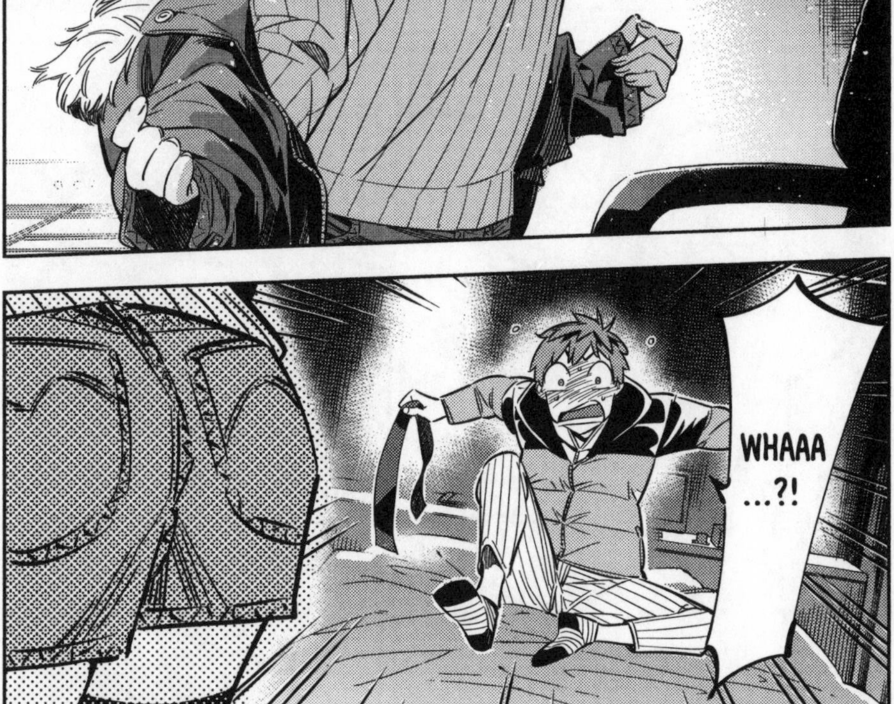
WHAAA
...?!

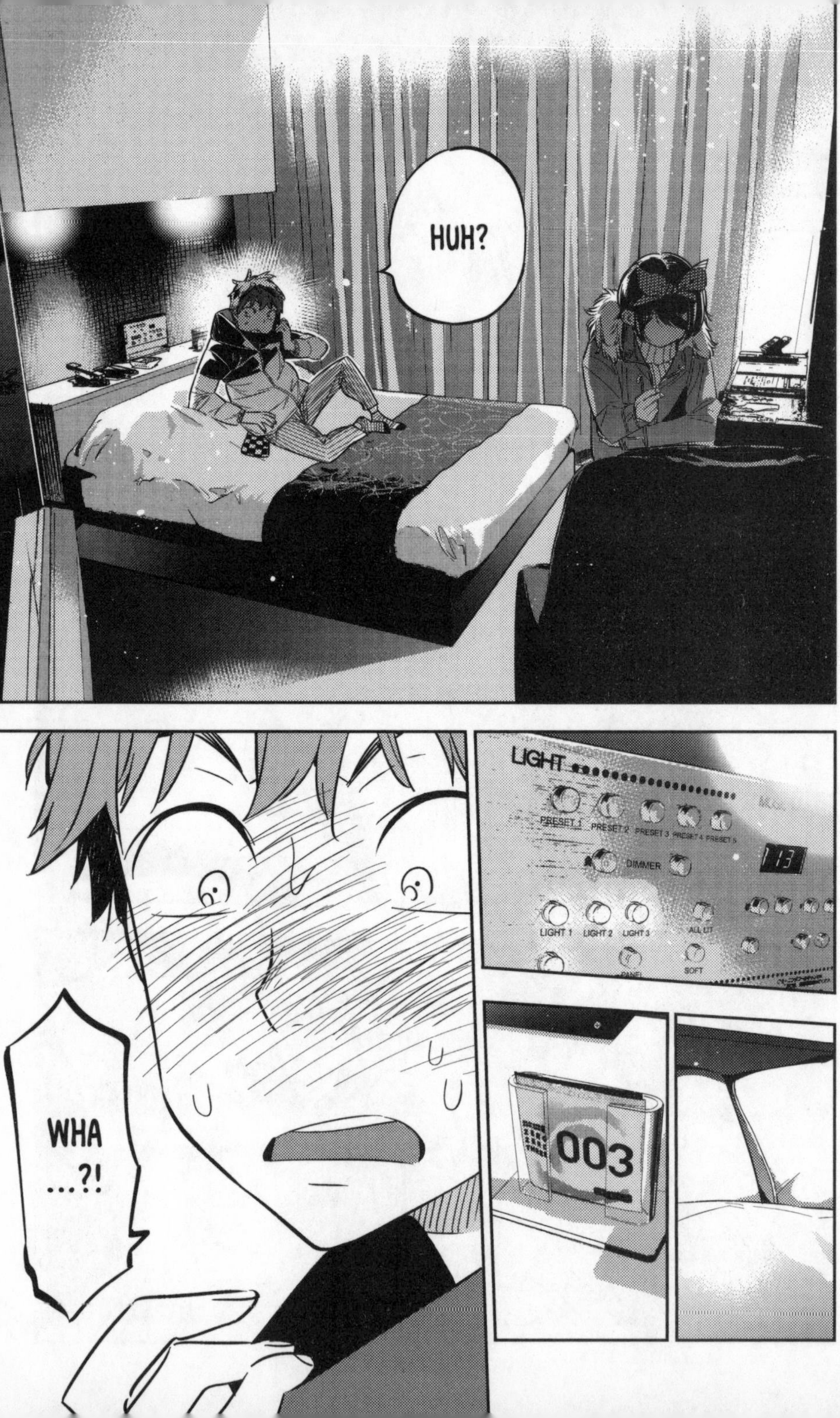
HUH?
LIGHT
PRESET 1
PRESET 2
PRESET 3
PRESET 4
PRESET 5
DIMMER
LIGHT 1
LIGHT 2
LIGHT 3
ALL LIT
SOFT
003
WHA ...?!

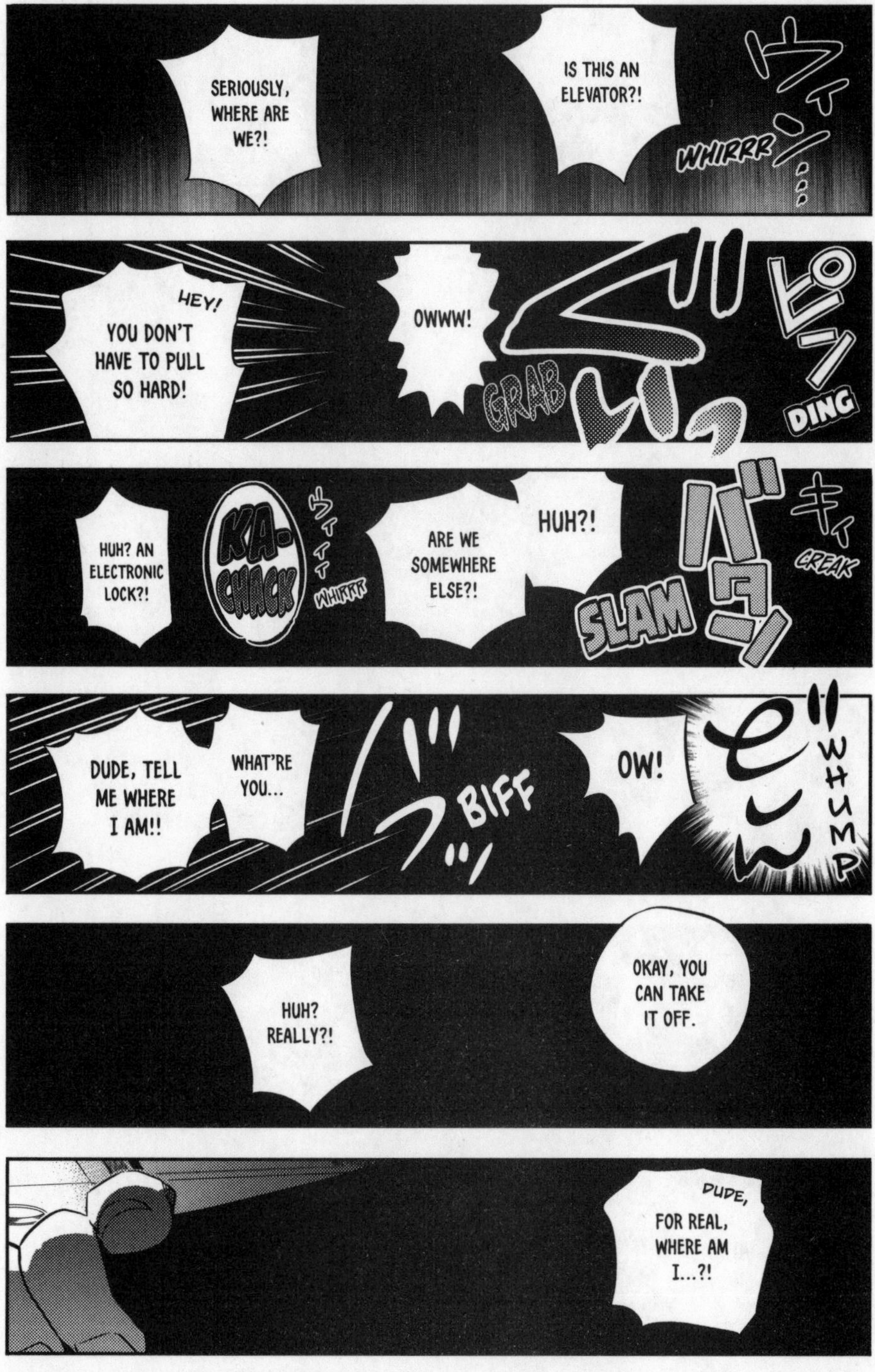
ウィン…
WHIRRR
IS THIS AN ELEVATOR?!
SERIOUSLY, WHERE ARE WE?!
ピン
DING
GRAB
OWWW!
HEY! YOU DON'T HAVE TO PULL SO HARD!
キィ
CREAK
SLAM
HUH?!
ARE WE SOMEWHERE ELSE?!
WHIRRR
KA-CHACK
HUH? AN ELECTRONIC LOCK?!
WHUMP
OW!
BIFF
WHAT'RE YOU...
DUDE, TELL ME WHERE I AM!!
OKAY, YOU CAN TAKE IT OFF.
HUH? REALLY?!
DUDE, FOR REAL, WHERE AM I...?!

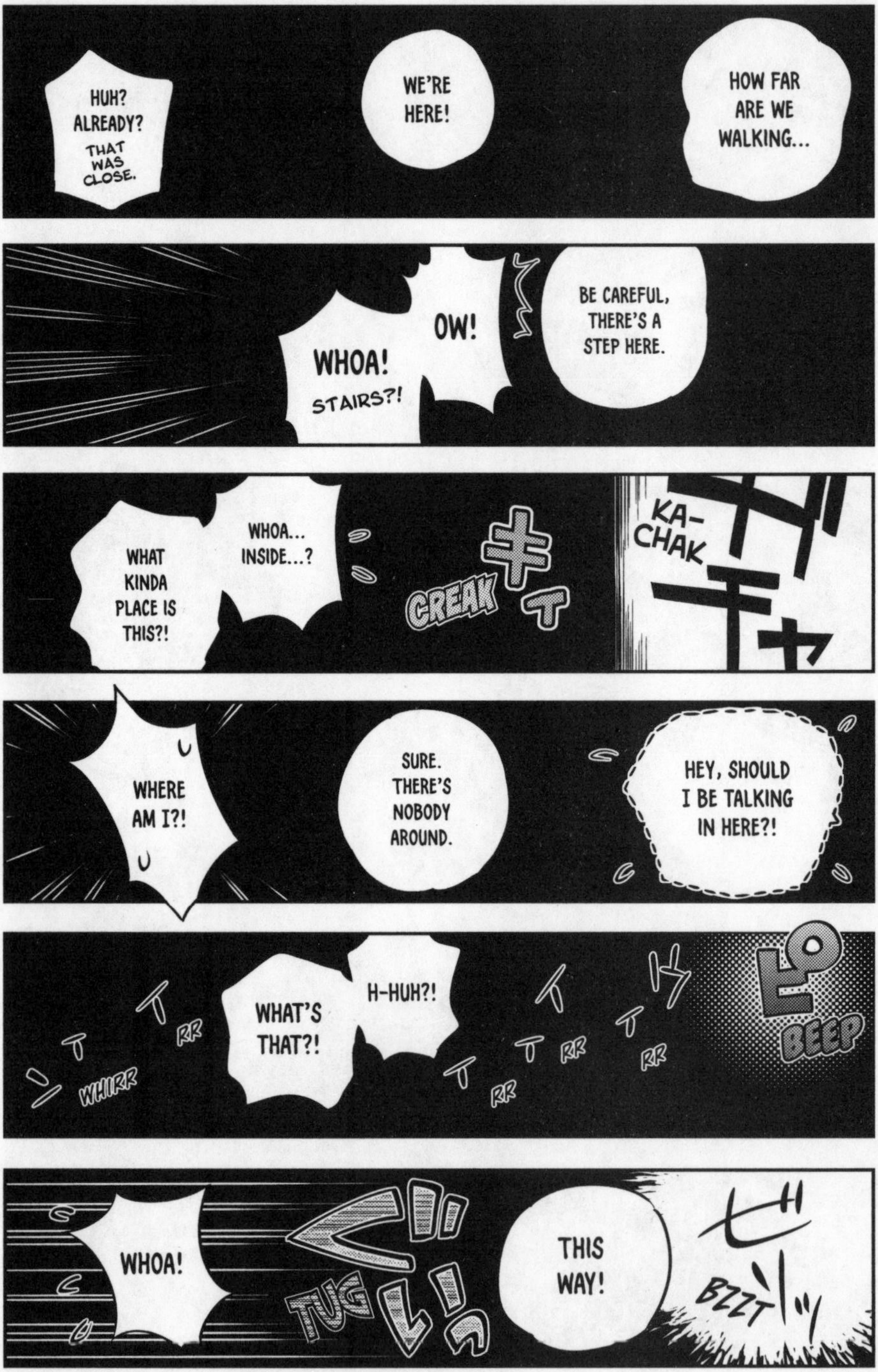
HOW FAR ARE WE WALKING...
WE'RE HERE!
HUH? ALREADY? THAT WAS CLOSE.
BE CAREFUL, THERE'S A STEP HERE.
OW!
WHOA! STAIRS?!
KA-CHAK
CREAK
WHOA... INSIDE...?
WHAT KINDA PLACE IS THIS?!
HEY, SHOULD I BE TALKING IN HERE?!
SURE. THERE'S NOBODY AROUND.
WHERE AM I?!
BEEP
RR
RR
RR
RR
H-HUH?!
WHAT'S THAT?!
RR
WHIRR
BZZT
THIS WAY!
TUG
WHOA!

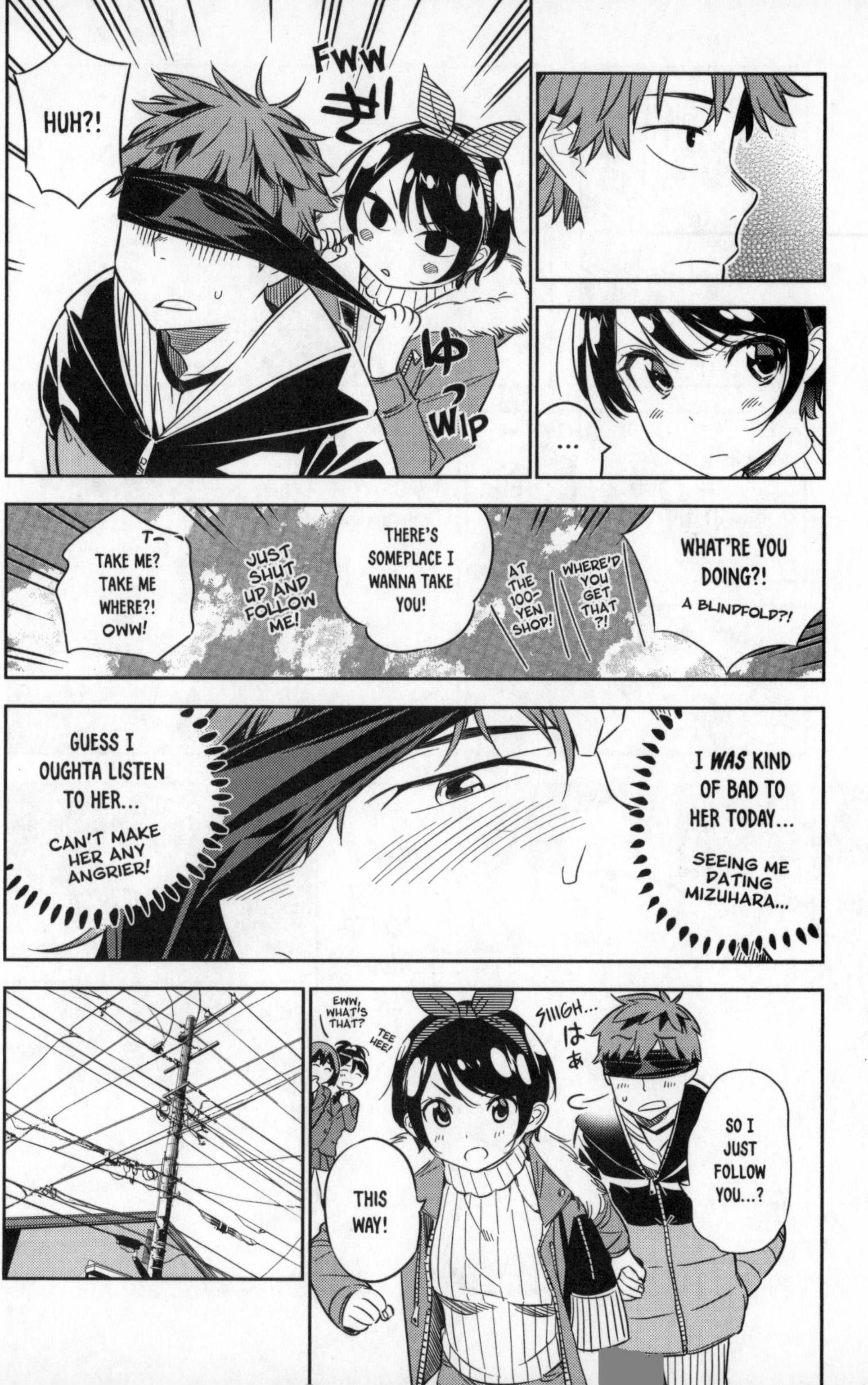
...
HUH?!
FWW
ぎっ
ゆっ
WIP
WHAT'RE YOU DOING?!
A BLINDFOLD?!
WHERE'D YOU GET THAT?!
AT THE 100-YEN SHOP!
THERE'S SOMEPLACE I WANNA TAKE YOU!
JUST SHUT UP AND FOLLOW ME!
T- TAKE ME? TAKE ME WHERE?! OWW!
I *WAS* KIND OF BAD TO HER TODAY...
SEEING ME DATING MIZUHARA...
GUESS I OUGHTA LISTEN TO HER...
CAN'T MAKE HER ANY ANGRIER!
SIIIGH...
はぁ
SO I JUST FOLLOW YOU...?
THIS WAY!
EWW, WHAT'S THAT?
TEE HEE!

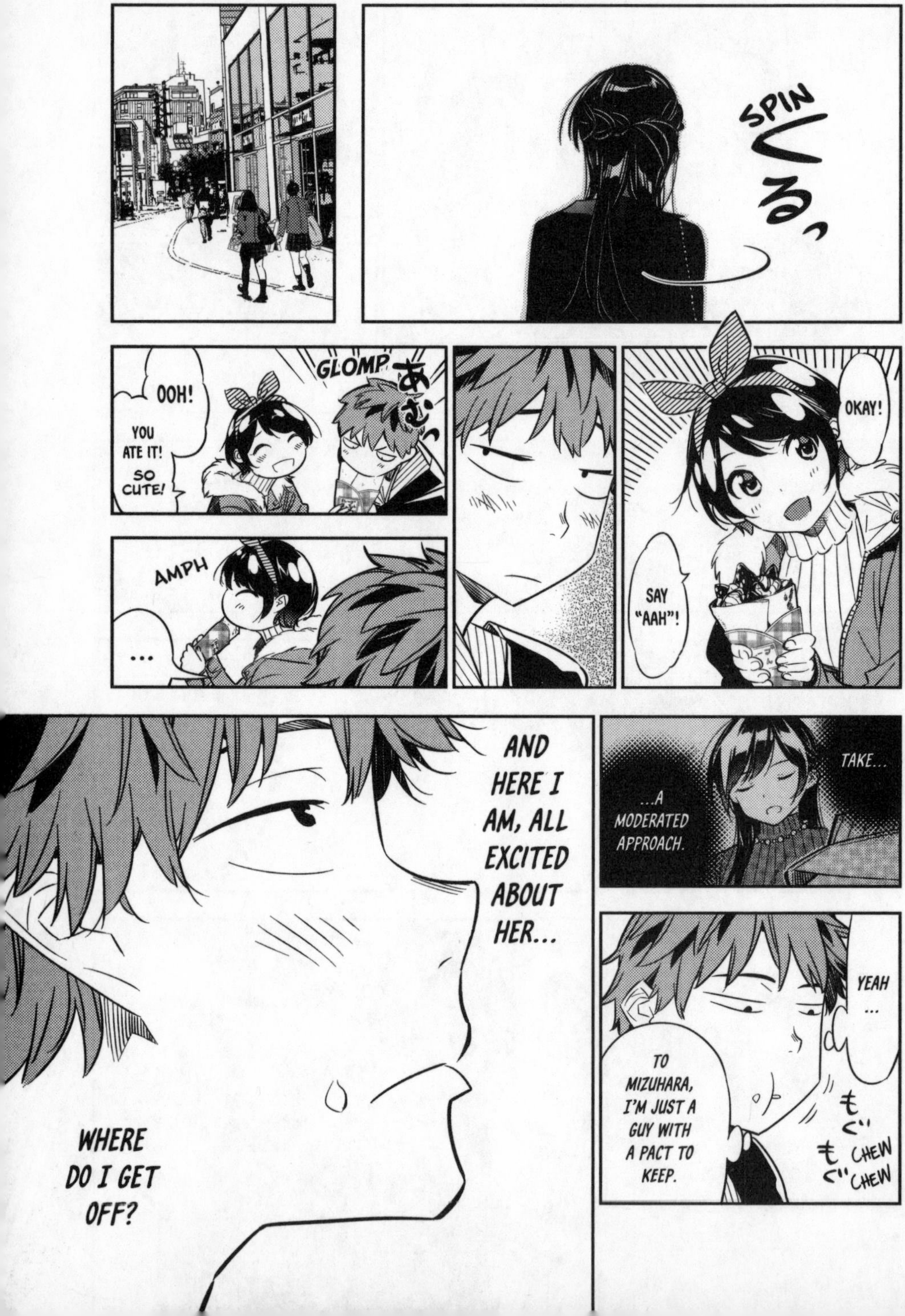

SPIN
くるっ
OKAY!
SAY "AAH"!
GLOMP
あむっ
OOH!
YOU ATE IT! SO CUTE!
AMPH
...
TAKE...
...A MODERATED APPROACH.
YEAH...
TO MIZUHARA, I'M JUST A GUY WITH A PACT TO KEEP.
もぐ もぐ
CHEW CHEW
AND HERE I AM, ALL EXCITED ABOUT HER...
WHERE DO I GET OFF?

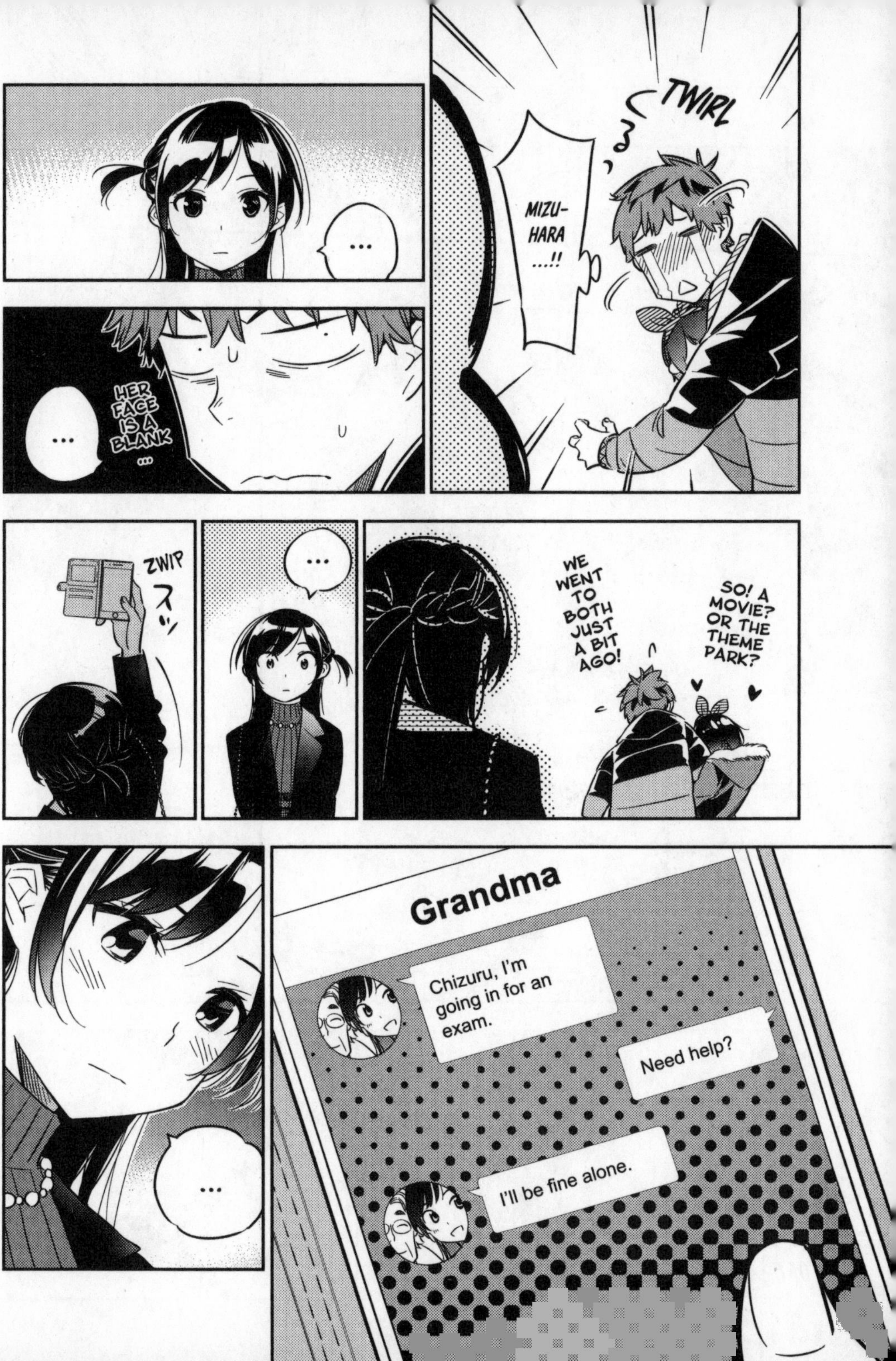
TWIRL
MIZU-HARA...!!
...
HER FACE IS A BLANK...
...
SO! A MOVIE? OR THE THEME PARK?
WE WENT TO BOTH JUST A BIT AGO!
...
ZWIP
Grandma
Chizuru, I'm going in for an exam.
Need help?
I'll be fine alone.
...

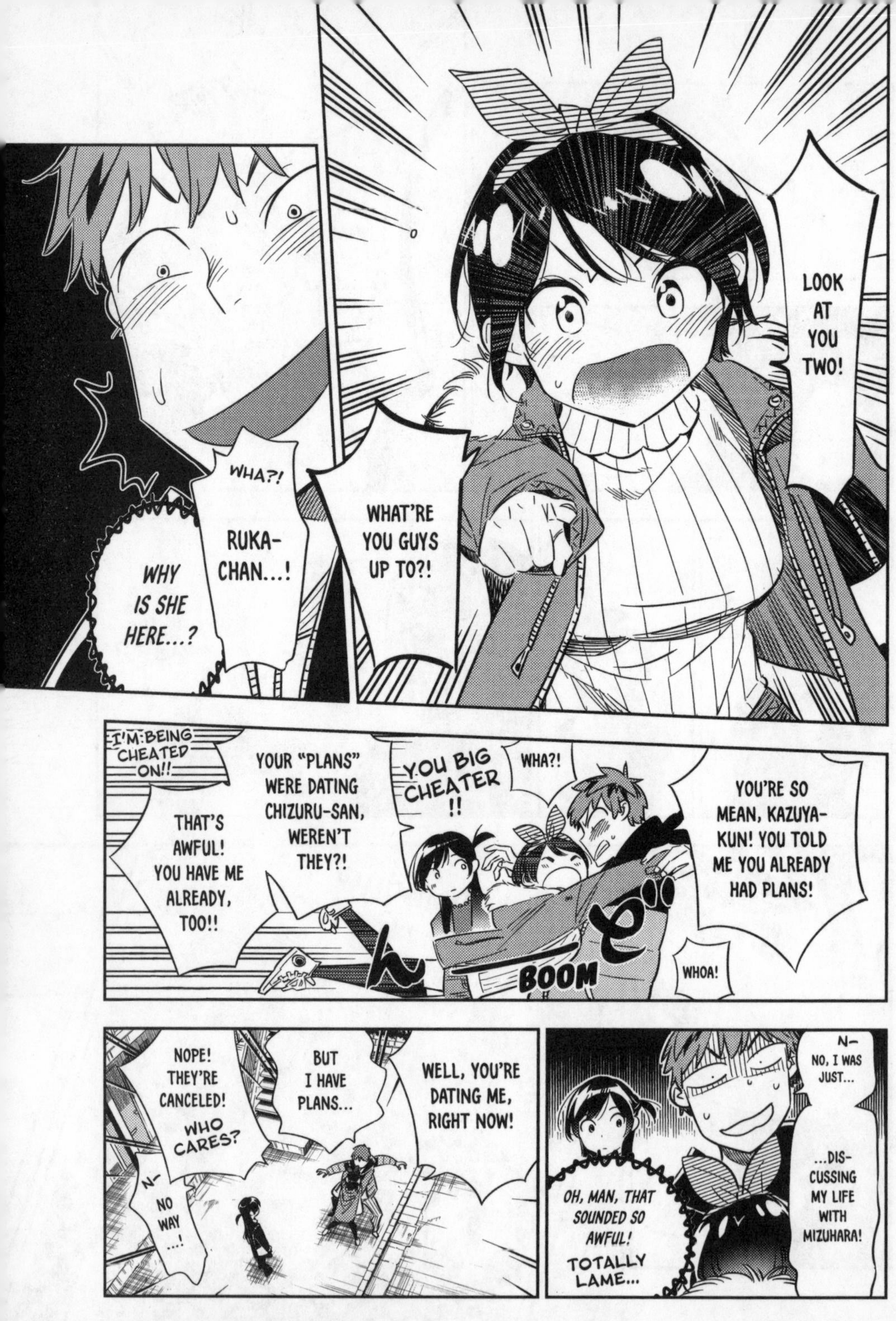
LOOK AT YOU TWO!
WHAT'RE YOU GUYS UP TO?!
WHA?!
RUKA-CHAN...!
WHY IS SHE HERE...?
YOU'RE SO MEAN, KAZUYA-KUN! YOU TOLD ME YOU ALREADY HAD PLANS!
WHA?!
YOU BIG CHEATER!!
YOUR "PLANS" WERE DATING CHIZURU-SAN, WEREN'T THEY?!
I'M BEING CHEATED ON!!
THAT'S AWFUL! YOU HAVE ME ALREADY, TOO!!
WHOA!
BOOM
N- NO, I WAS JUST...
...DIS-CUSSING MY LIFE WITH MIZUHARA!
OH, MAN, THAT SOUNDED SO AWFUL!
TOTALLY LAME...
WELL, YOU'RE DATING ME, RIGHT NOW!
BUT I HAVE PLANS...
NOPE! THEY'RE CANCELED!
WHO CARES?
N- NO WAY...!

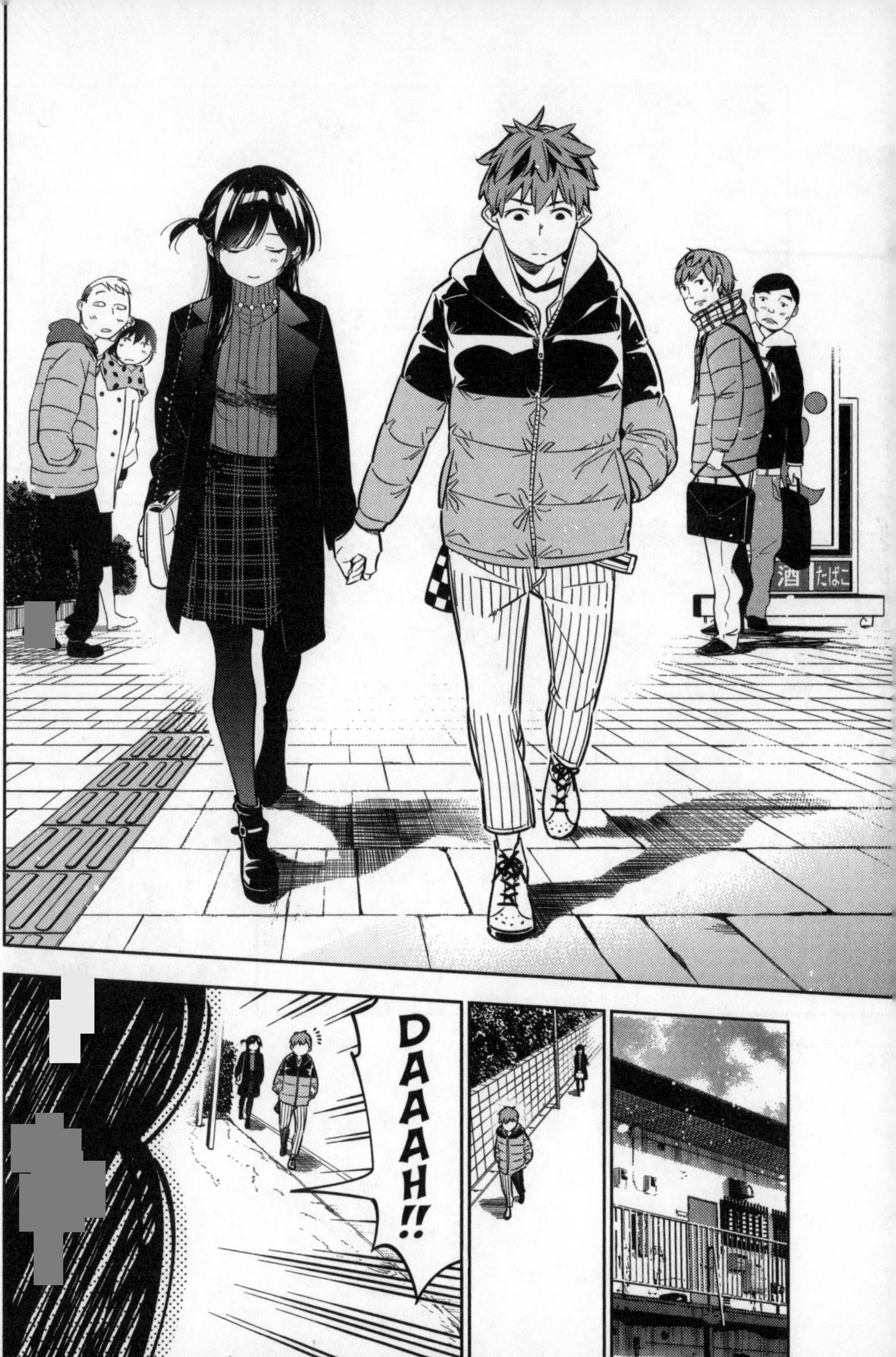
酒 たばこ
DAAAH!!

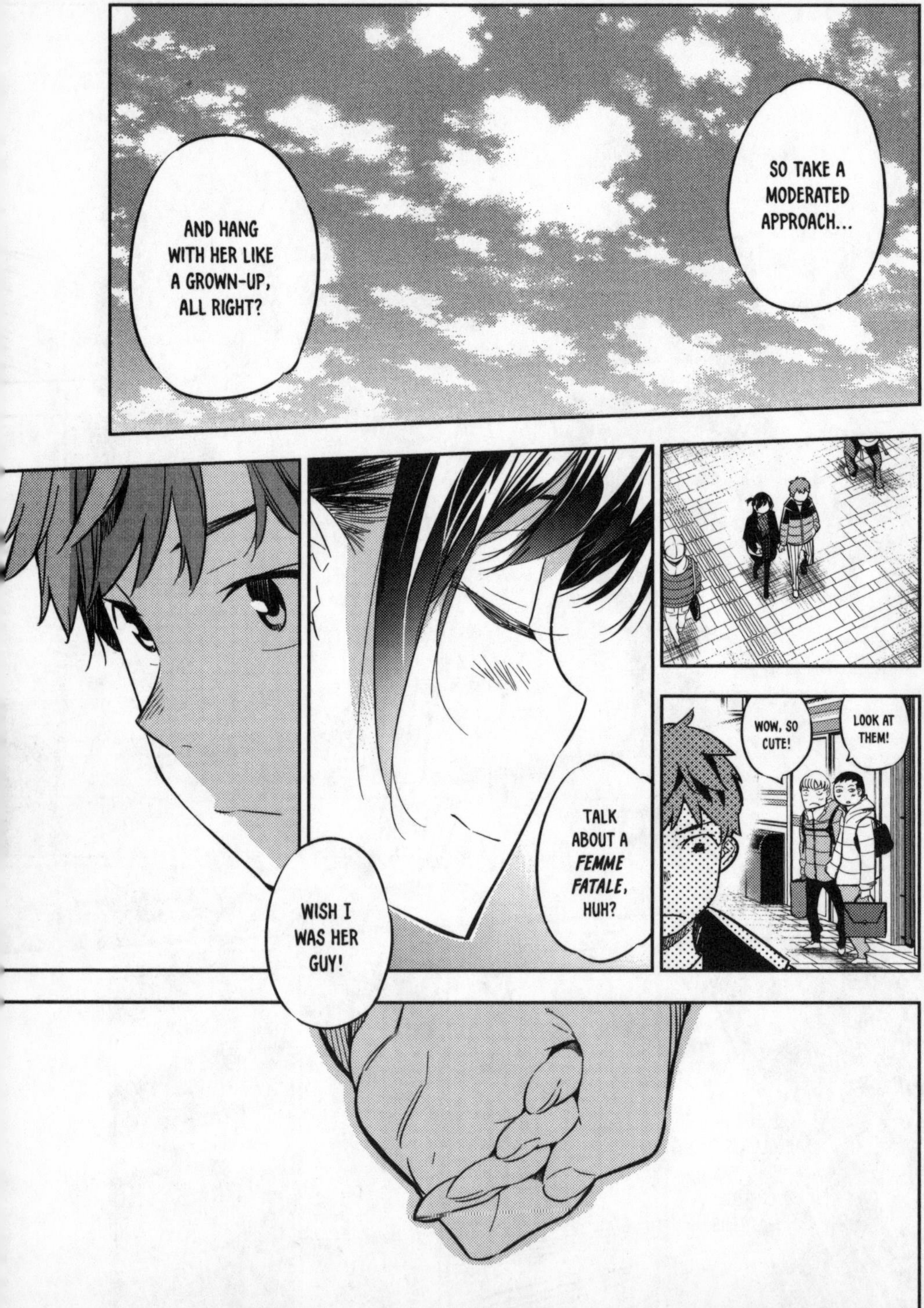
SO TAKE A MODERATED APPROACH...
AND HANG WITH HER LIKE A GROWN-UP, ALL RIGHT?
LOOK AT THEM!
WOW, SO CUTE!
TALK ABOUT A *FEMME FATALE*, HUH?
WISH I WAS HER GUY!

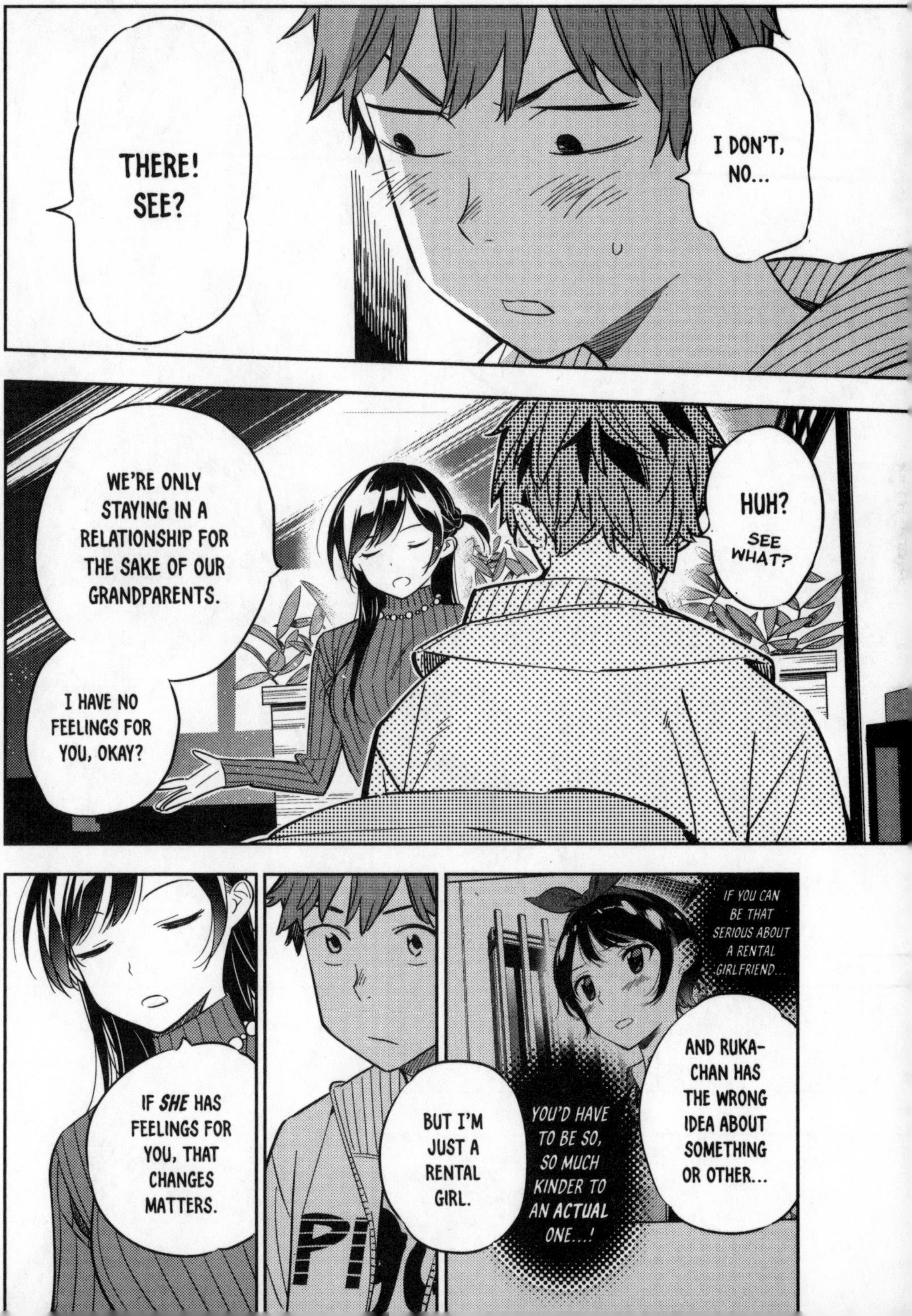
I DON'T, NO...
THERE! SEE?
HUH? SEE WHAT?
WE'RE ONLY STAYING IN A RELATIONSHIP FOR THE SAKE OF OUR GRANDPARENTS.
I HAVE NO FEELINGS FOR YOU, OKAY?
IF YOU CAN BE THAT SERIOUS ABOUT A RENTAL GIRLFRIEND...
AND RUKA-CHAN HAS THE WRONG IDEA ABOUT SOMETHING OR OTHER...
YOU'D HAVE TO BE SO, SO MUCH KINDER TO AN ACTUAL ONE...!
BUT I'M JUST A RENTAL GIRL.
IF SHE HAS FEELINGS FOR YOU, THAT CHANGES MATTERS.

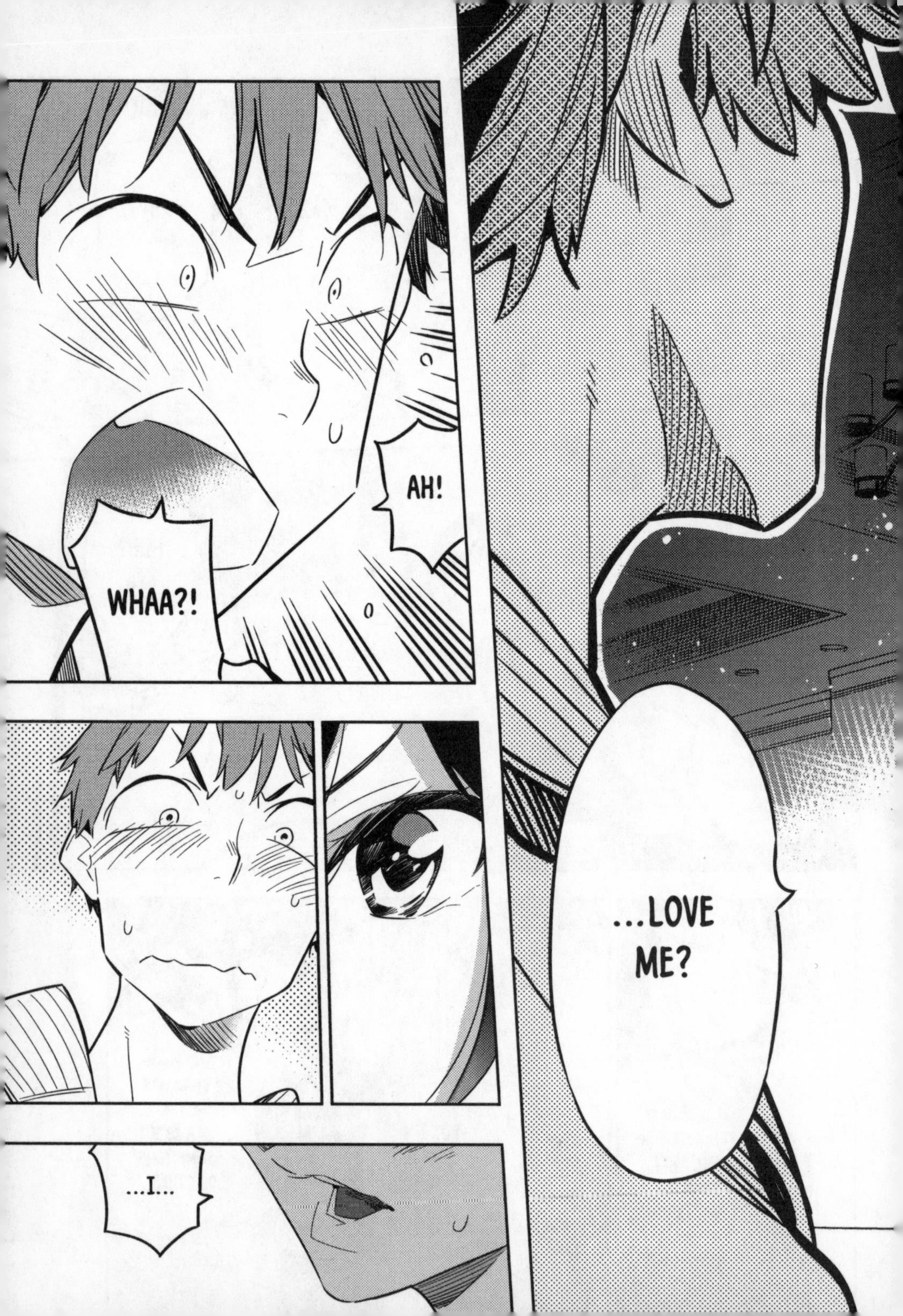
...LOVE ME?
AH!
WHAA?!
...I...

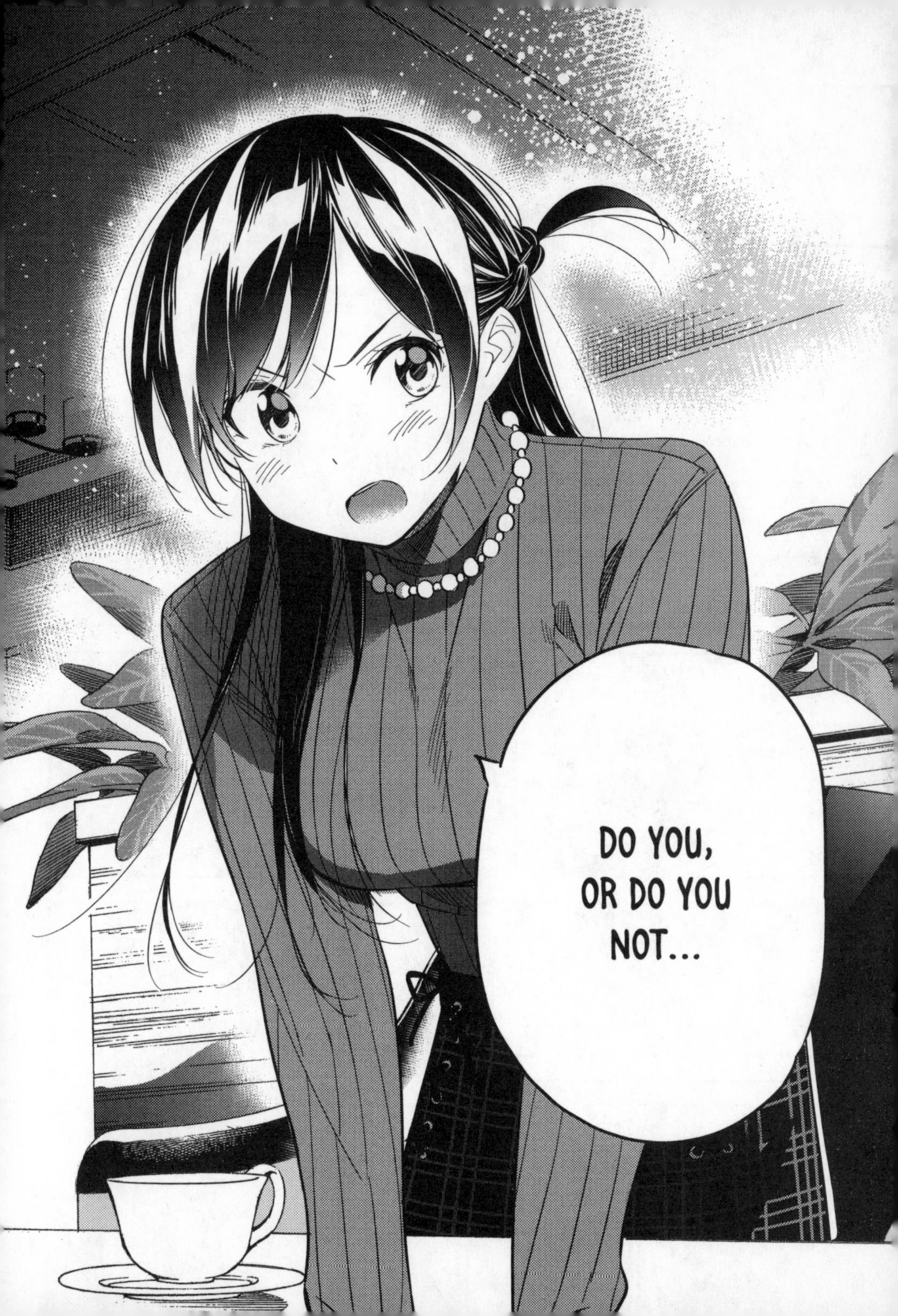
DO YOU, OR DO YOU NOT...

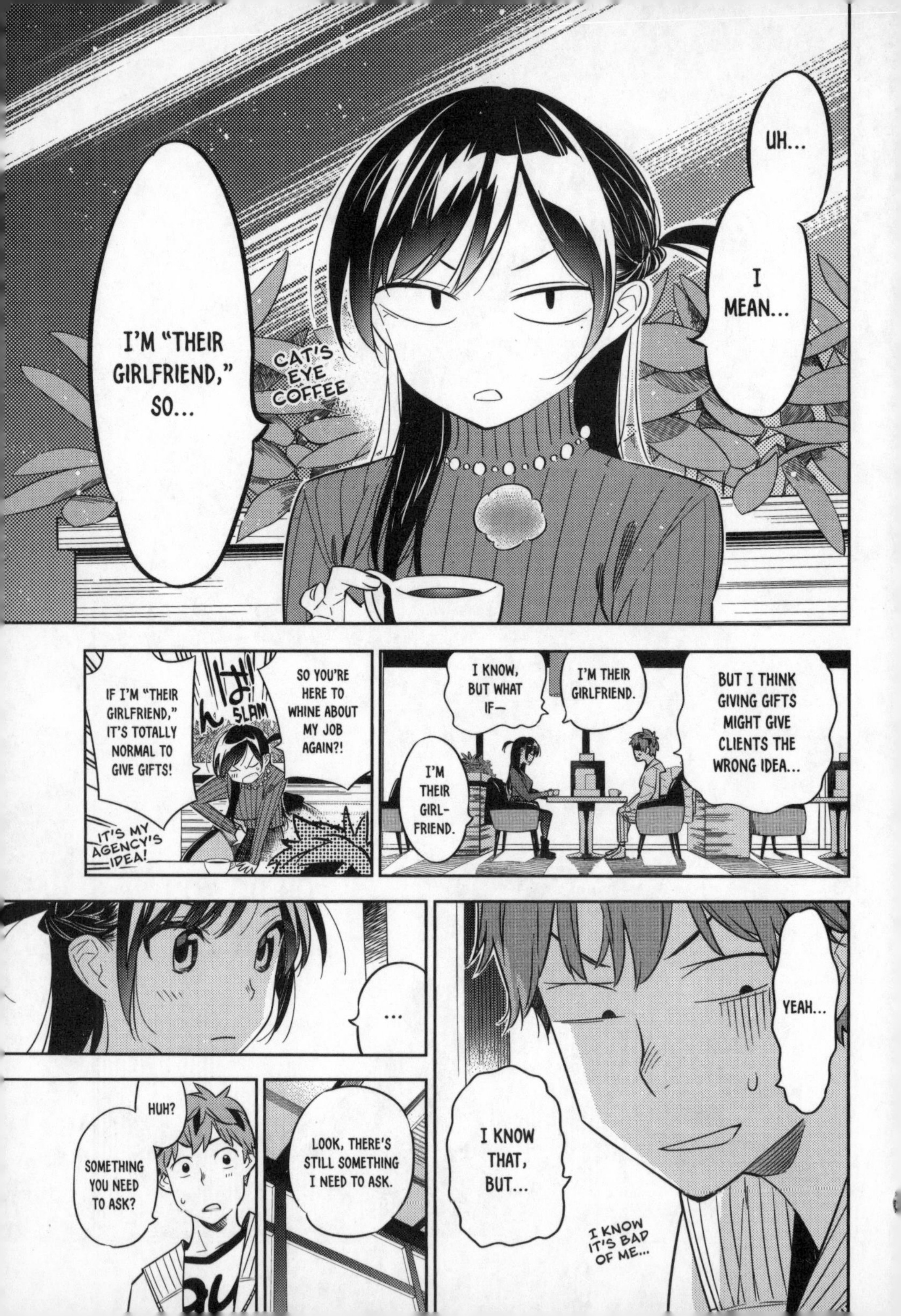
UH...
I MEAN...
CAT'S EYE COFFEE
I'M "THEIR GIRLFRIEND," SO...
BUT I THINK GIVING GIFTS MIGHT GIVE CLIENTS THE WRONG IDEA...
I'M THEIR GIRLFRIEND.
I KNOW, BUT WHAT IF—
I'M THEIR GIRL-FRIEND.
SO YOU'RE HERE TO WHINE ABOUT MY JOB AGAIN?!
ばん
SLAM
IF I'M "THEIR GIRLFRIEND," IT'S TOTALLY NORMAL TO GIVE GIFTS!
IT'S MY AGENCY'S IDEA!
YEAH...
I KNOW THAT, BUT...
I KNOW IT'S BAD OF ME...
...
LOOK, THERE'S STILL SOMETHING I NEED TO ASK.
HUH?
SOMETHING YOU NEED TO ASK?

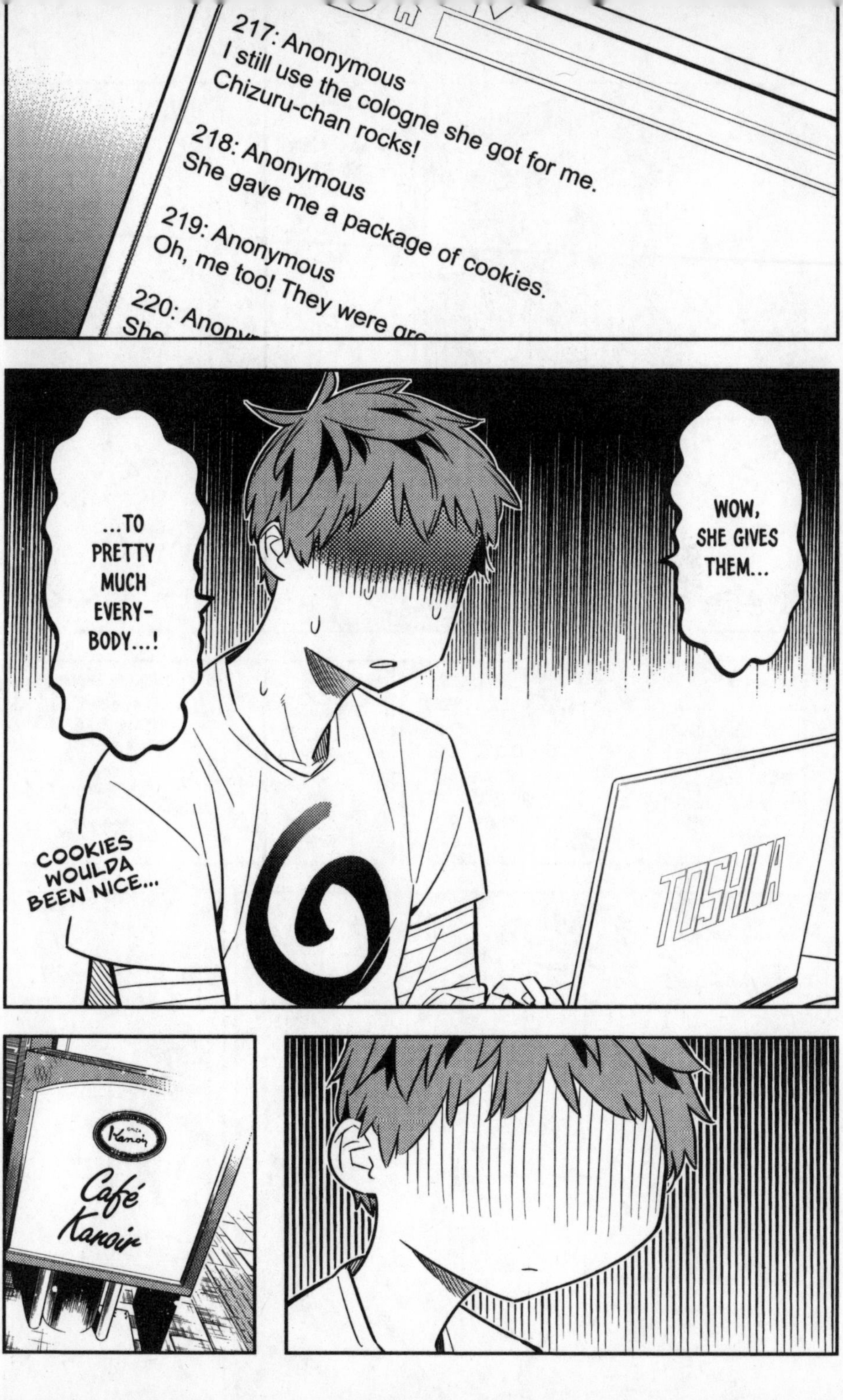
217: Anonymous
I still use the cologne she got for me.
Chizuru-chan rocks!
218: Anonymous
She gave me a package of cookies.
219: Anonymous
Oh, me too! They were
220:
WOW, SHE GIVES THEM...
...TO PRETTY MUCH EVERY-BODY...!
COOKIES WOULDA BEEN NICE...
TOSHI
Kanoir
Café Kanoir

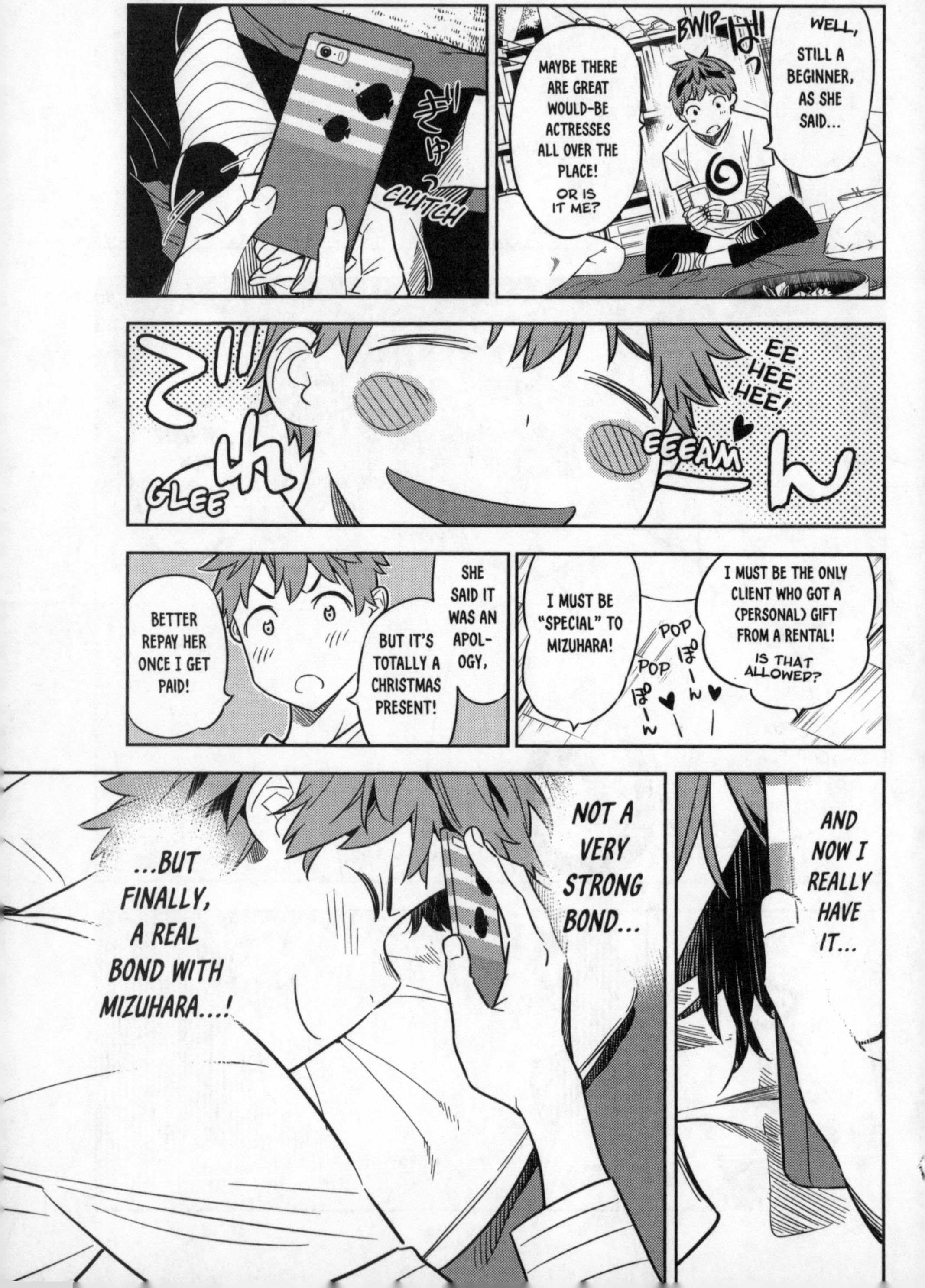
WELL, STILL A BEGINNER, AS SHE SAID...
BWIP
MAYBE THERE ARE GREAT WOULD-BE ACTRESSES ALL OVER THE PLACE!
OR IS IT ME?
CLUTCH
EE HEE HEE!
EEEAM
GLEE
I MUST BE THE ONLY CLIENT WHO GOT A (PERSONAL) GIFT FROM A RENTAL!
IS THAT ALLOWED?
I MUST BE "SPECIAL" TO MIZUHARA!
POP
POP
SHE SAID IT WAS AN APOL-OGY,
BUT IT'S TOTALLY A CHRISTMAS PRESENT!
BETTER REPAY HER ONCE I GET PAID!
AND NOW I REALLY HAVE IT...
NOT A VERY STRONG BOND...
...BUT FINALLY, A REAL BOND WITH MIZUHARA...!

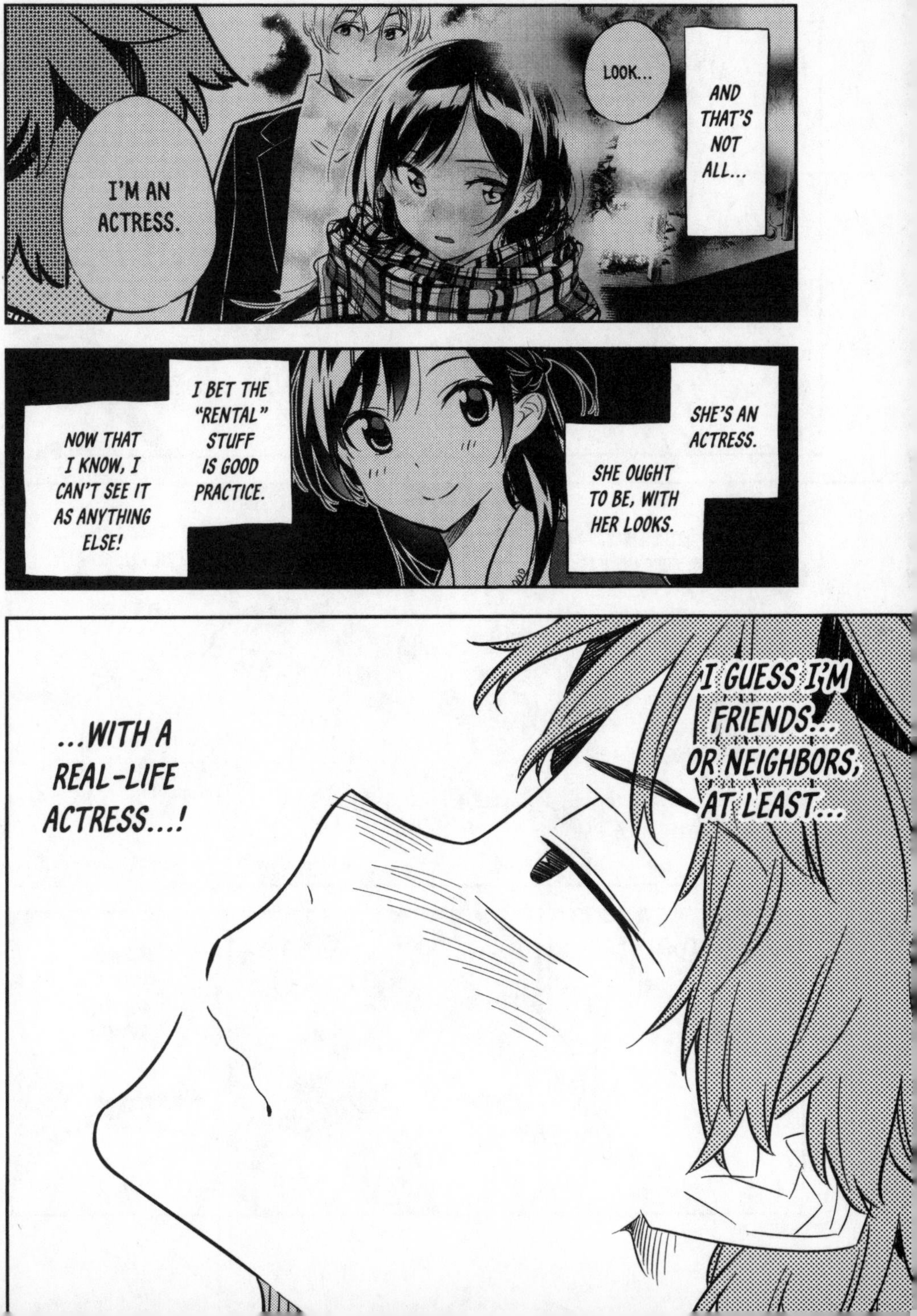
AND THAT'S NOT ALL...
LOOK...
I'M AN ACTRESS.
SHE'S AN ACTRESS.
SHE OUGHT TO BE, WITH HER LOOKS.
I BET THE "RENTAL" STUFF IS GOOD PRACTICE.
NOW THAT I KNOW, I CAN'T SEE IT AS ANYTHING ELSE!
I GUESS I'M FRIENDS... OR NEIGHBORS, AT LEAST...
...WITH A REAL-LIFE ACTRESS...!

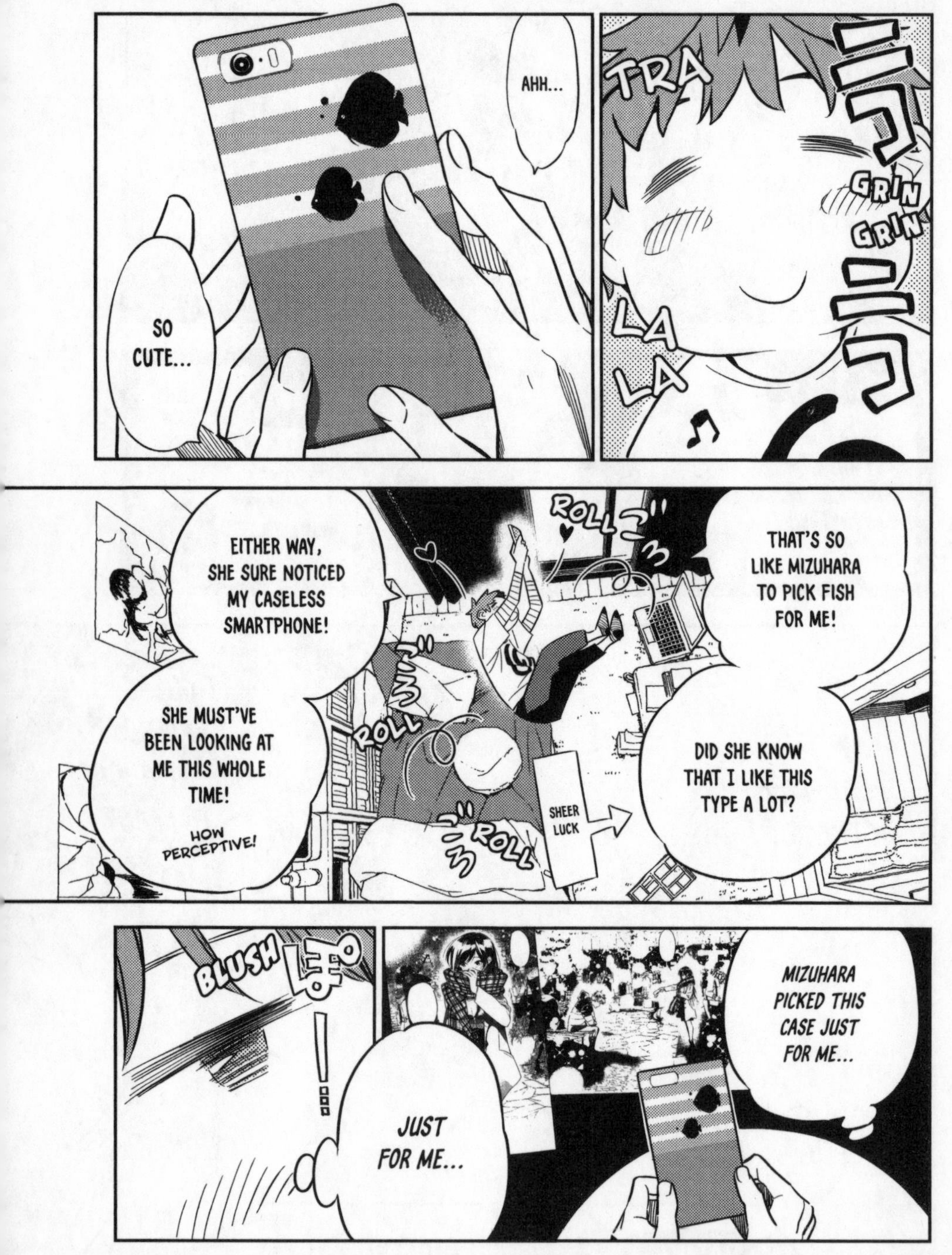
TRA
LA
LA
GRIN
GRIN
ニコニコ
AHH...
SO CUTE...
THAT'S SO LIKE MIZUHARA TO PICK FISH FOR ME!
DID SHE KNOW THAT I LIKE THIS TYPE A LOT?
SHEER LUCK
ROLL ごろ
ROLL ごろ
ROLL ごろ
EITHER WAY, SHE SURE NOTICED MY CASELESS SMARTPHONE!
SHE MUST'VE BEEN LOOKING AT ME THIS WHOLE TIME!
HOW PERCEPTIVE!
MIZUHARA PICKED THIS CASE JUST FOR ME...
JUST FOR ME...
BLUSH
ぽー!!!

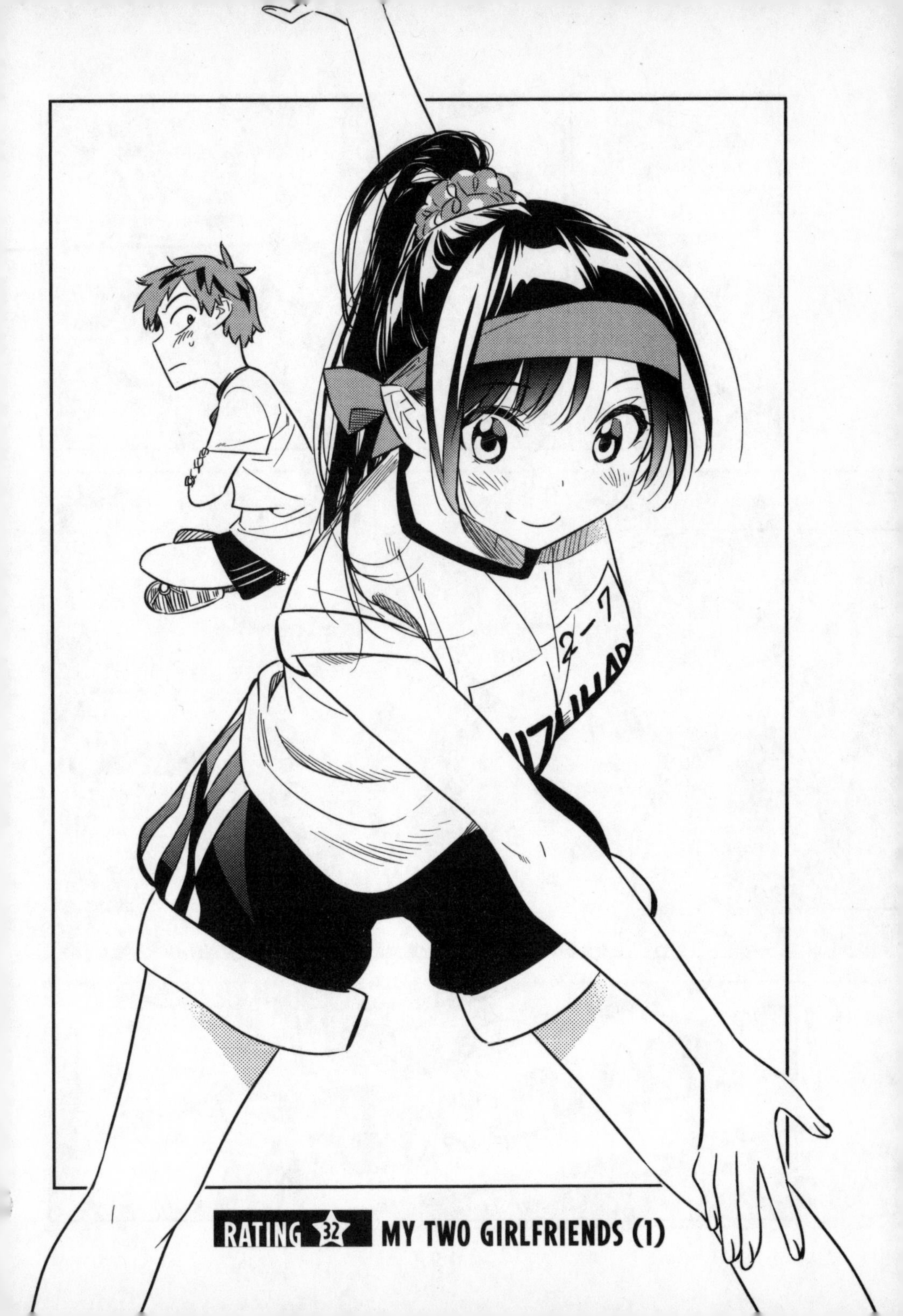
2-7

RATING 32 MY TWO GIRLFRIENDS (1)

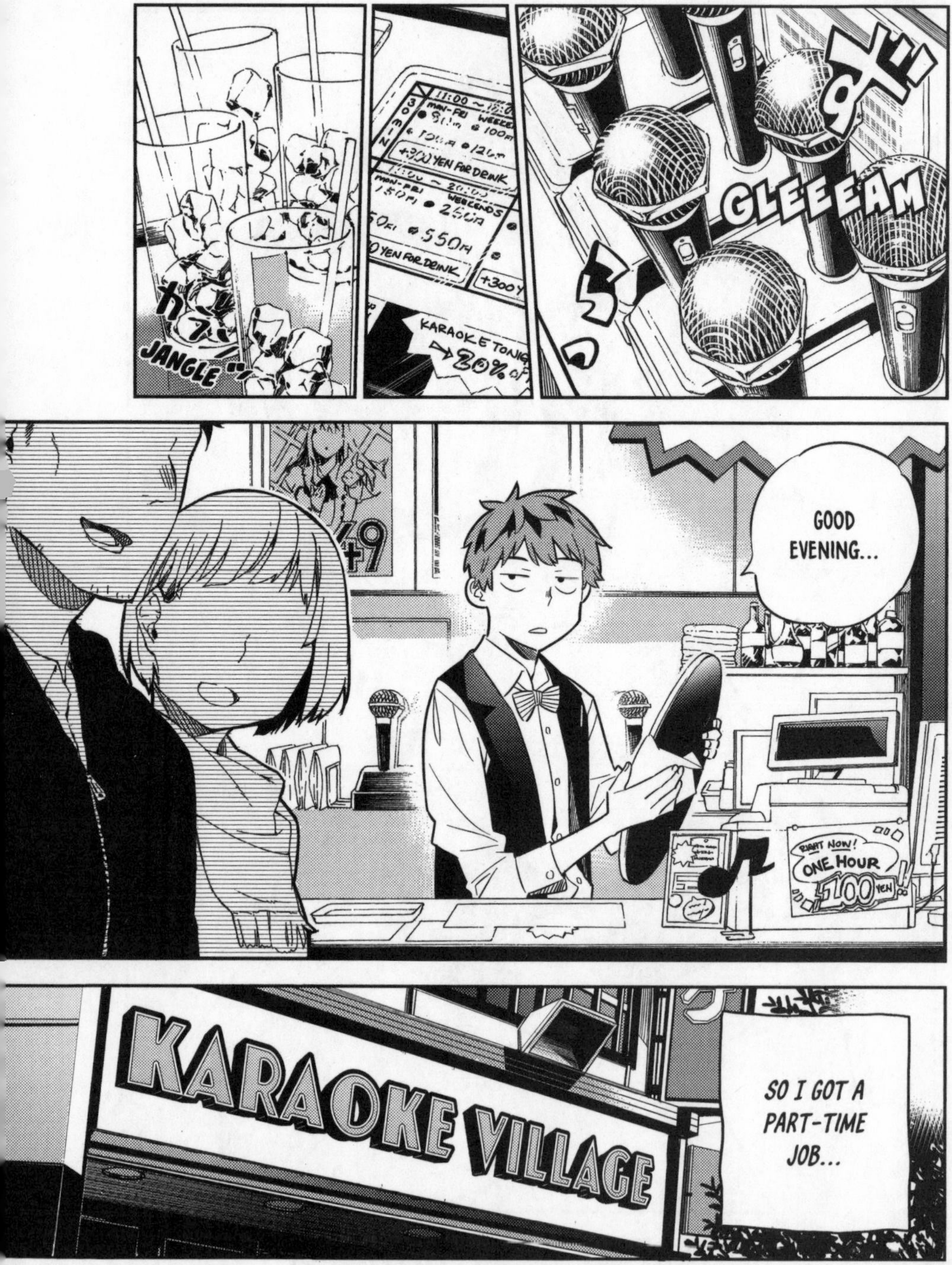
GLEEEAM
+300 YEN FOR DRINK
JANGLE
GOOD EVENING...
RIGHT NOW! ONE HOUR 100 YEN
KARAOKE VILLAGE
SO I GOT A PART-TIME JOB...

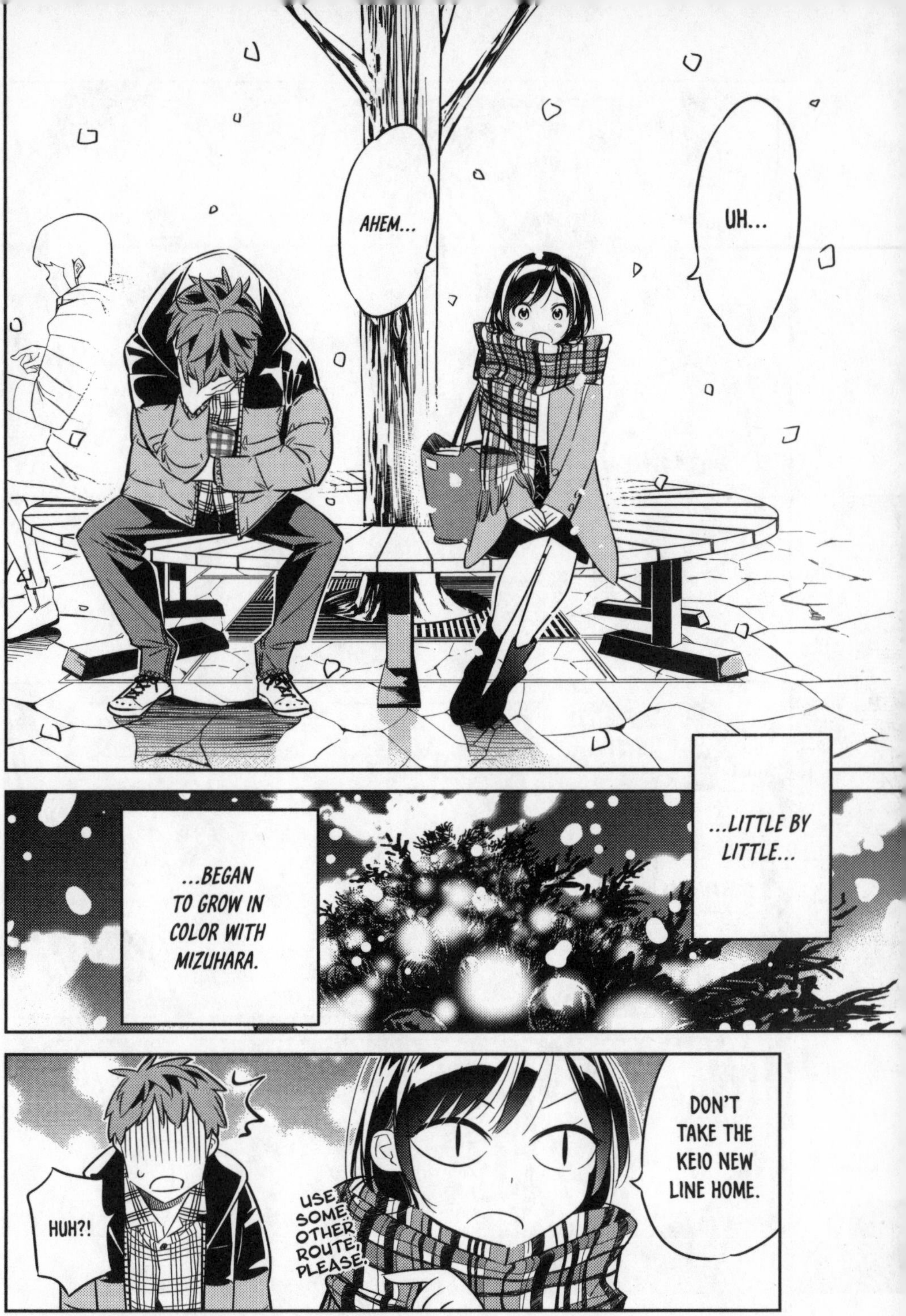
UH...
AHEM...
...LITTLE BY LITTLE...
...BEGAN TO GROW IN COLOR WITH MIZUHARA.
DON'T TAKE THE KEIO NEW LINE HOME.
USE SOME OTHER ROUTE, PLEASE.
HUH?!

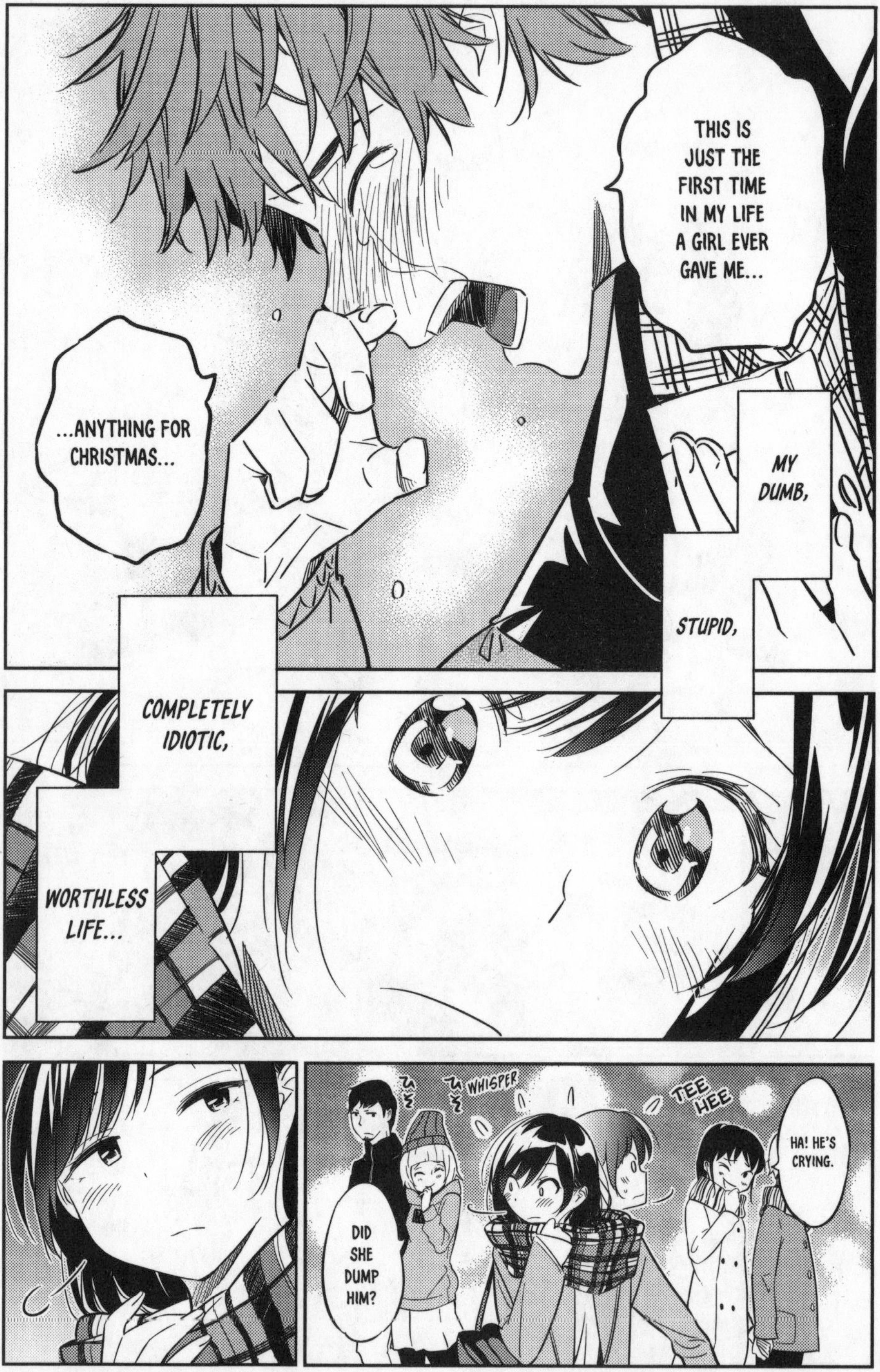
THIS IS JUST THE FIRST TIME IN MY LIFE A GIRL EVER GAVE ME...
...ANYTHING FOR CHRISTMAS...
MY DUMB,
STUPID,
COMPLETELY IDIOTIC,
WORTHLESS LIFE...
HA! HE'S CRYING.
TEE HEE
WHISPER
DID SHE DUMP HIM?

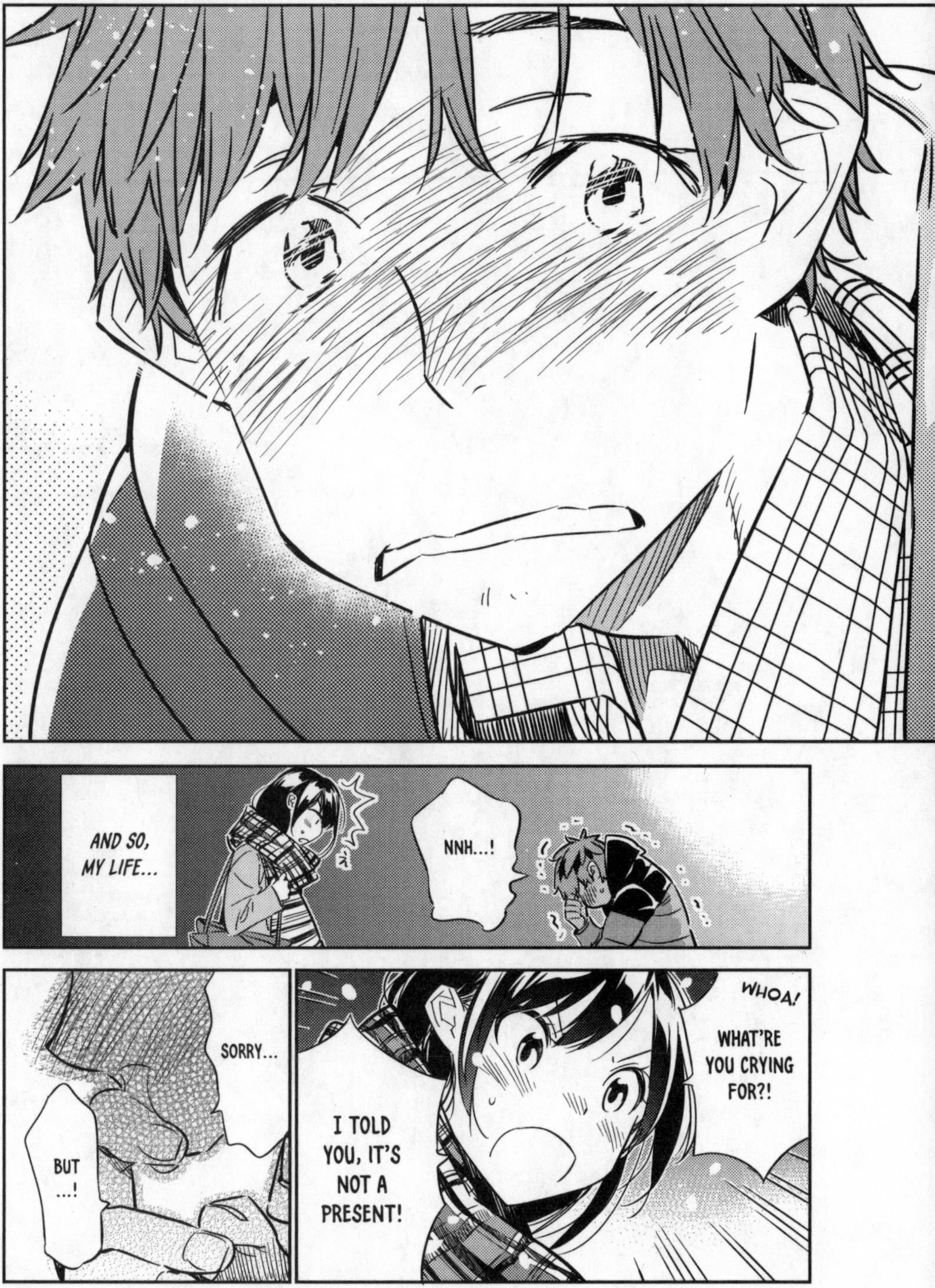
NNH...!
AND SO, MY LIFE...
WHOA!
WHAT'RE YOU CRYING FOR?!
I TOLD YOU, IT'S NOT A PRESENT!
SORRY...
BUT ...!

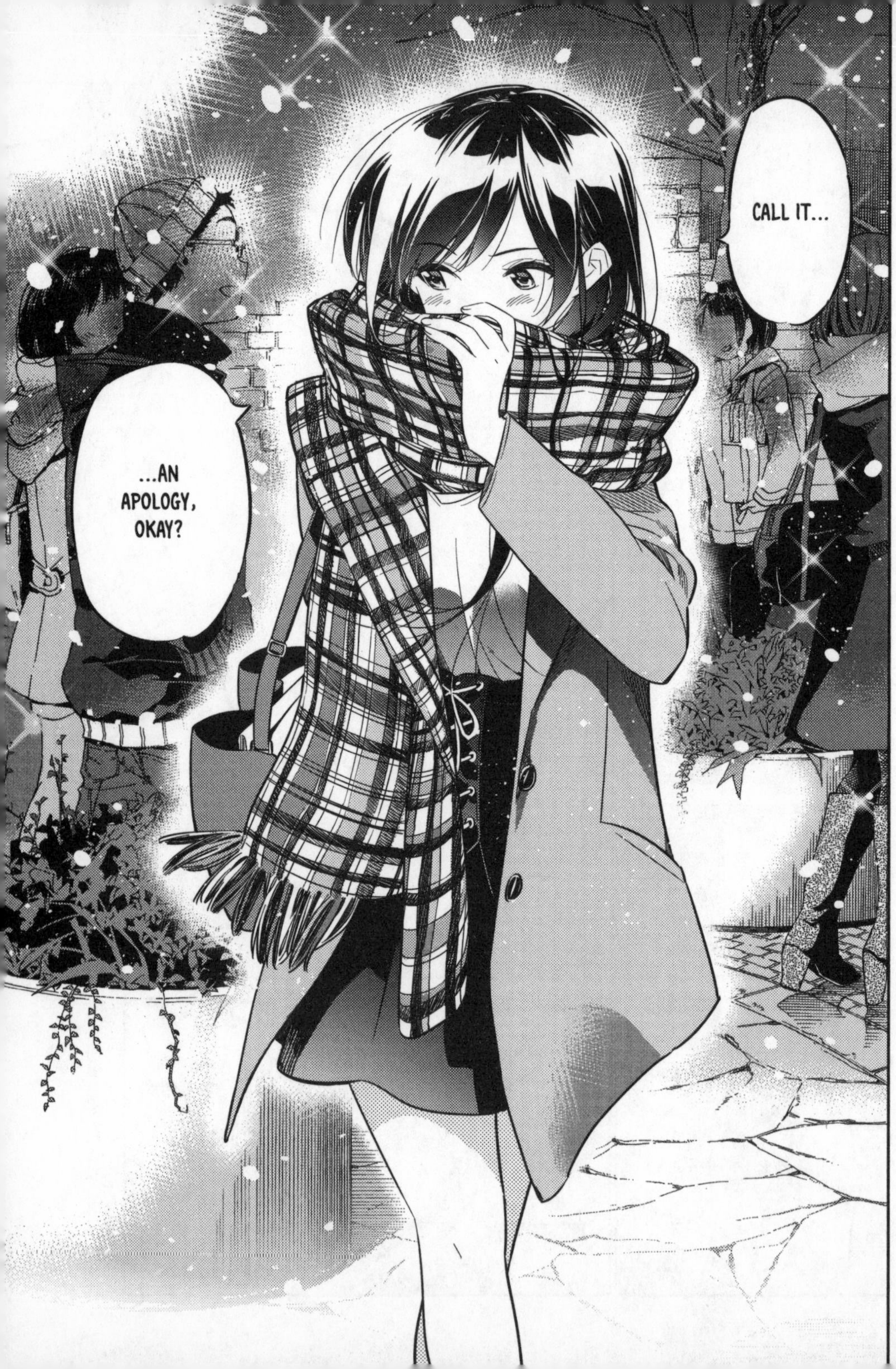
CALL IT...
...AN APOLOGY, OKAY?

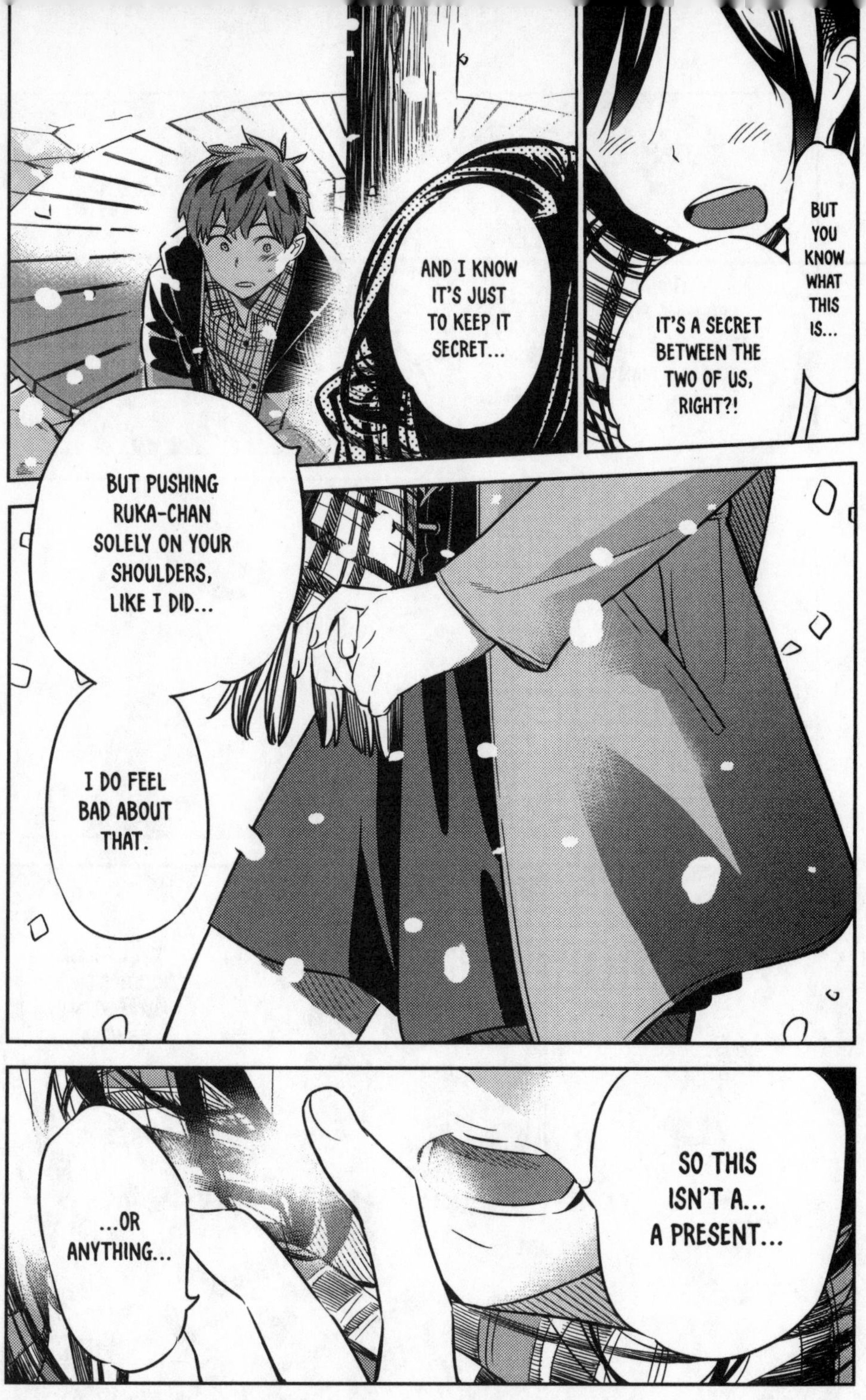
BUT YOU KNOW WHAT THIS IS...
IT'S A SECRET BETWEEN THE TWO OF US, RIGHT?!
AND I KNOW IT'S JUST TO KEEP IT SECRET...
BUT PUSHING RUKA-CHAN SOLELY ON YOUR SHOULDERS, LIKE I DID...
I DO FEEL BAD ABOUT THAT.
SO THIS ISN'T A... A PRESENT...
...OR ANYTHING...

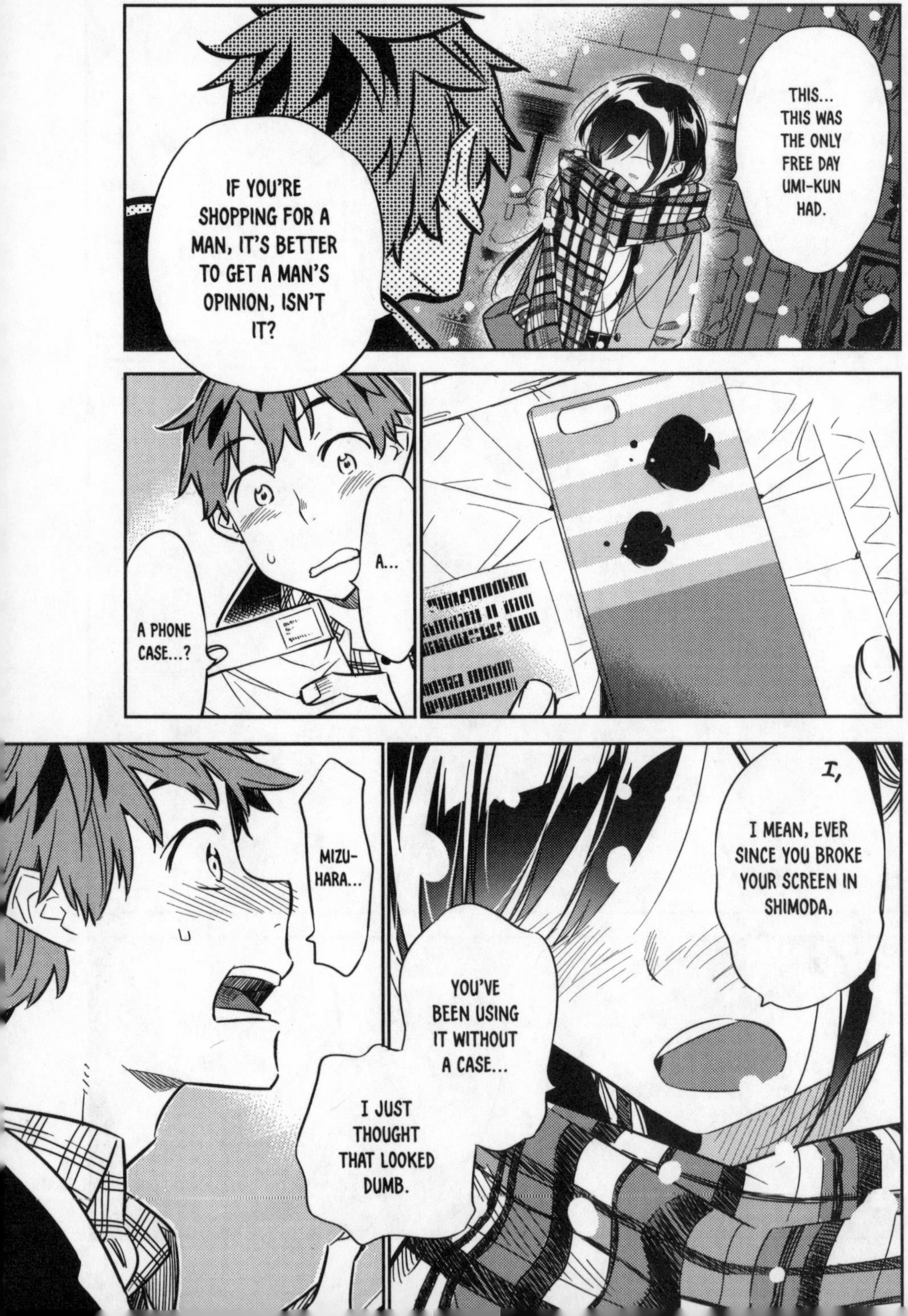
THIS... THIS WAS THE ONLY FREE DAY UMI-KUN HAD.
IF YOU'RE SHOPPING FOR A MAN, IT'S BETTER TO GET A MAN'S OPINION, ISN'T IT?
A...
A PHONE CASE...?
I,
I MEAN, EVER SINCE YOU BROKE YOUR SCREEN IN SHIMODA,
YOU'VE BEEN USING IT WITHOUT A CASE...
I JUST THOUGHT THAT LOOKED DUMB.
MIZU-HARA...

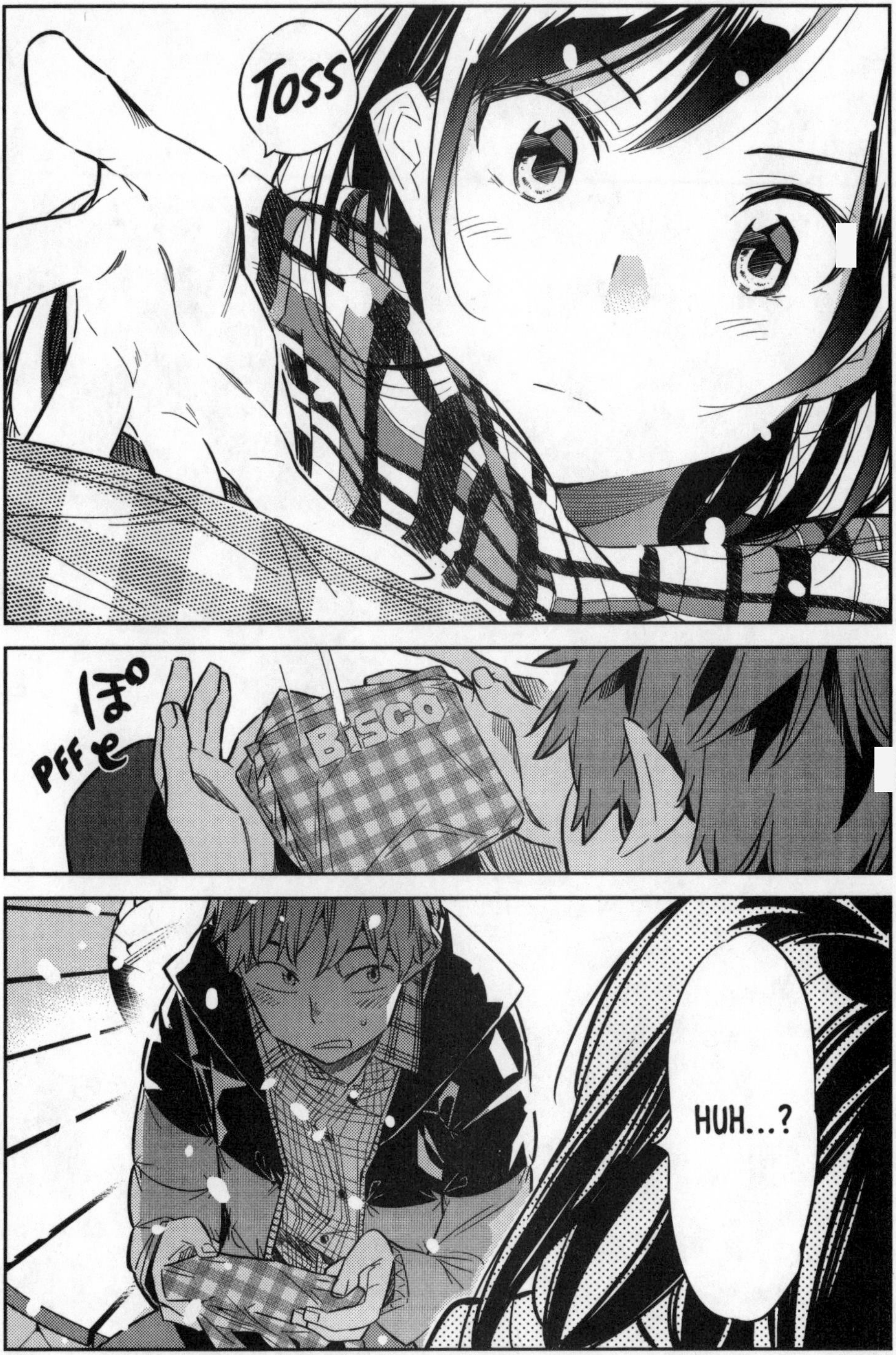
TOSS
ぽそ
PFF
BISCO
HUH...?

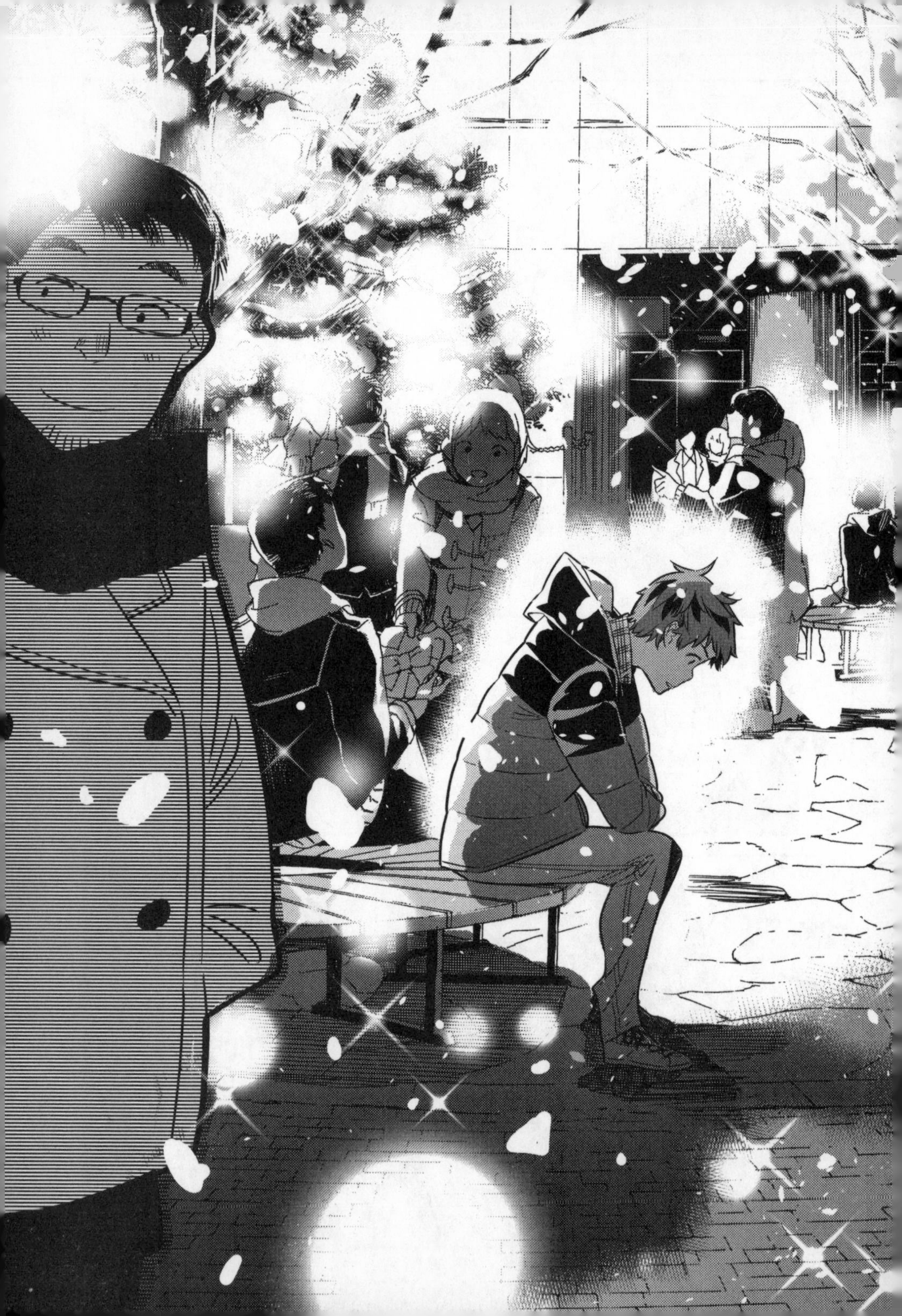

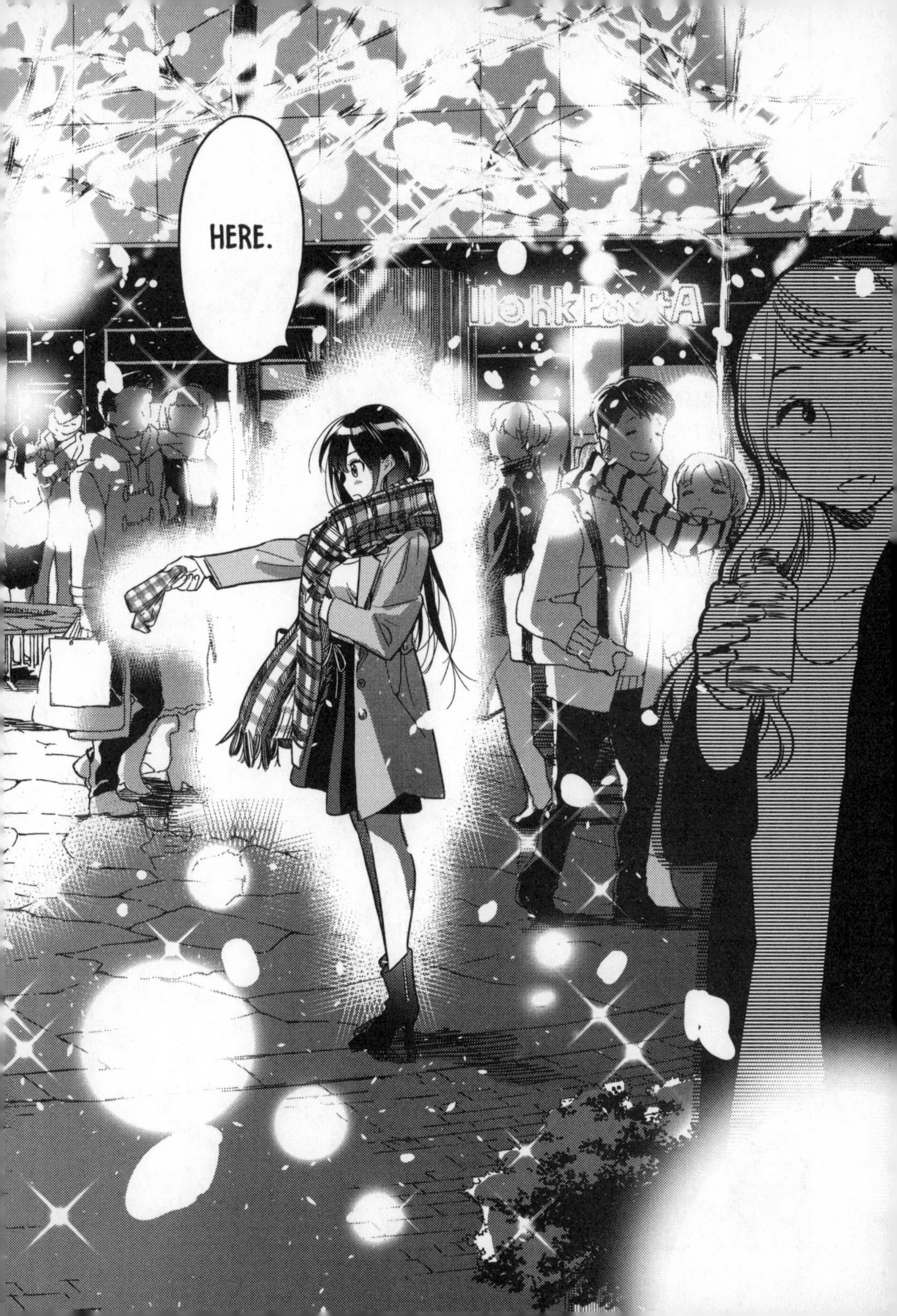
HERE.

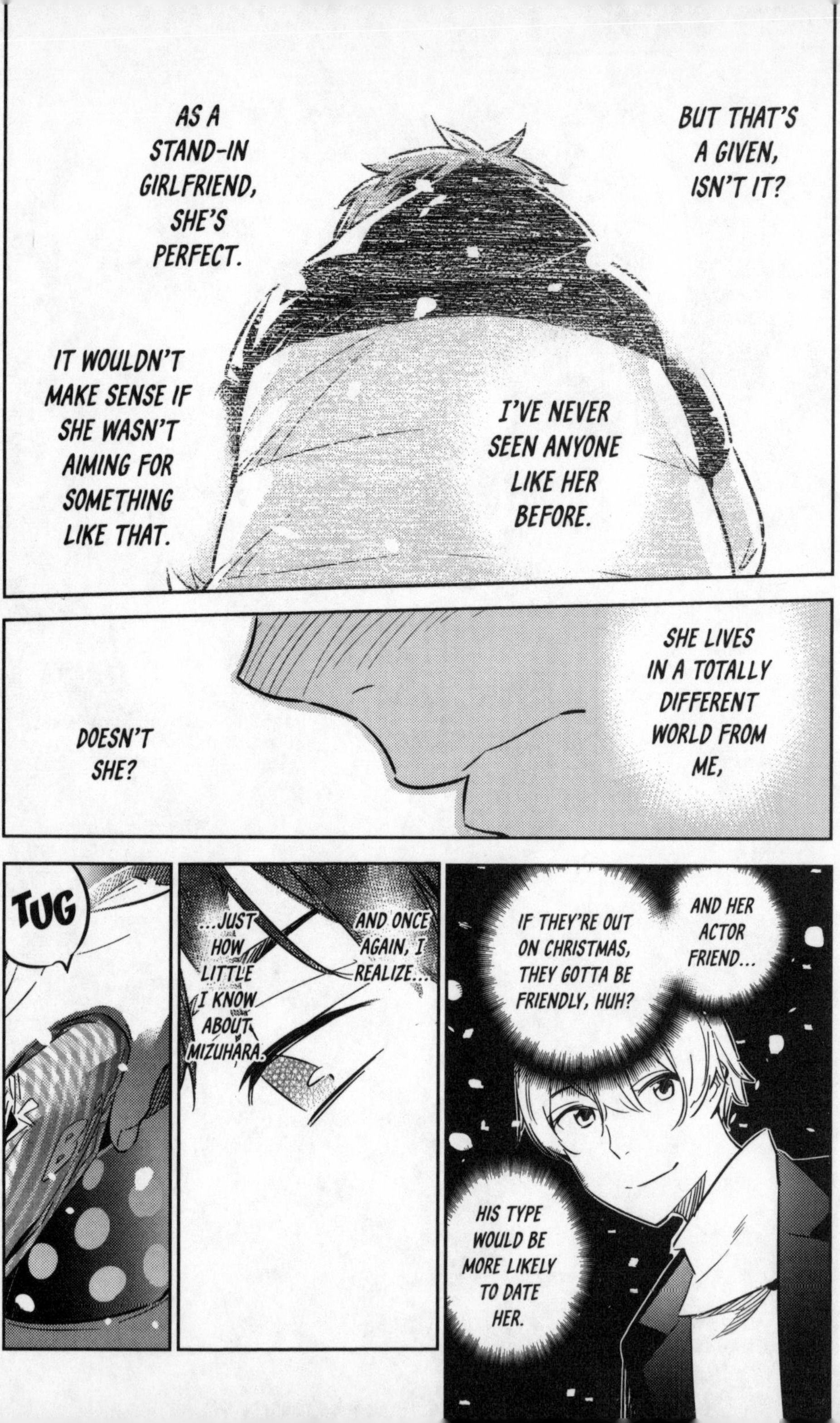
BUT THAT'S A GIVEN, ISN'T IT?
AS A STAND-IN GIRLFRIEND, SHE'S PERFECT.
I'VE NEVER SEEN ANYONE LIKE HER BEFORE.
IT WOULDN'T MAKE SENSE IF SHE WASN'T AIMING FOR SOMETHING LIKE THAT.
SHE LIVES IN A TOTALLY DIFFERENT WORLD FROM ME,
DOESN'T SHE?
AND HER ACTOR FRIEND...
IF THEY'RE OUT ON CHRISTMAS, THEY GOTTA BE FRIENDLY, HUH?
HIS TYPE WOULD BE MORE LIKELY TO DATE HER.
AND ONCE AGAIN, I REALIZE...
...JUST HOW LITTLE I KNOW ABOUT MIZUHARA.
TUG

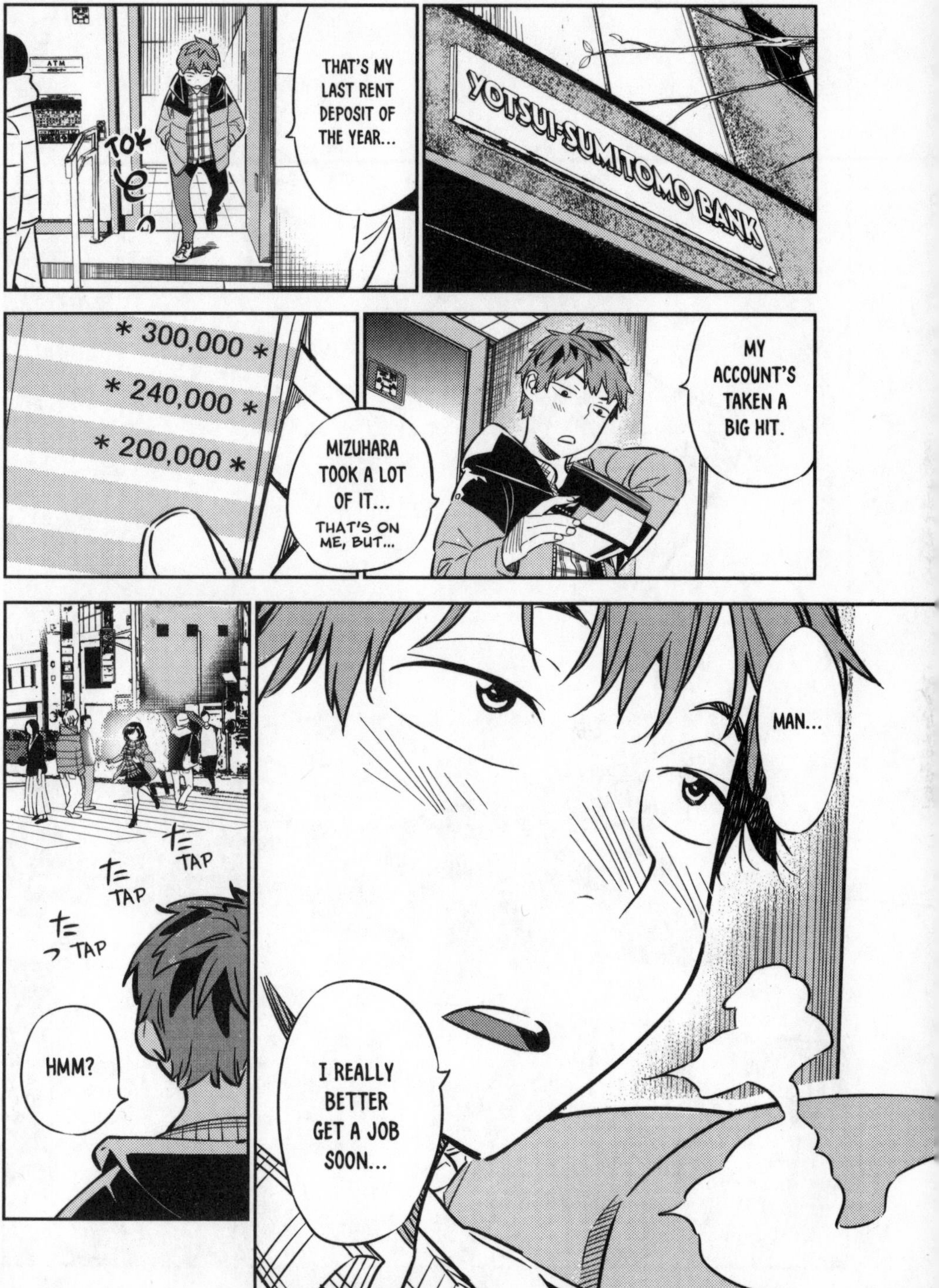
YOTSUI-SUMITOMO BANK
THAT'S MY LAST RENT DEPOSIT OF THE YEAR...
TOK
MY ACCOUNT'S TAKEN A BIG HIT.
MIZUHARA TOOK A LOT OF IT...
THAT'S ON ME, BUT...
* 300,000 *
* 240,000 *
* 200,000 *
MAN...
I REALLY BETTER GET A JOB SOON...
TAP
TAP
TAP
HMM?

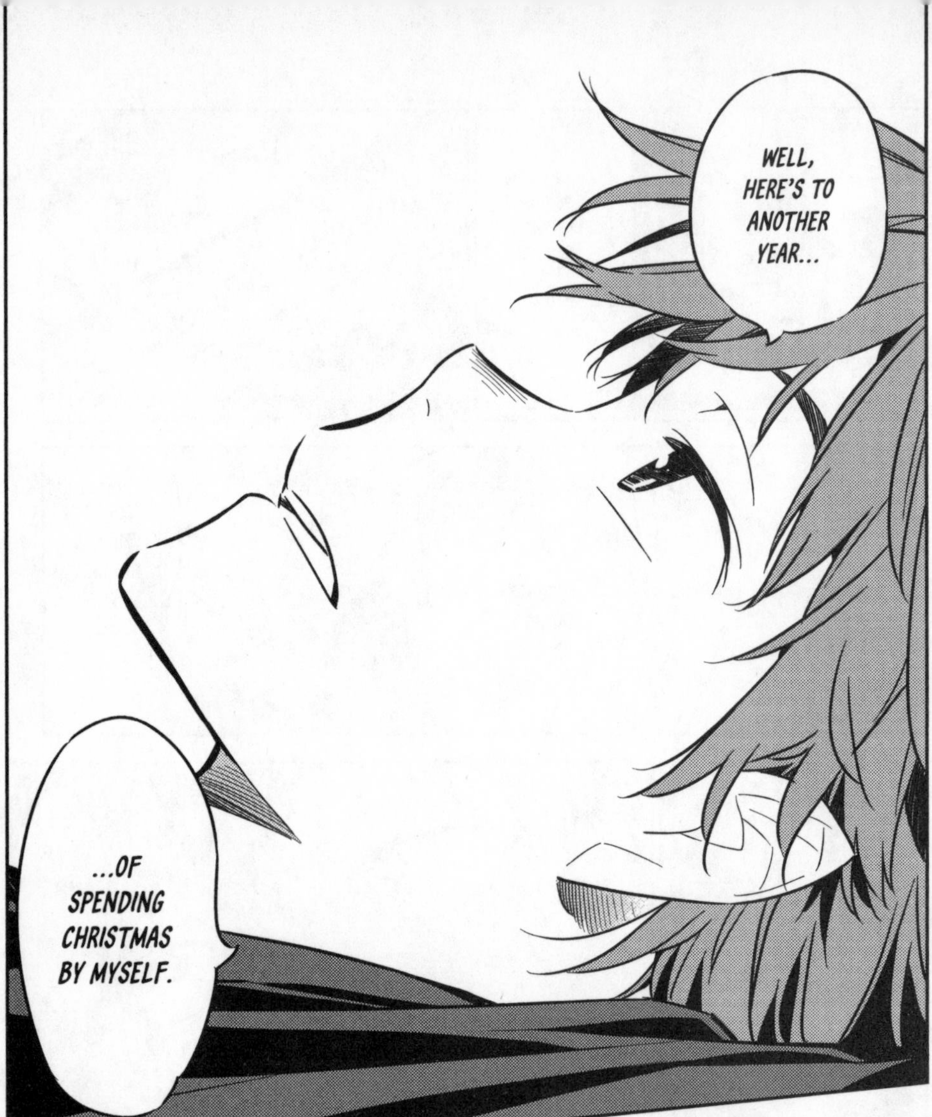
WELL, HERE'S TO ANOTHER YEAR...
...OF SPENDING CHRISTMAS BY MYSELF.
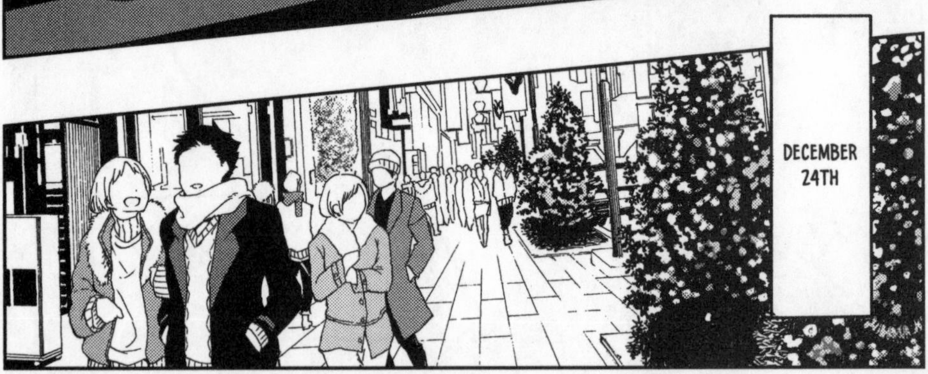
DECEMBER 24TH

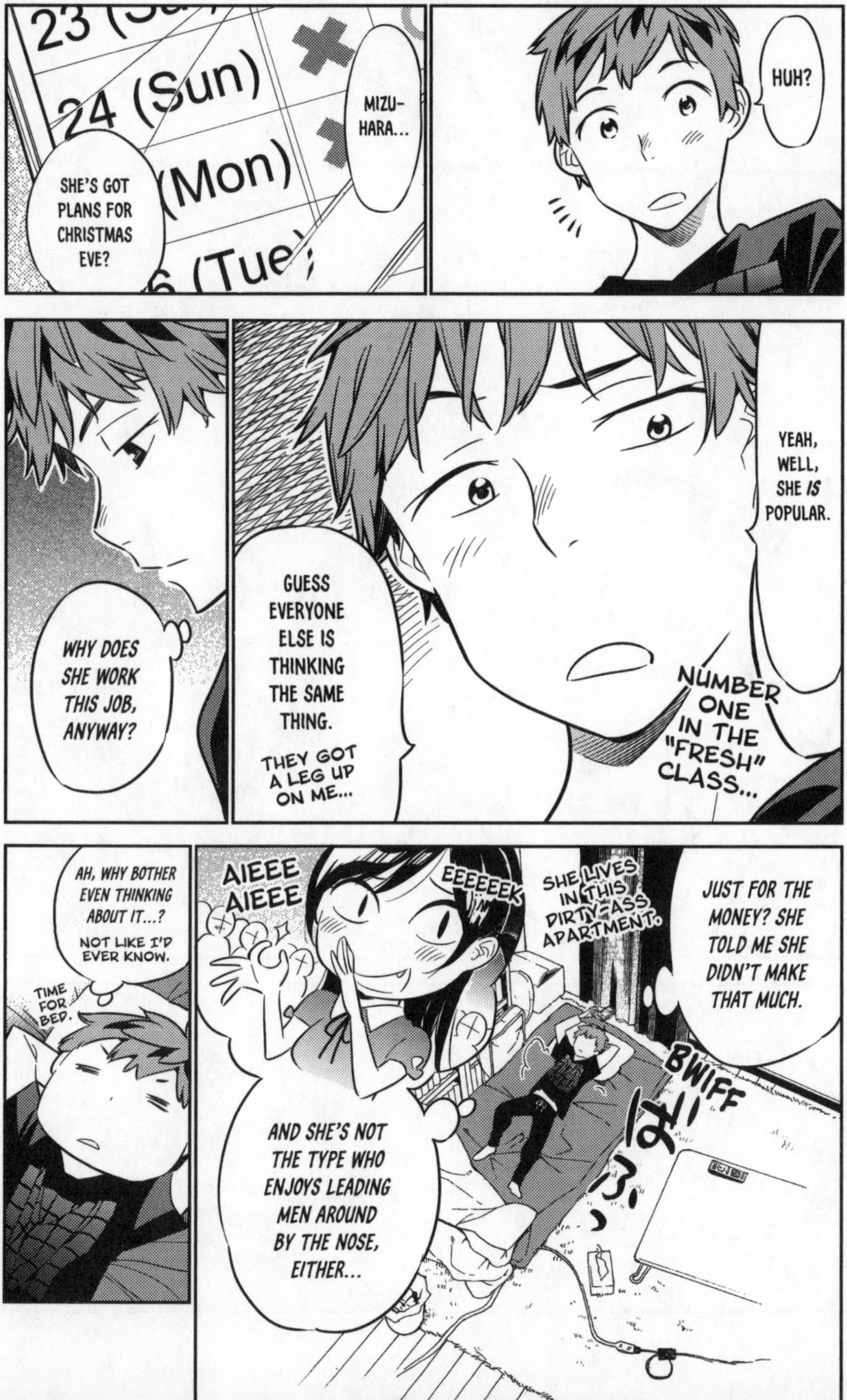
HUH?
MIZU-HARA...
24 (Sun)
(Mon)
SHE'S GOT PLANS FOR CHRISTMAS EVE?
YEAH, WELL, SHE *IS* POPULAR.
NUMBER ONE IN THE "FRESH" CLASS...
GUESS EVERYONE ELSE IS THINKING THE SAME THING.
THEY GOT A LEG UP ON ME...
WHY DOES SHE WORK THIS JOB, ANYWAY?
JUST FOR THE MONEY? SHE TOLD ME SHE DIDN'T MAKE THAT MUCH.
SHE LIVES IN THIS DIRTY-ASS APARTMENT.
EEEEEEK
AIEEE AIEEE
AND SHE'S NOT THE TYPE WHO ENJOYS LEADING MEN AROUND BY THE NOSE, EITHER...
BWIFF
ばふっ
AH, WHY BOTHER EVEN THINKING ABOUT IT...?
NOT LIKE I'D EVER KNOW.
TIME FOR BED.

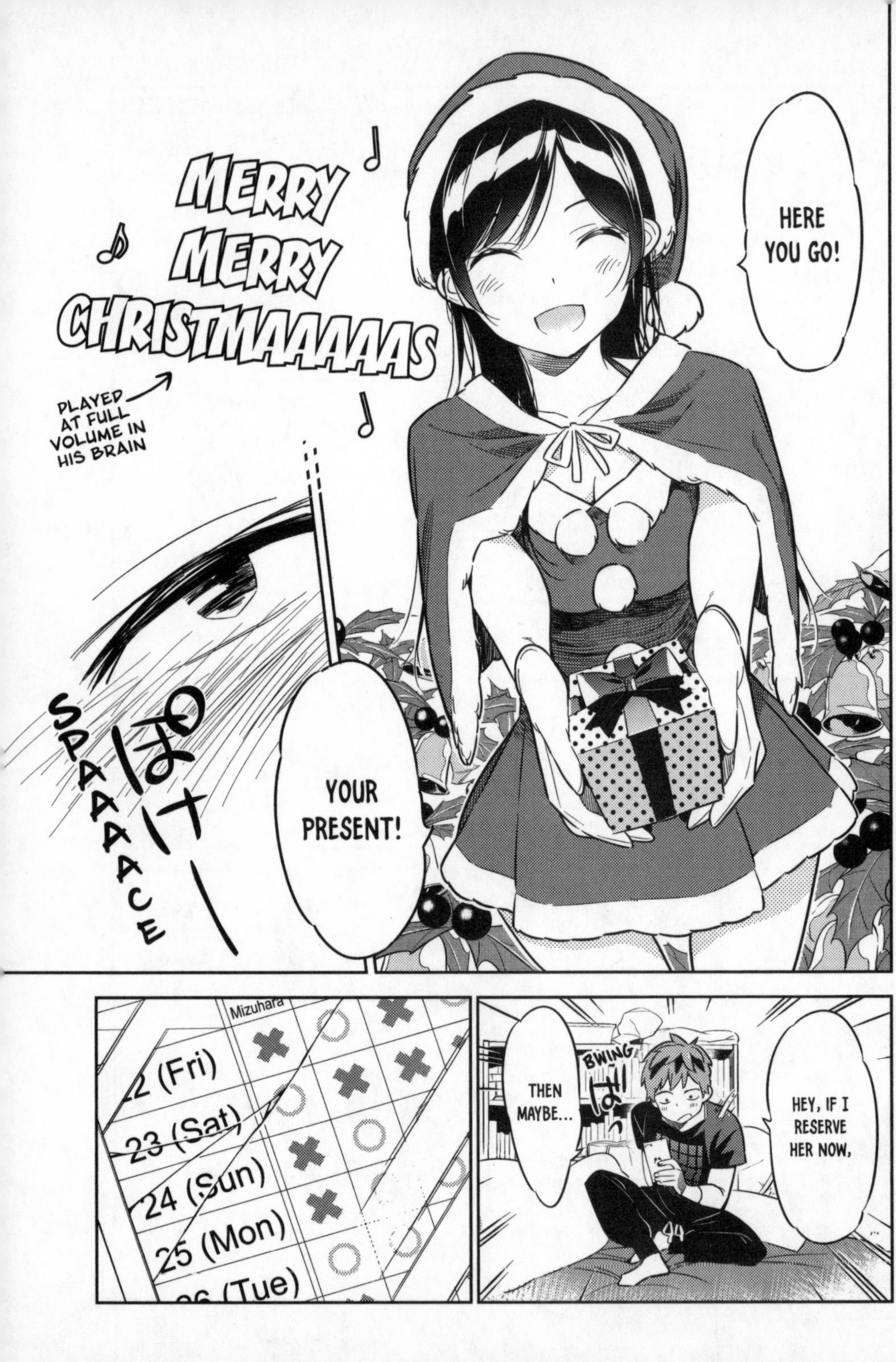
HERE YOU GO!
MERRY MERRY CHRISTMAAAAAAS
PLAYED AT FULL VOLUME IN HIS BRAIN
YOUR PRESENT!
ぽけー
SPAAAACE
HEY, IF I RESERVE HER NOW,
BWING
ぱっ
THEN MAYBE...
Mizuhara
2 (Fri)
23 (Sat)
24 (Sun)
25 (Mon)
(Tue)

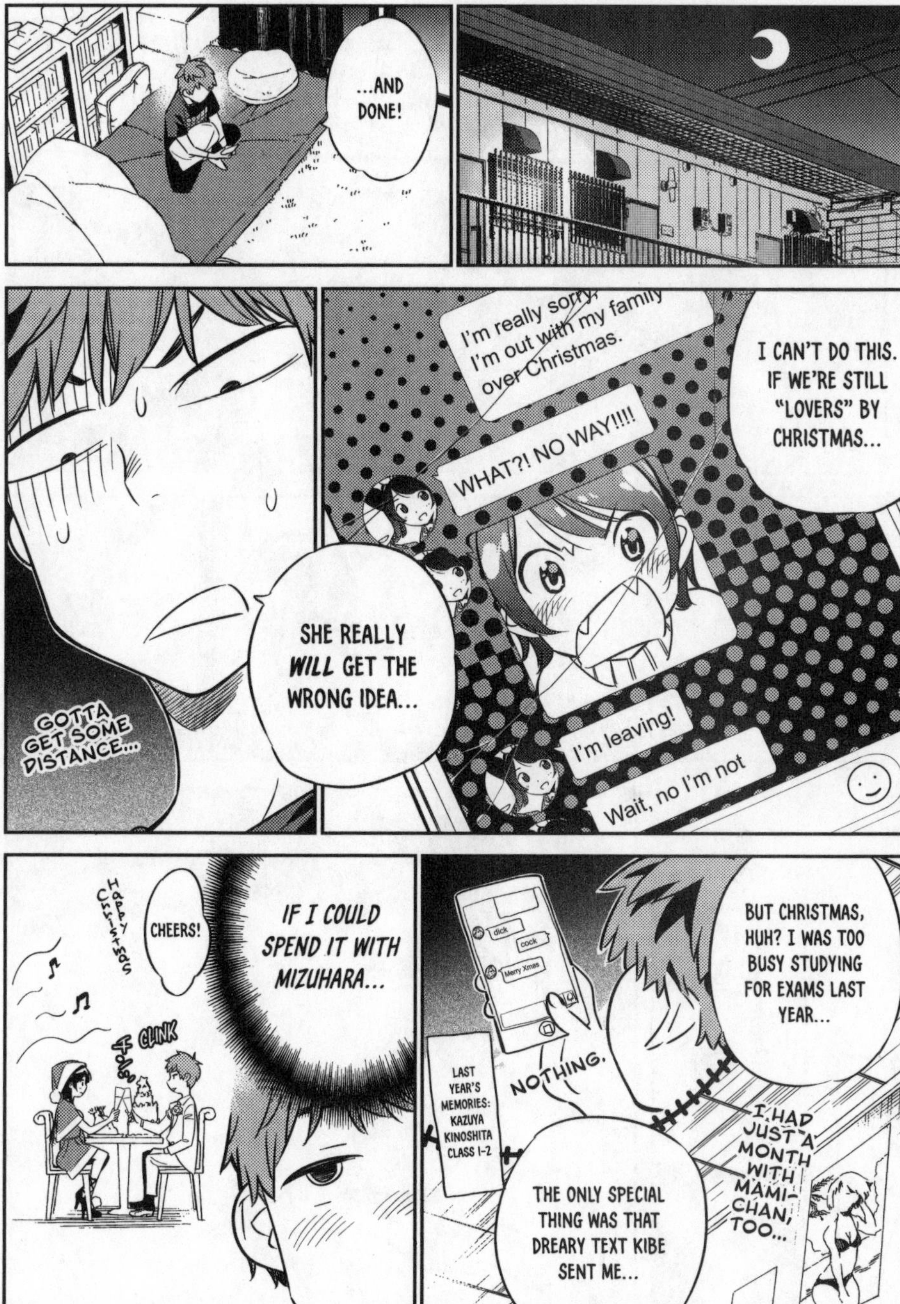
...AND DONE!
I'm really sorry, I'm out with my family over Christmas.
WHAT?! NO WAY!!!!
I'm leaving!
Wait, no I'm not
I CAN'T DO THIS. IF WE'RE STILL "LOVERS" BY CHRISTMAS...
SHE REALLY WILL GET THE WRONG IDEA...
GOTTA GET SOME DISTANCE...
BUT CHRISTMAS, HUH? I WAS TOO BUSY STUDYING FOR EXAMS LAST YEAR...
dick
cock
Merry Xmas
NOTHING.
I HAD JUST A MONTH WITH MAMI-CHAN, TOO...
THE ONLY SPECIAL THING WAS THAT DREARY TEXT KIBE SENT ME...
LAST YEAR'S MEMORIES: KAZUYA KINOSHITA CLASS 1-2
IF I COULD SPEND IT WITH MIZUHARA...
CHEERS!
Happy Christmas
CLINK

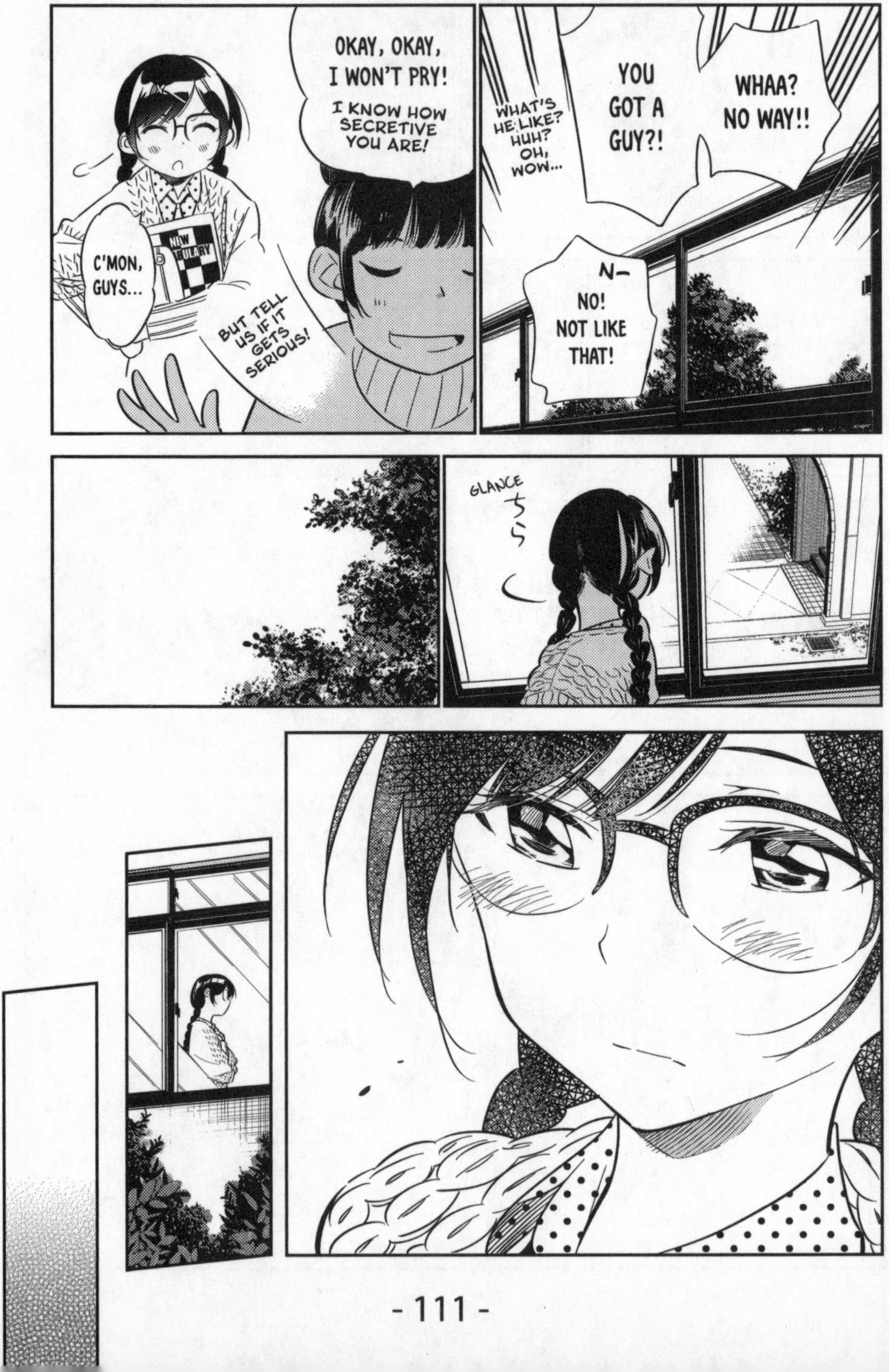
WHAA? NO WAY!!
YOU GOT A GUY?!
WHAT'S HE LIKE? HUH? OH, WOW...
N— NO! NOT LIKE THAT!
OKAY, OKAY, I WON'T PRY!
I KNOW HOW SECRETIVE YOU ARE!
BUT TELL US IF IT GETS SERIOUS!
C'MON, GUYS...
GLANCE
ちら

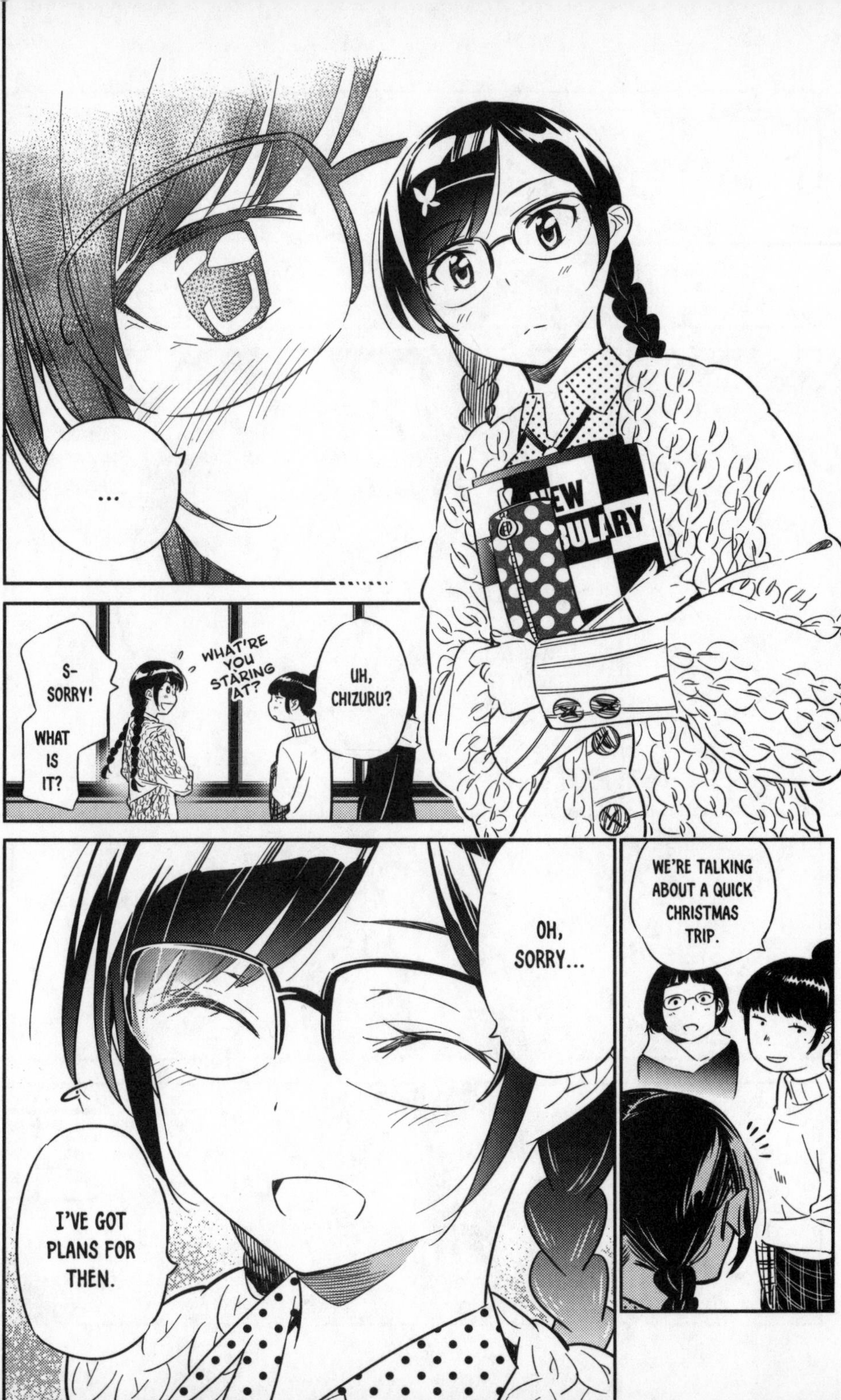
...
UH, CHIZURU?
WHAT'RE YOU STARING AT?
S- SORRY!
WHAT IS IT?
WE'RE TALKING ABOUT A QUICK CHRISTMAS TRIP.
OH, SORRY...
I'VE GOT PLANS FOR THEN.

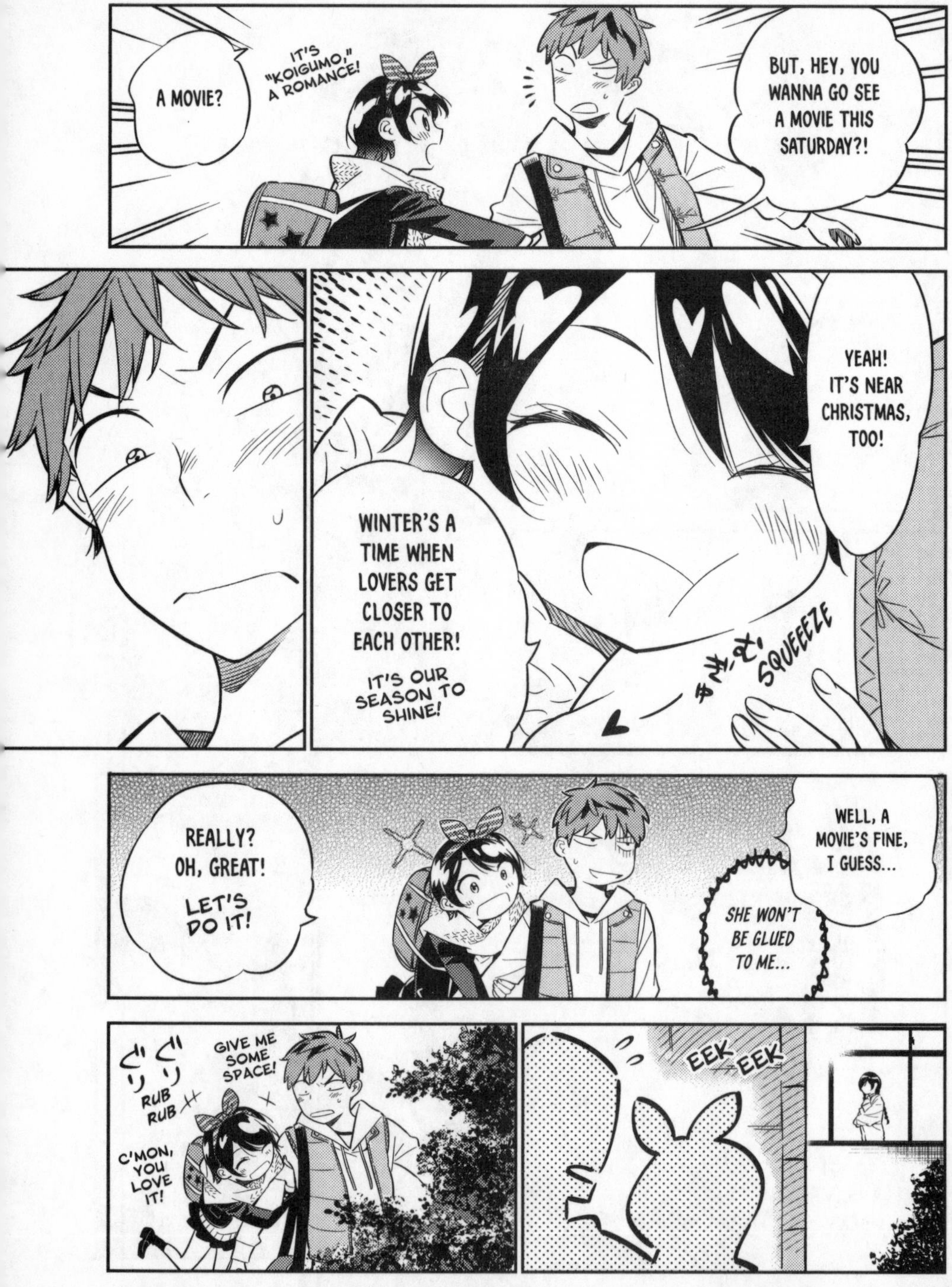
BUT, HEY, YOU WANNA GO SEE A MOVIE THIS SATURDAY?!
IT'S "KOIGUMO," A ROMANCE!
A MOVIE?
YEAH! IT'S NEAR CHRISTMAS, TOO!
WINTER'S A TIME WHEN LOVERS GET CLOSER TO EACH OTHER!
IT'S OUR SEASON TO SHINE!
ぎゅむ
SQUEEEZE
WELL, A MOVIE'S FINE, I GUESS...
SHE WON'T BE GLUED TO ME...
REALLY? OH, GREAT!
LET'S DO IT!
EEK EEK
GIVE ME SOME SPACE!
ぐりぐり
RUB RUB
C'MON, YOU LOVE IT!

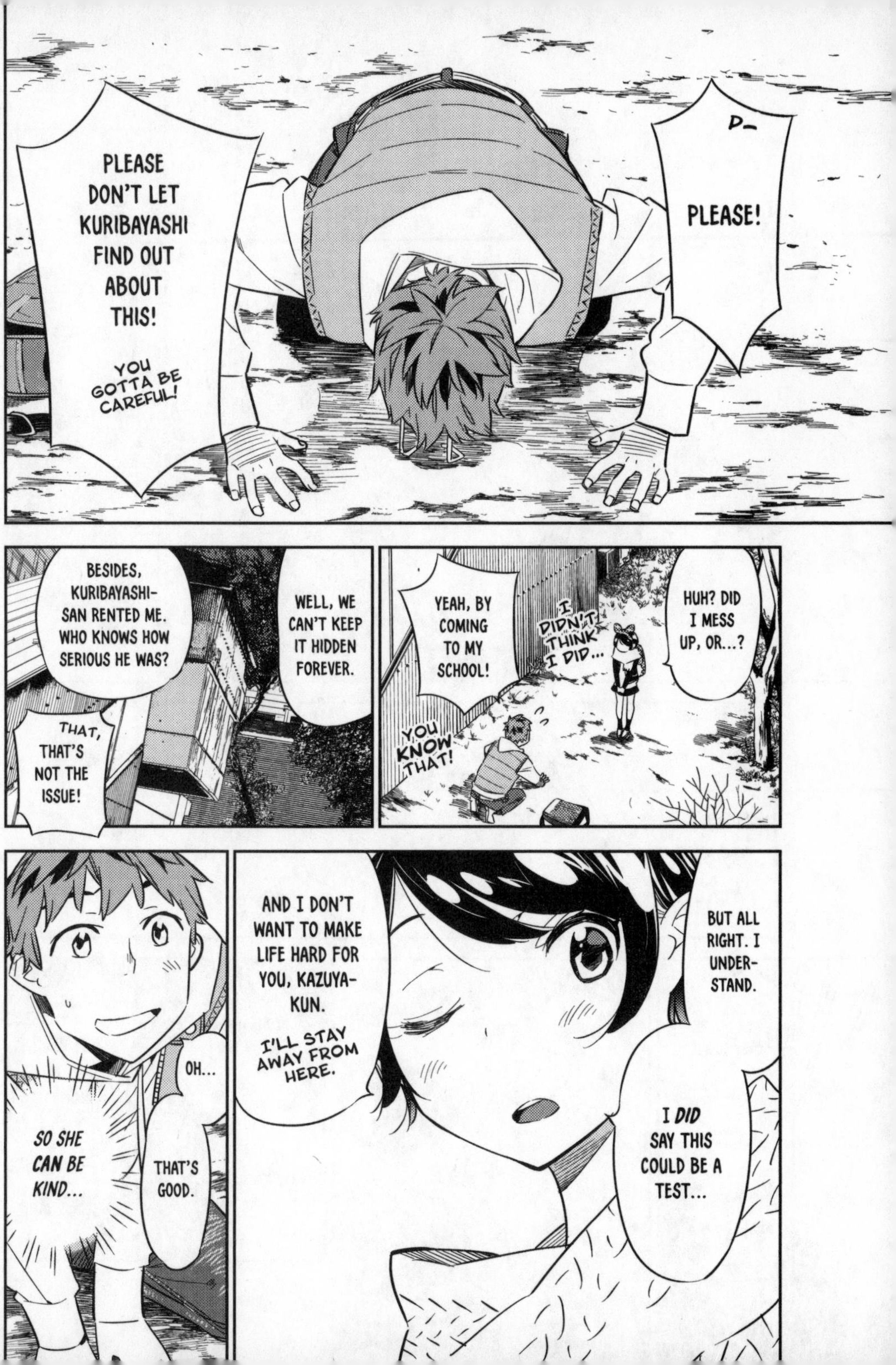
P—
PLEASE!
PLEASE DON'T LET KURIBAYASHI FIND OUT ABOUT THIS!
YOU GOTTA BE CAREFUL!
HUH? DID I MESS UP, OR...?
I DIDN'T THINK I DID...
YEAH, BY COMING TO MY SCHOOL!
YOU KNOW THAT!
WELL, WE CAN'T KEEP IT HIDDEN FOREVER.
BESIDES, KURIBAYASHI-SAN RENTED ME. WHO KNOWS HOW SERIOUS HE WAS?
THAT, THAT'S NOT THE ISSUE!
BUT ALL RIGHT. I UNDER-STAND.
AND I DON'T WANT TO MAKE LIFE HARD FOR YOU, KAZUYA-KUN.
I'LL STAY AWAY FROM HERE.
I *DID* SAY THIS COULD BE A TEST...
OH...
THAT'S GOOD.
SO SHE CAN BE KIND...

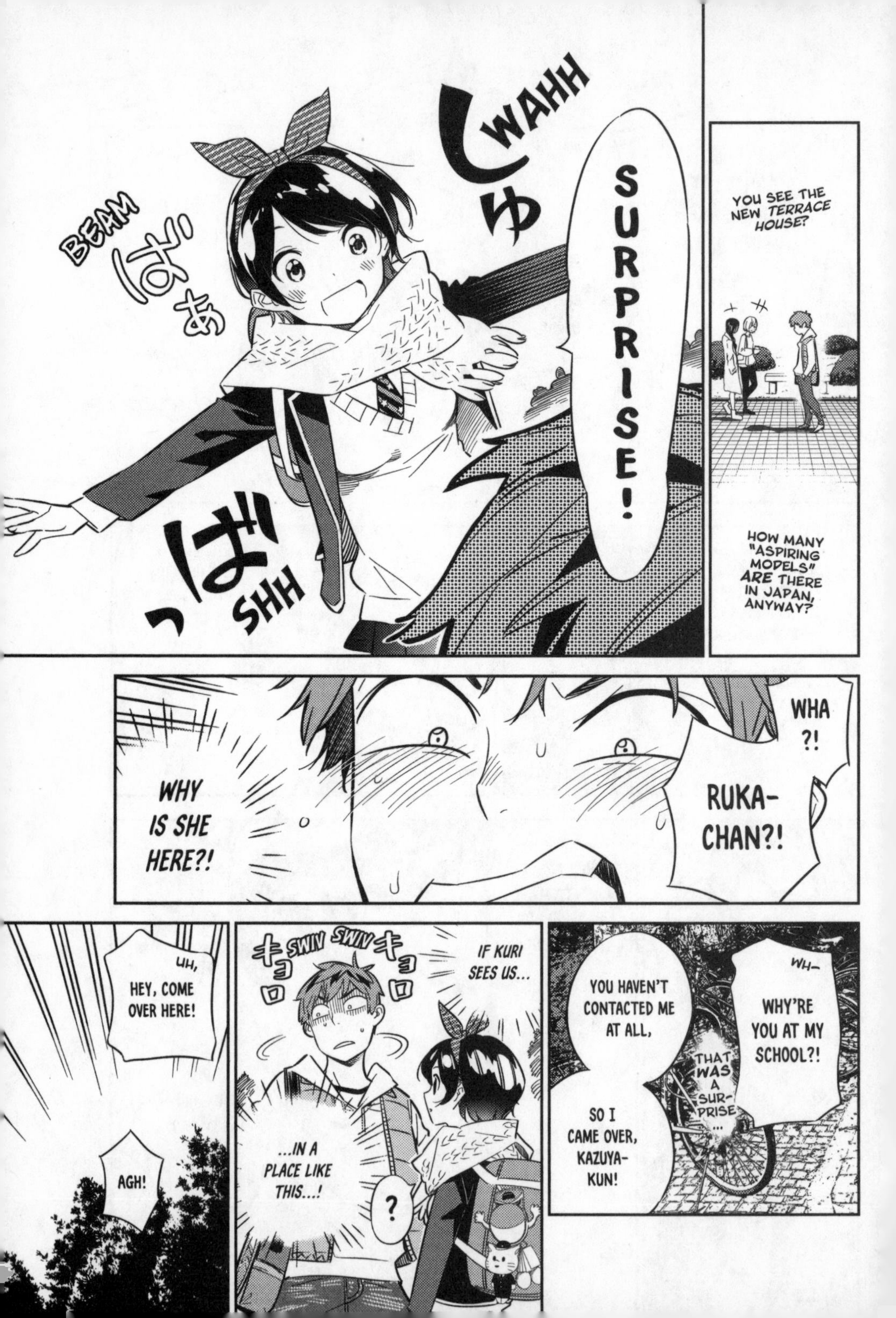
YOU SEE THE NEW TERRACE HOUSE?
HOW MANY "ASPIRING MODELS" ARE THERE IN JAPAN, ANYWAY?
しゅ WAHH
SURPRISE!
ぱぁ BEAM
ばっ SHH
WHA?!
RUKA-CHAN?!
WHY IS SHE HERE?!
WH-
WHY'RE YOU AT MY SCHOOL?!
THAT WAS A SUR-PRISE...
YOU HAVEN'T CONTACTED ME AT ALL,
SO I CAME OVER, KAZUYA-KUN!
IF KURI SEES US...
キョロ SWIV
キョロ SWIV
...IN A PLACE LIKE THIS...!
?
UH,
HEY, COME OVER HERE!
AGH!

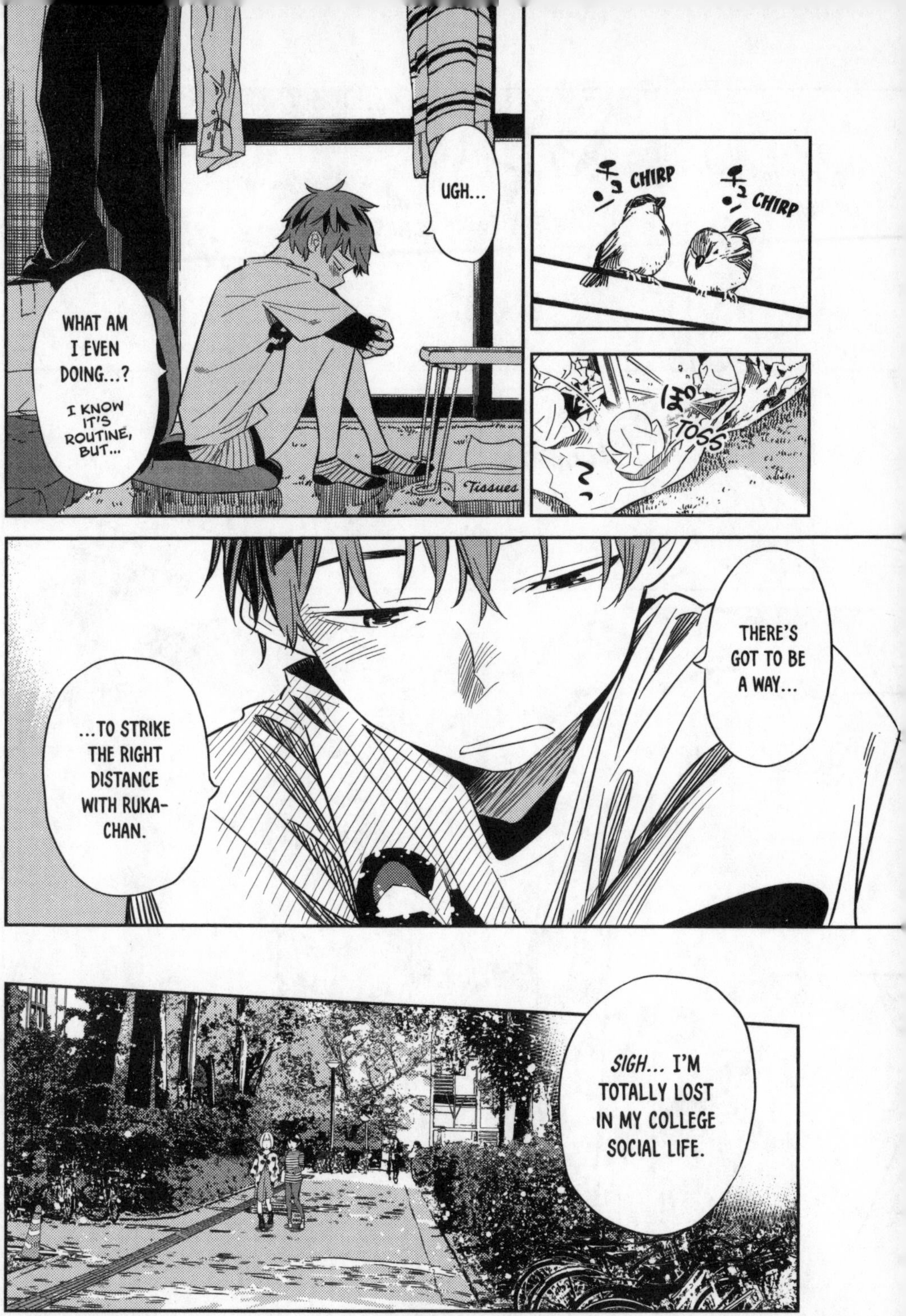
CHIRP
CHIRP
TOSS
UGH...
WHAT AM I EVEN DOING...?
I KNOW IT'S ROUTINE, BUT...
Tissues
THERE'S GOT TO BE A WAY...
...TO STRIKE THE RIGHT DISTANCE WITH RUKA-CHAN.
SIGH... I'M TOTALLY LOST IN MY COLLEGE SOCIAL LIFE.

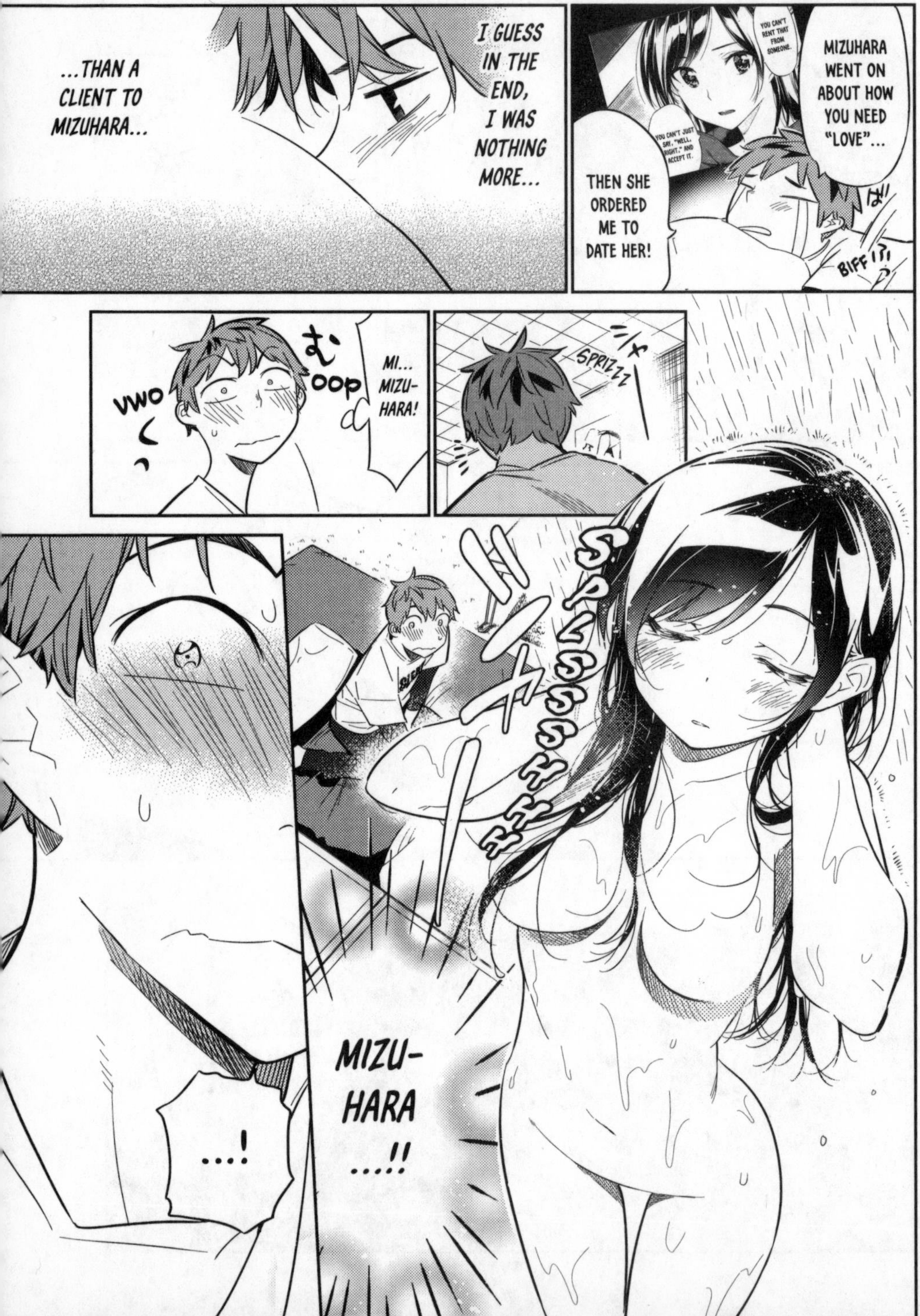
MIZUHARA WENT ON ABOUT HOW YOU NEED "LOVE"...
YOU CAN'T RENT THAT FROM SOMEONE.
YOU CAN'T JUST SAY, "WELL, RIGHT," AND ACCEPT IT.
THEN SHE ORDERED ME TO DATE HER!
BIFF
I GUESS IN THE END, I WAS NOTHING MORE...
...THAN A CLIENT TO MIZUHARA...
SPRIZZZ
MI... MIZUHARA!
VWOOP
SPLSSSHHH
MIZU-HARA ...!!
...!

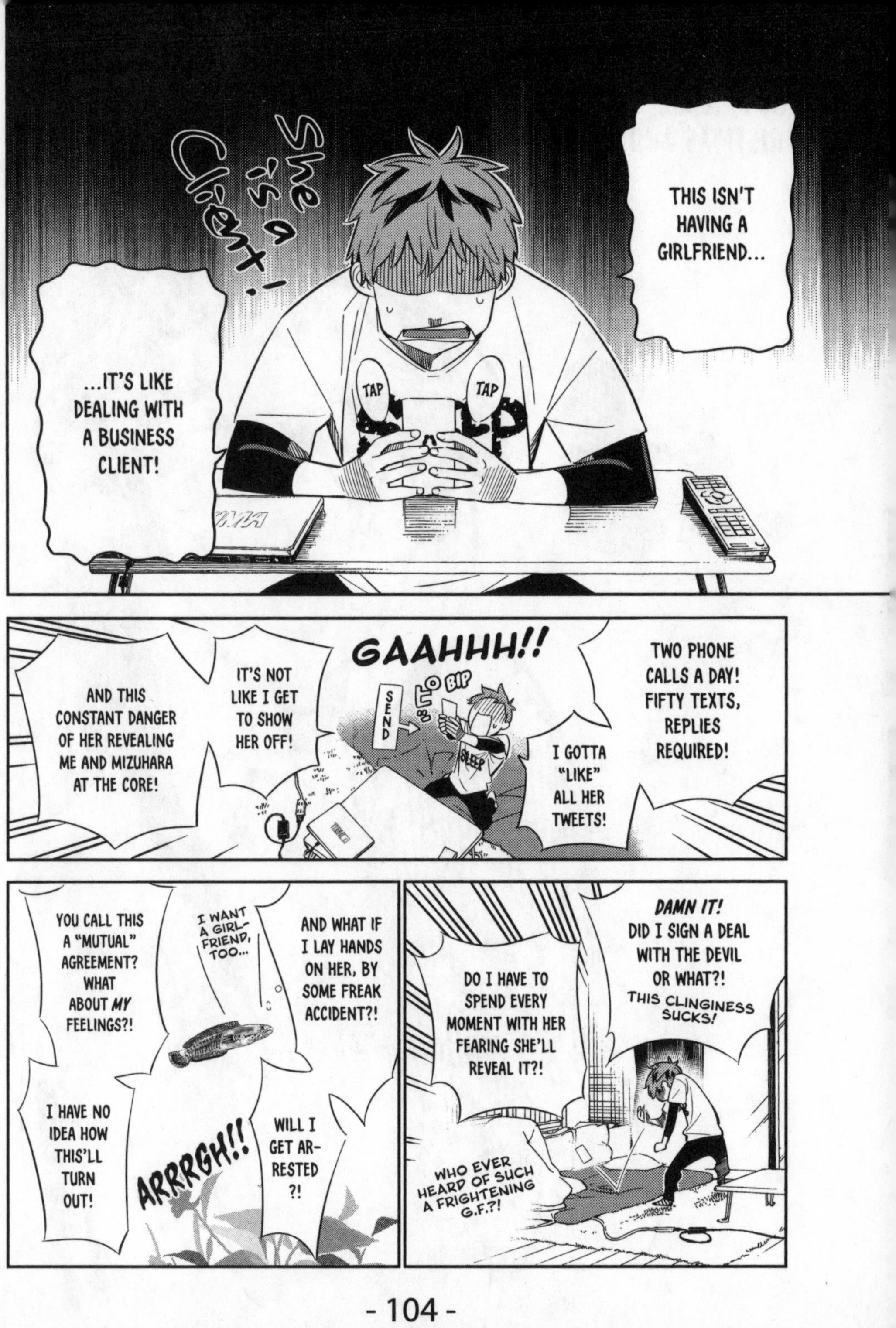
THIS ISN'T HAVING A GIRLFRIEND...
She is a Client!
TAP
TAP
...IT'S LIKE DEALING WITH A BUSINESS CLIENT!
TWO PHONE CALLS A DAY! FIFTY TEXTS, REPLIES REQUIRED!
I GOTTA "LIKE" ALL HER TWEETS!
GAAHHH!!
BIP
SEND
IT'S NOT LIKE I GET TO SHOW HER OFF!
AND THIS CONSTANT DANGER OF HER REVEALING ME AND MIZUHARA AT THE CORE!
DAMN IT! DID I SIGN A DEAL WITH THE DEVIL OR WHAT?!
THIS CLINGINESS SUCKS!
DO I HAVE TO SPEND EVERY MOMENT WITH HER FEARING SHE'LL REVEAL IT?!
WHO EVER HEARD OF SUCH A FRIGHTENING G.F.?!
AND WHAT IF I LAY HANDS ON HER, BY SOME FREAK ACCIDENT?!
I WANT A GIRL-FRIEND, TOO...
YOU CALL THIS A "MUTUAL" AGREEMENT? WHAT ABOUT *MY* FEELINGS?!
WILL I GET AR-RESTED?!
ARRRGH!!
I HAVE NO IDEA HOW THIS'LL TURN OUT!

RATING 29
CHRISTMAS AND MY GIRLFRIEND (1)

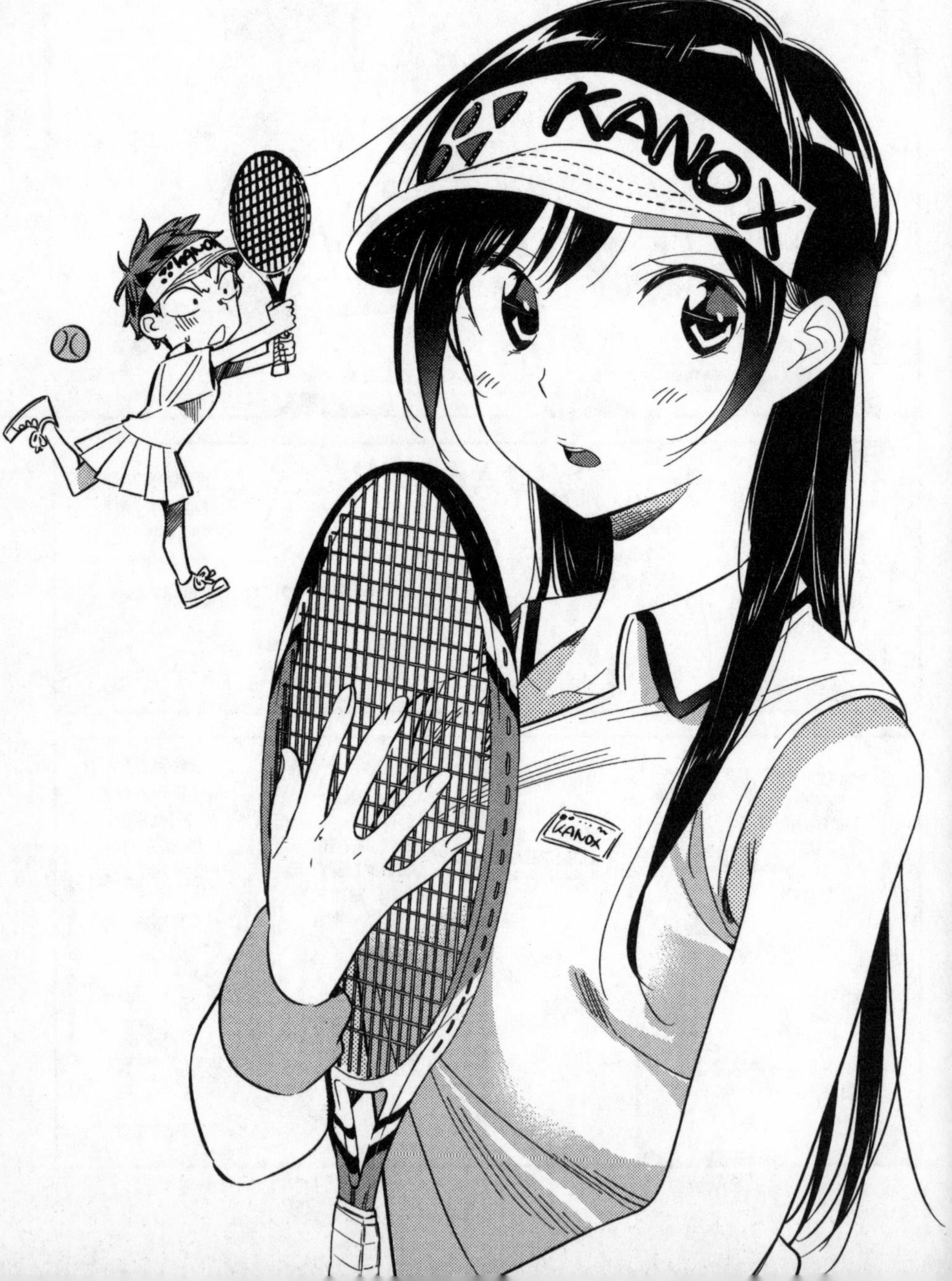
KANOX
KANOX
KANOX

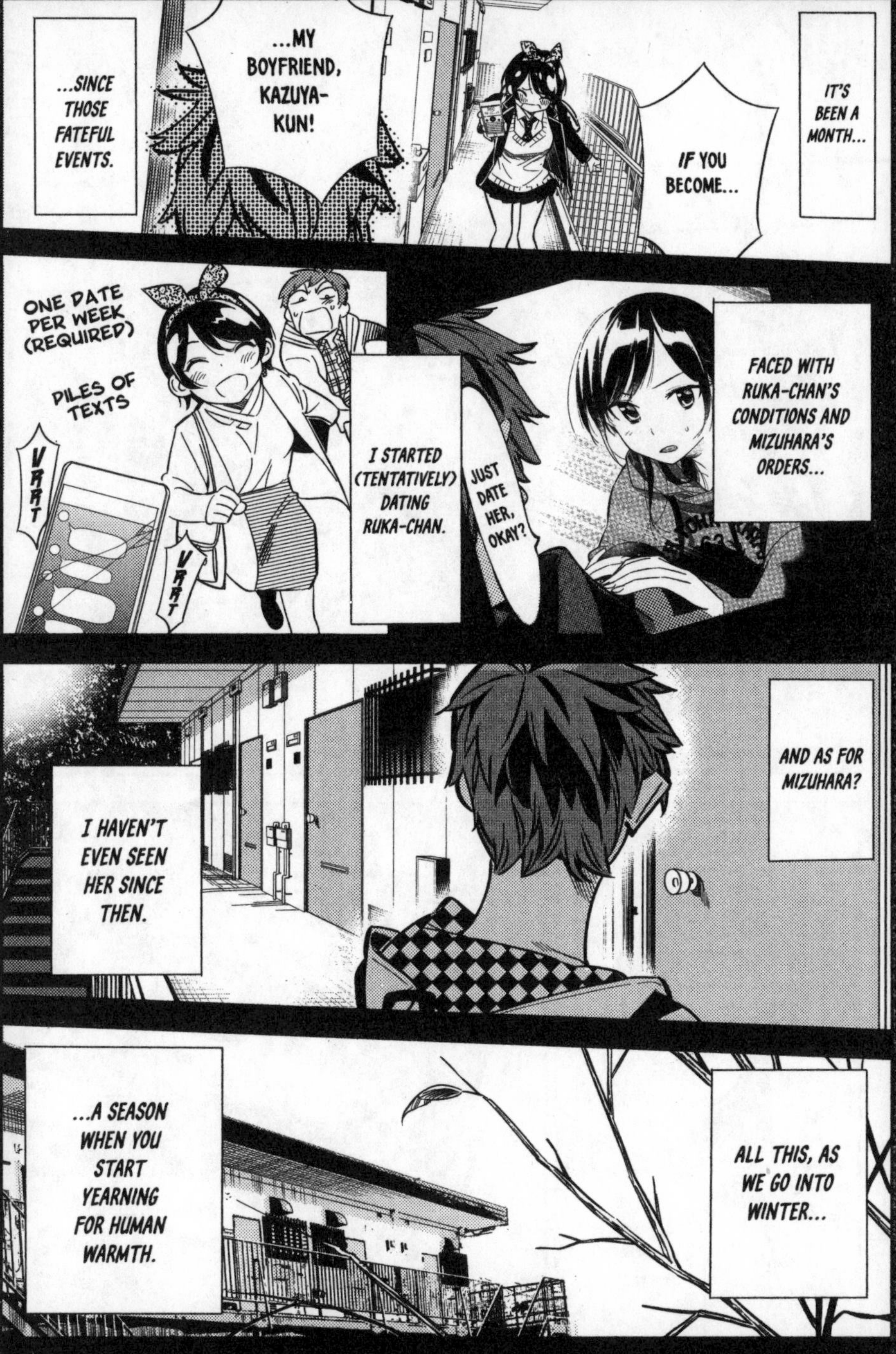
IT'S BEEN A MONTH...
IF YOU BECOME...
...MY BOYFRIEND, KAZUYA-KUN!
...SINCE THOSE FATEFUL EVENTS.
FACED WITH RUKA-CHAN'S CONDITIONS AND MIZUHARA'S ORDERS...
JUST DATE HER, OKAY?
I STARTED (TENTATIVELY) DATING RUKA-CHAN.
ONE DATE PER WEEK (REQUIRED)
PILES OF TEXTS
VRRT
VRRT
AND AS FOR MIZUHARA?
I HAVEN'T EVEN SEEN HER SINCE THEN.
ALL THIS, AS WE GO INTO WINTER...
...A SEASON WHEN YOU START YEARNING FOR HUMAN WARMTH.

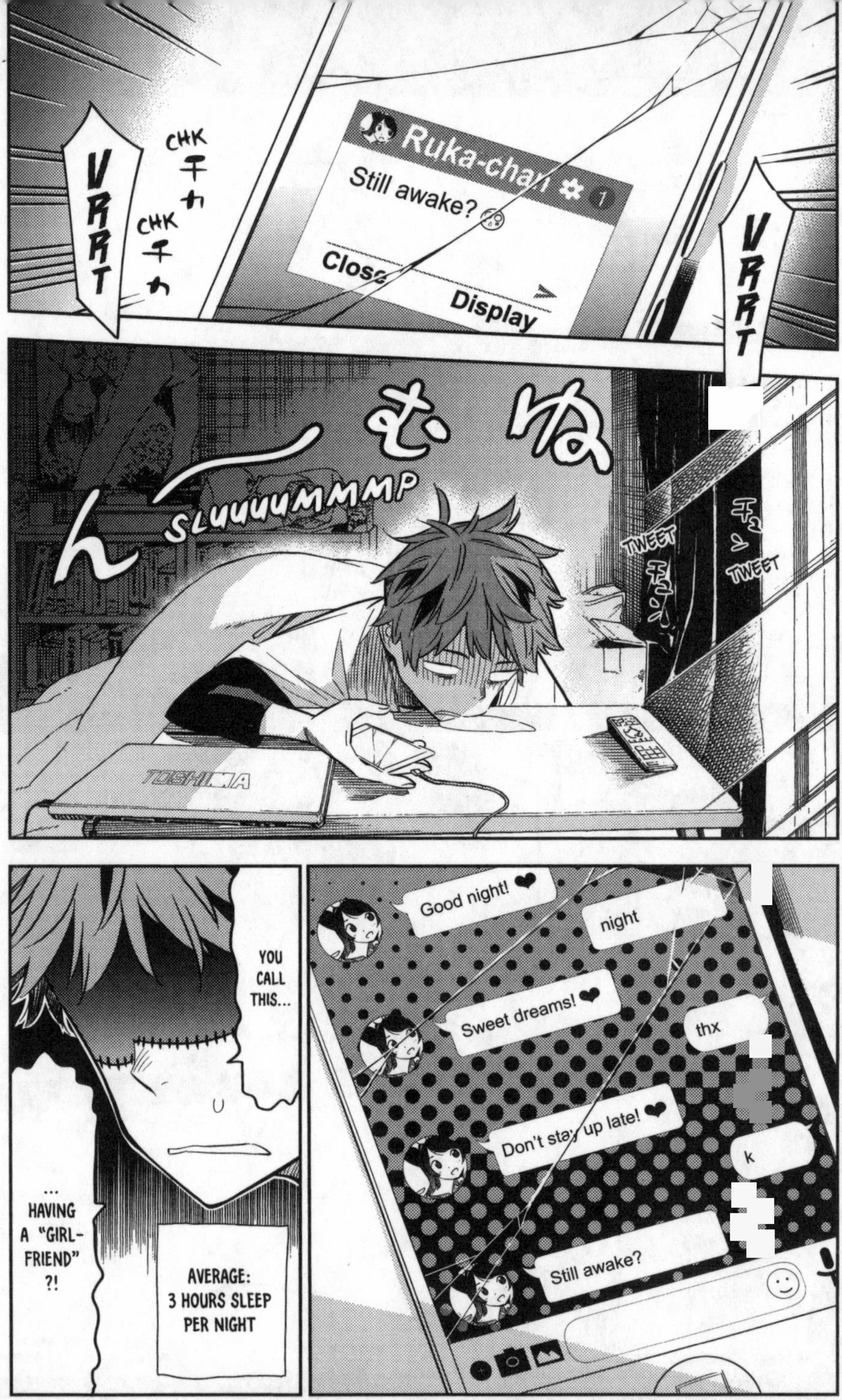
VRRT
Ruka-chan
1
Still awake?
Close
Display
CHK
CHK
VRRT
SLUUUUMMMP
TWEET
TWEET
TOSHIMA
Good night!
night
Sweet dreams!
thx
Don't stay up late!
k
Still awake?
YOU CALL THIS...
...HAVING A "GIRL-FRIEND"?!
AVERAGE: 3 HOURS SLEEP PER NIGHT

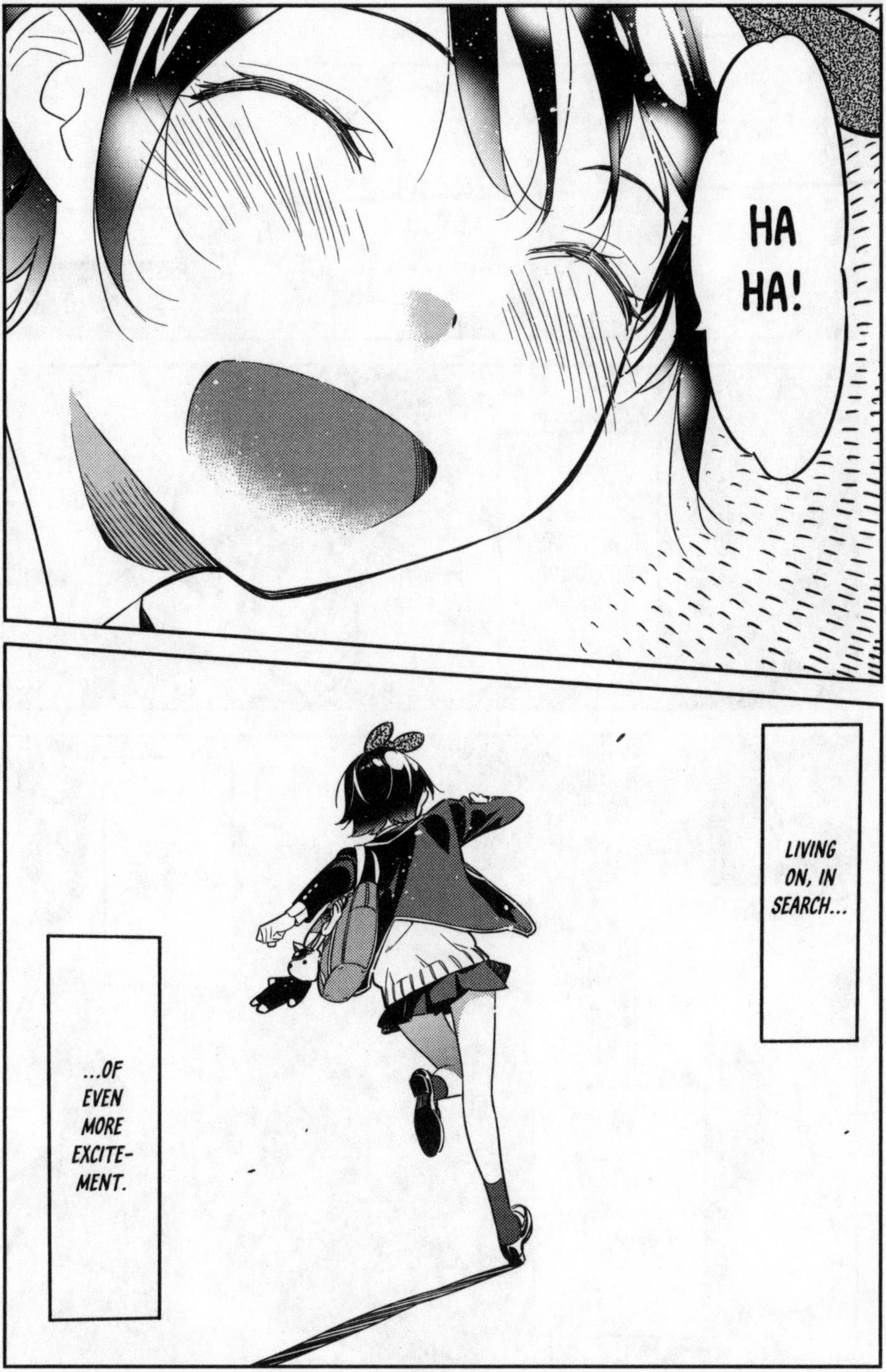
HA HA!
LIVING ON, IN SEARCH...
...OF EVEN MORE EXCITE-MENT.

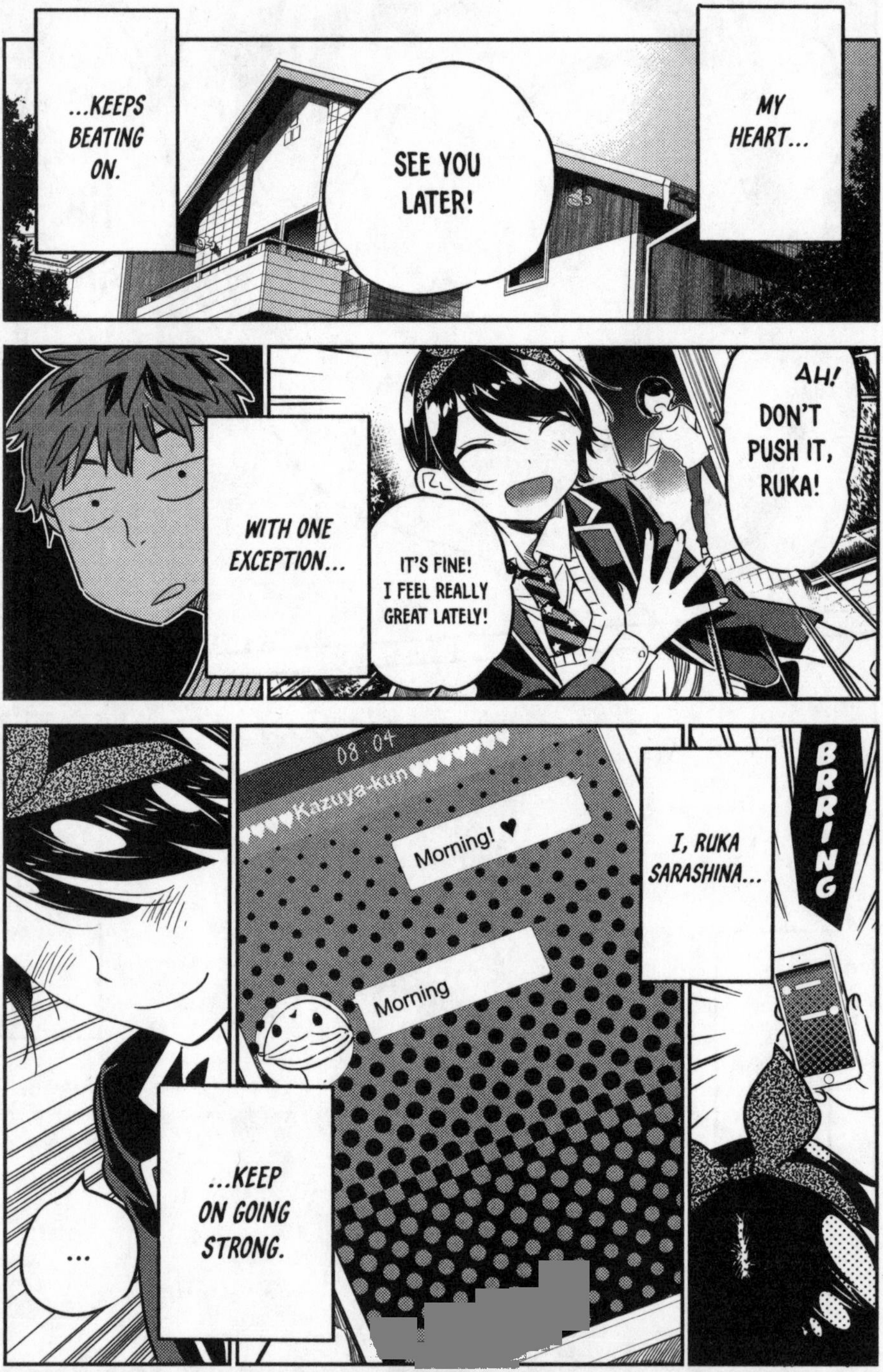
MY HEART...
SEE YOU LATER!
...KEEPS BEATING ON.
AH! DON'T PUSH IT, RUKA!
IT'S FINE! I FEEL REALLY GREAT LATELY!
WITH ONE EXCEPTION...
BRRING
I, RUKA SARASHINA...
08.04
♥♥♥Kazuya-kun♥♥♥♥♥♥
Morning! ♥
Morning
...KEEP ON GOING STRONG.
...

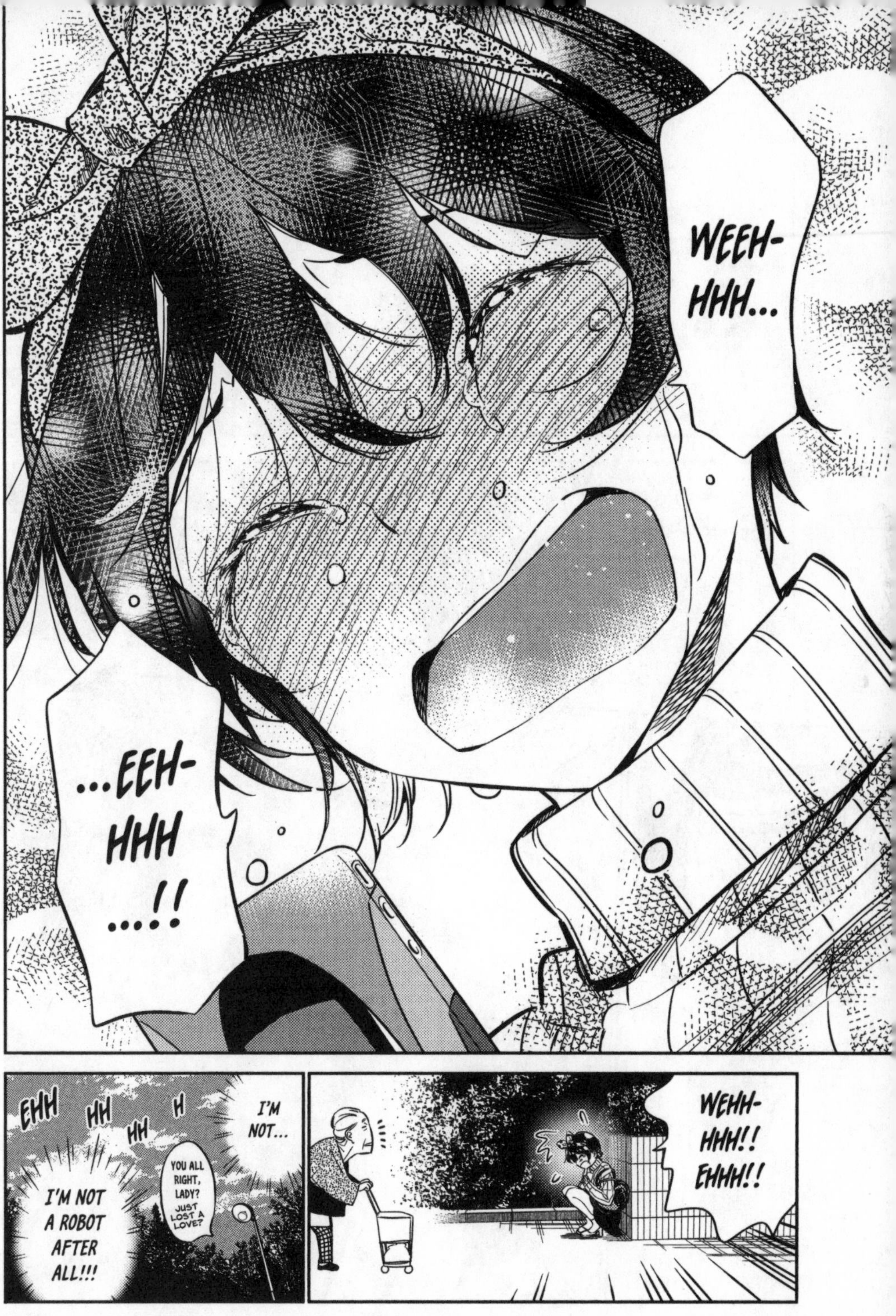
WEEH-HHH...
...EEH-HHH...!!
WEHH-HHH!! EHHH!!
I'M NOT...
EHH HH HH H
YOU ALL RIGHT, LADY? JUST LOST A LOVE?
I'M NOT A ROBOT AFTER ALL!!!

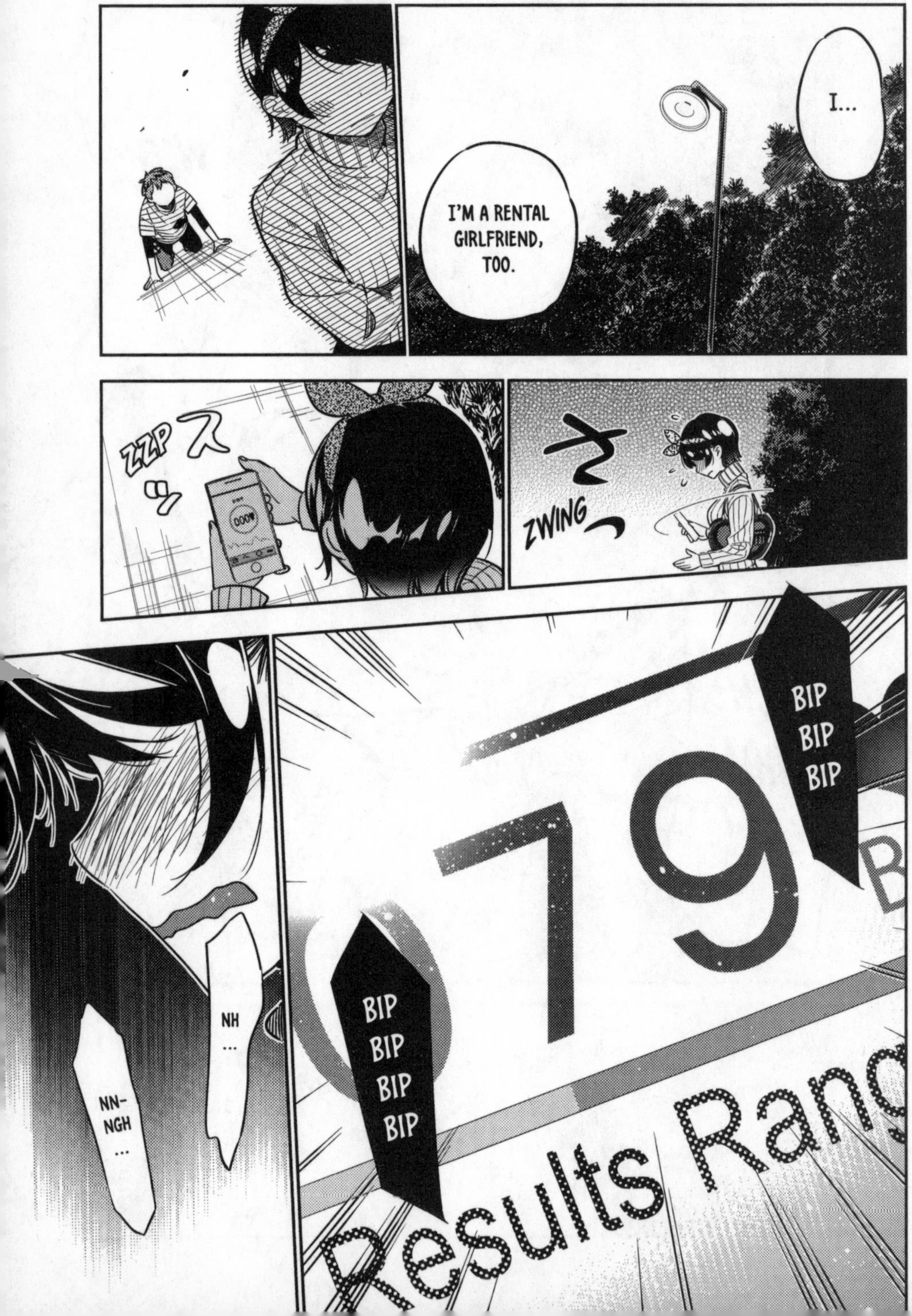
I...
I'M A RENTAL GIRLFRIEND, TOO.
さ
ZWING
ス
ッ
ZZP
BIP BIP BIP
79
Results Rang
BIP BIP BIP BIP
NH...
NN-NGH...

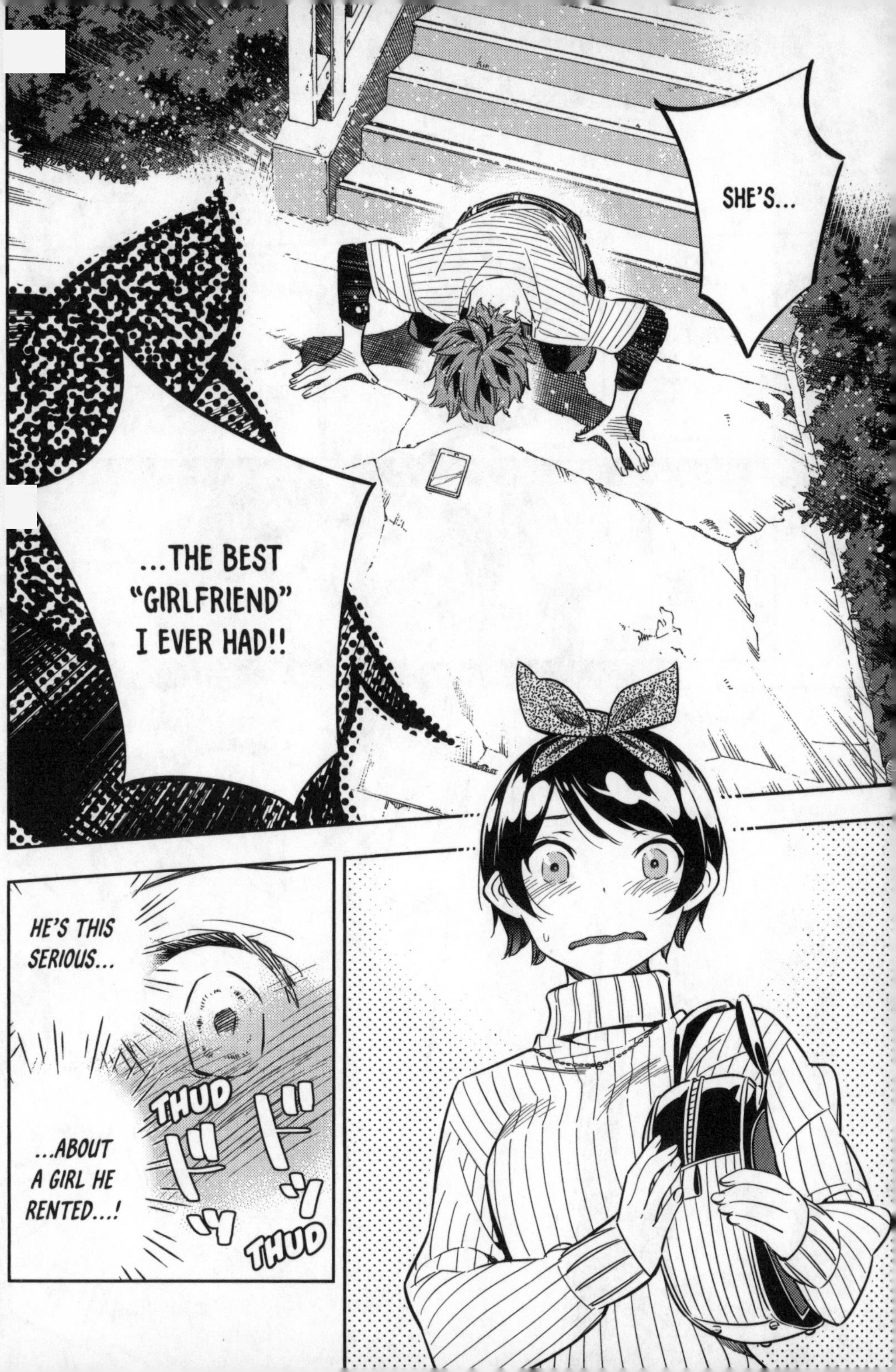
SHE'S...
..."THE BEST "GIRLFRIEND" I EVER HAD!!
HE'S THIS SERIOUS...
THUD
ドッ
ドッ
THUD
...ABOUT A GIRL HE RENTED...!

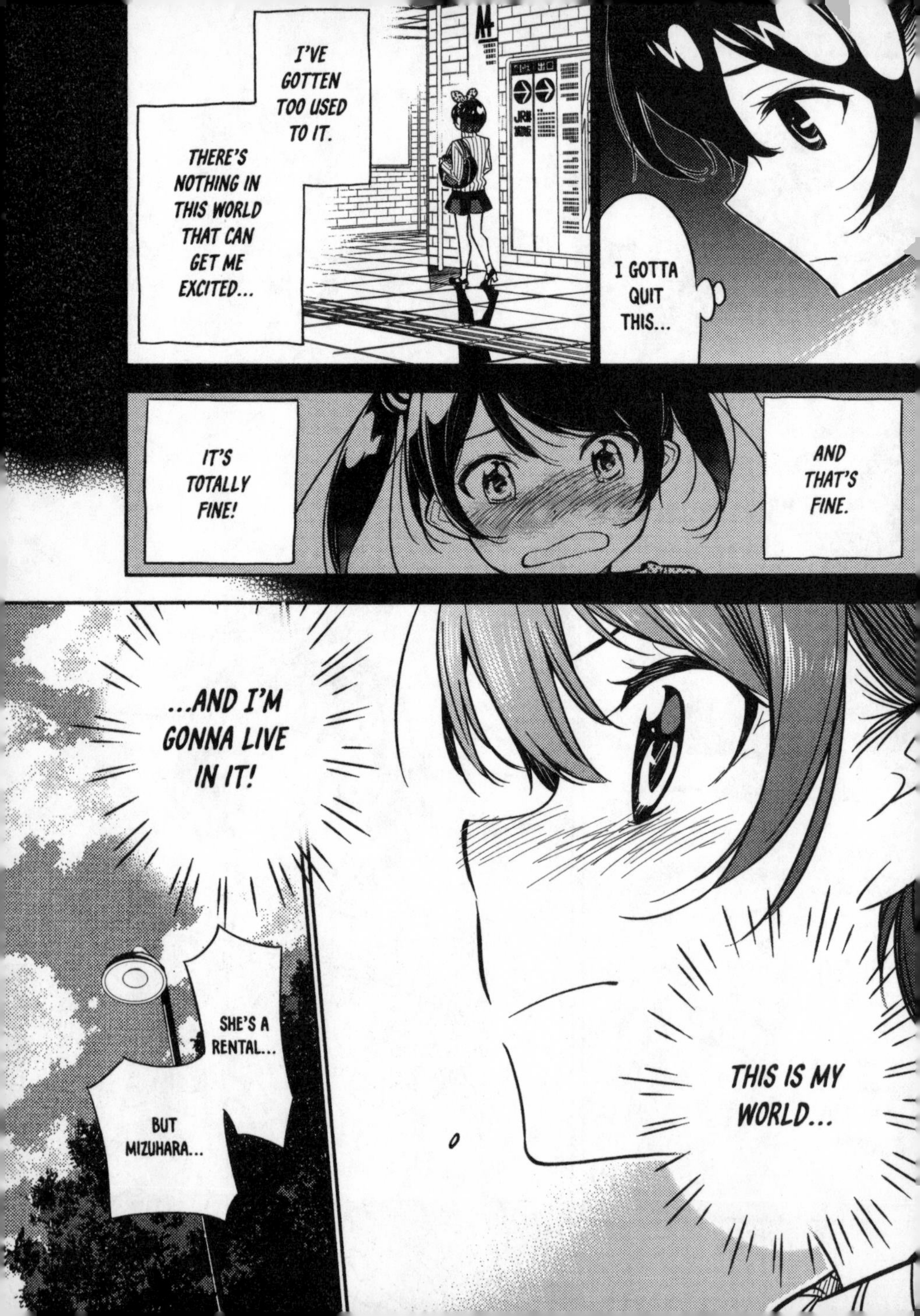
I GOTTA QUIT THIS...
I'VE GOTTEN TOO USED TO IT.
THERE'S NOTHING IN THIS WORLD THAT CAN GET ME EXCITED...
AND THAT'S FINE.
IT'S TOTALLY FINE!
THIS IS MY WORLD...
...AND I'M GONNA LIVE IN IT!
SHE'S A RENTAL...
BUT MIZUHARA...

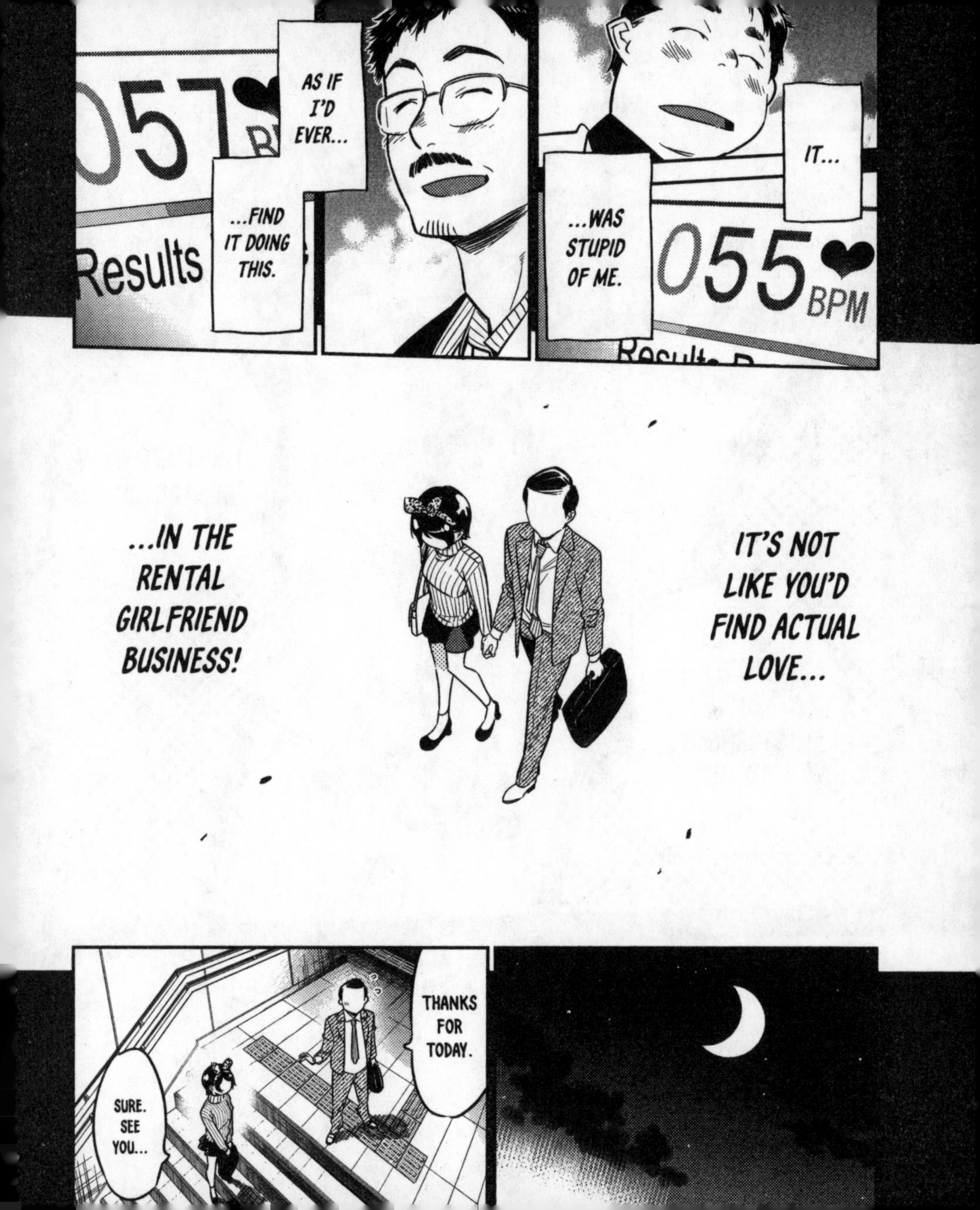
IT...
...WAS STUPID OF ME.
055 BPM
AS IF I'D EVER...
...FIND IT DOING THIS.
Results
IT'S NOT LIKE YOU'D FIND ACTUAL LOVE...
...IN THE RENTAL GIRLFRIEND BUSINESS!
THANKS FOR TODAY.
SURE. SEE YOU...

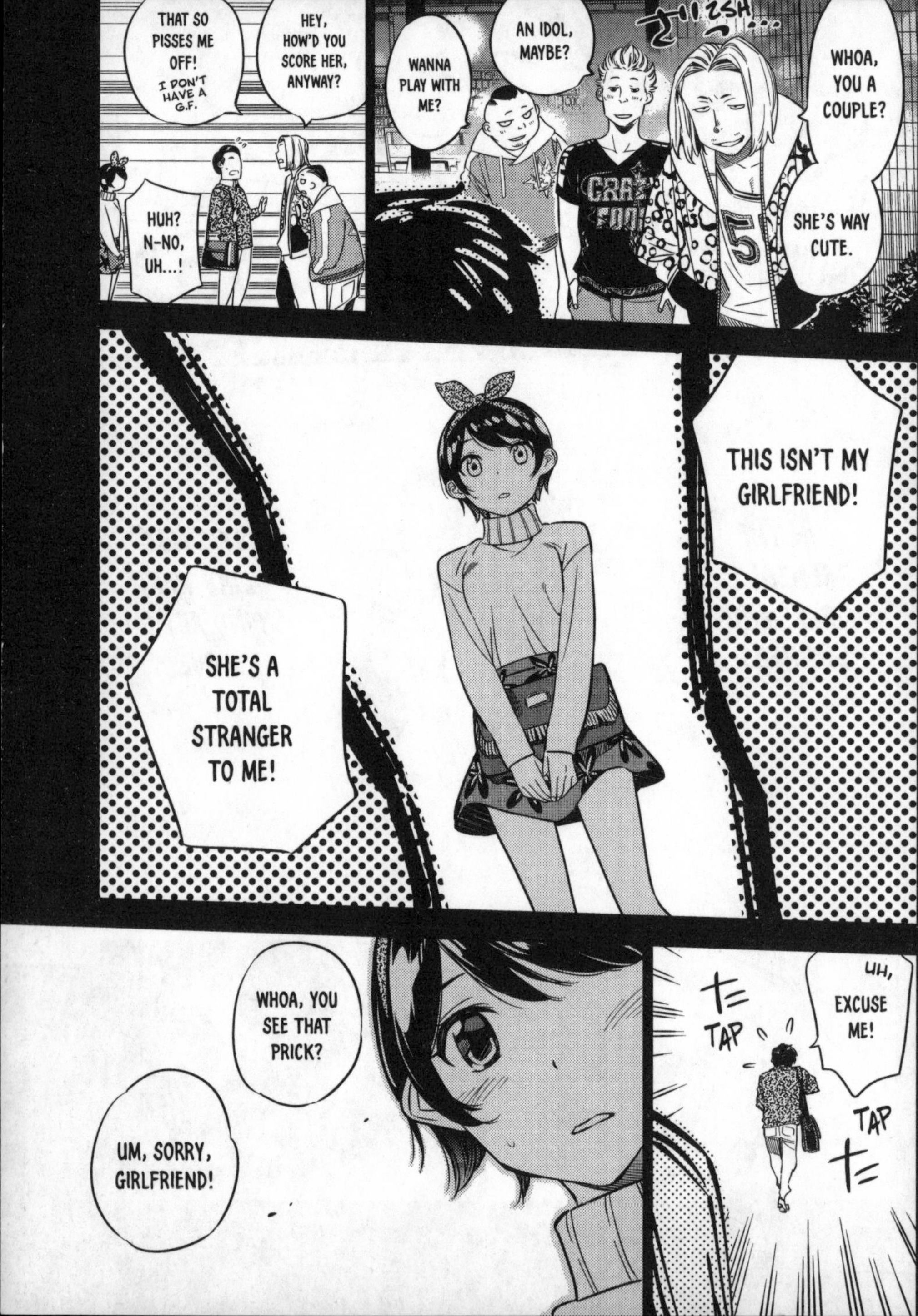
ZSH...
WHOA, YOU A COUPLE?
SHE'S WAY CUTE.
AN IDOL, MAYBE?
WANNA PLAY WITH ME?
HEY, HOW'D YOU SCORE HER, ANYWAY?
THAT SO PISSES ME OFF!
I DON'T HAVE A G.F.
HUH? N-NO, UH...!
THIS ISN'T MY GIRLFRIEND!
SHE'S A TOTAL STRANGER TO ME!
UH, EXCUSE ME!
TAP
TAP
WHOA, YOU SEE THAT PRICK?
UM, SORRY, GIRLFRIEND!

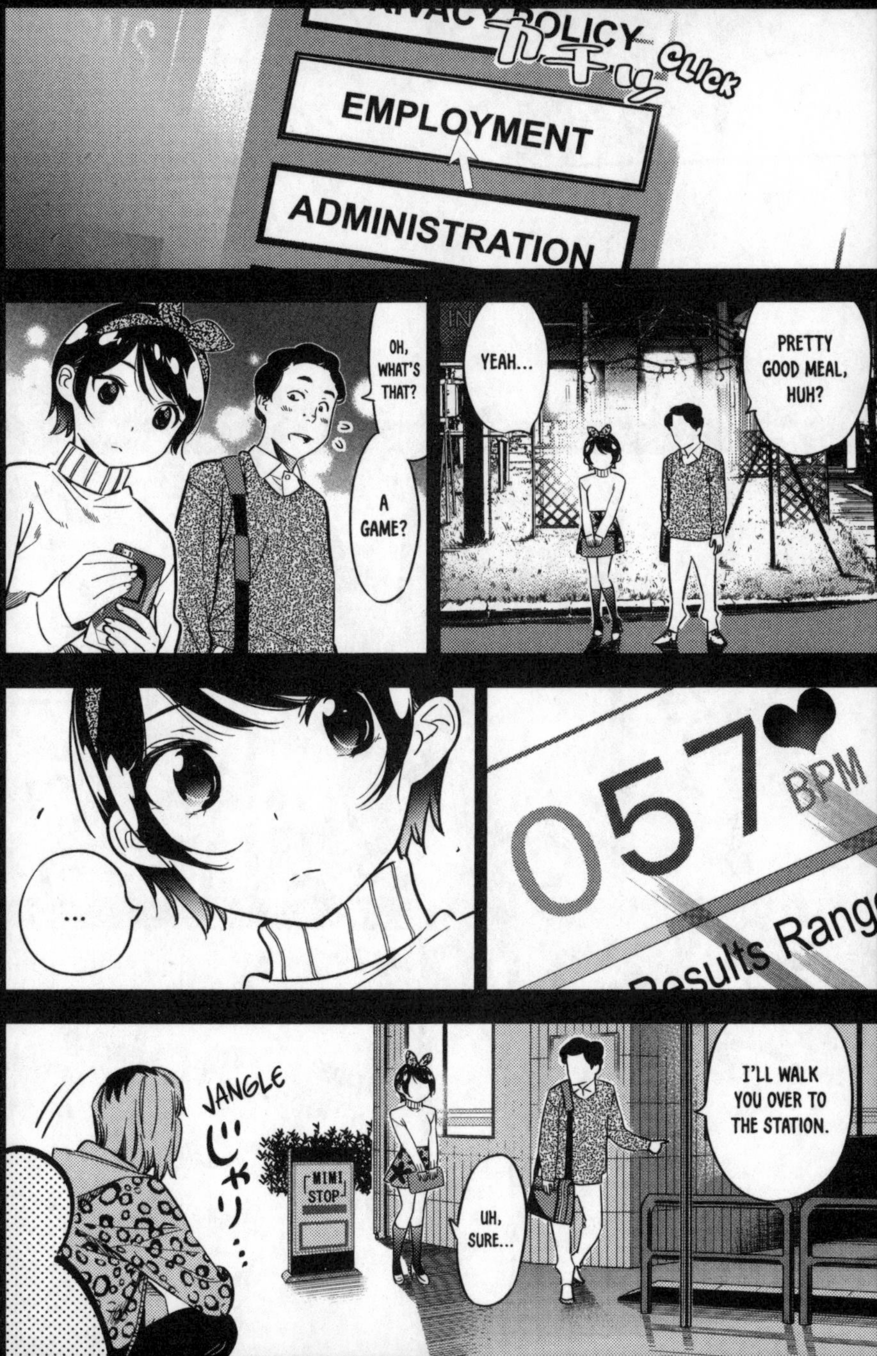
POLICY
カチッ
CLICK
EMPLOYMENT
ADMINISTRATION
PRETTY GOOD MEAL, HUH?
YEAH...
OH, WHAT'S THAT?
A GAME?
057
BPM
Results Rang
...
I'LL WALK YOU OVER TO THE STATION.
UH, SURE...
MINI STOP
JANGLE
じゃり...

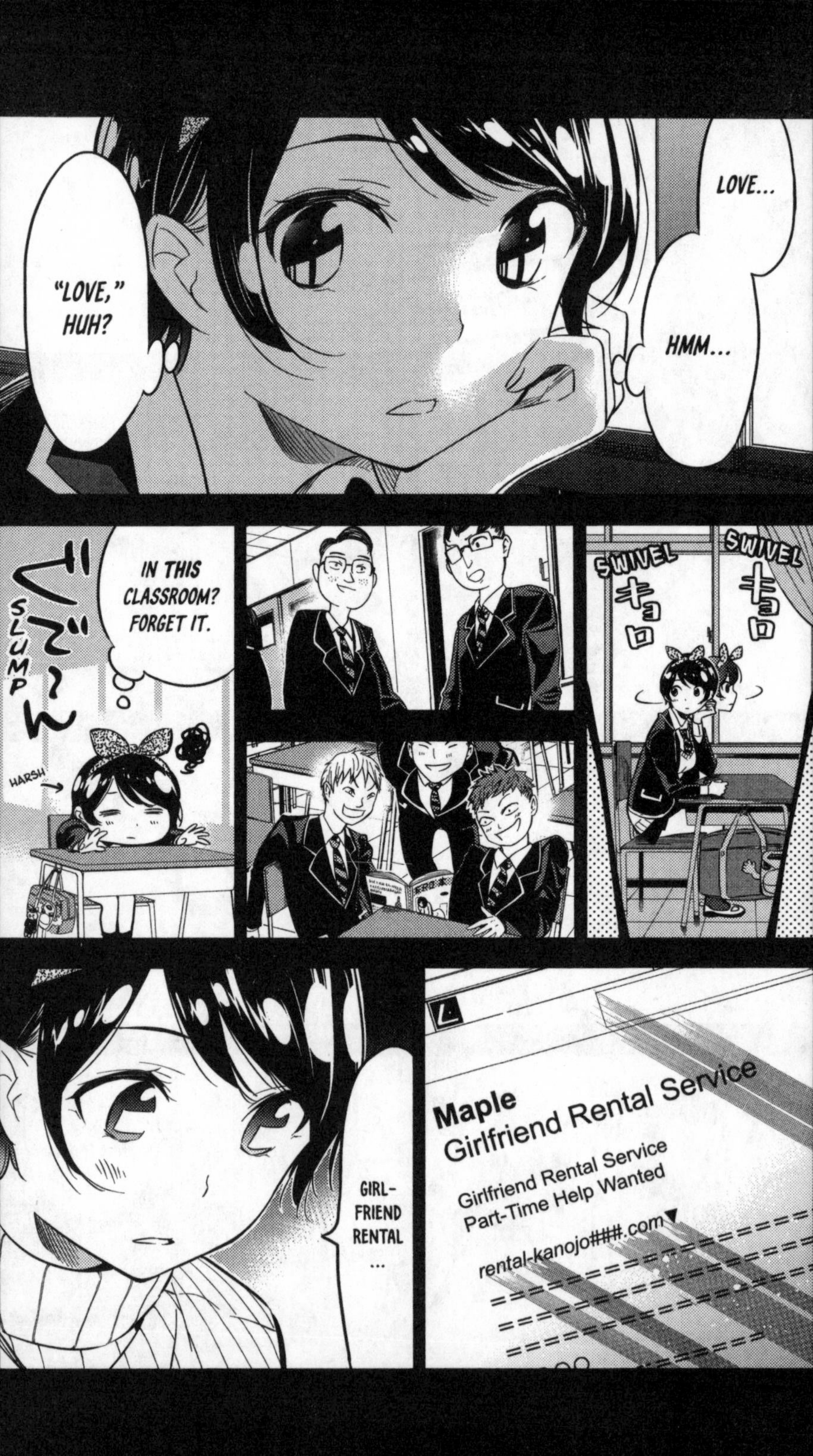
LOVE...
HMM...
"LOVE," HUH?
SWIVEL
キョロ
SWIVEL
キョロ
IN THIS CLASSROOM? FORGET IT.
でざ～ん
SLUMP
HARSH
Maple
Girlfriend Rental Service
Girlfriend Rental Service
Part-Time Help Wanted
rental-kanojo###.com
GIRL-FRIEND RENTAL ...

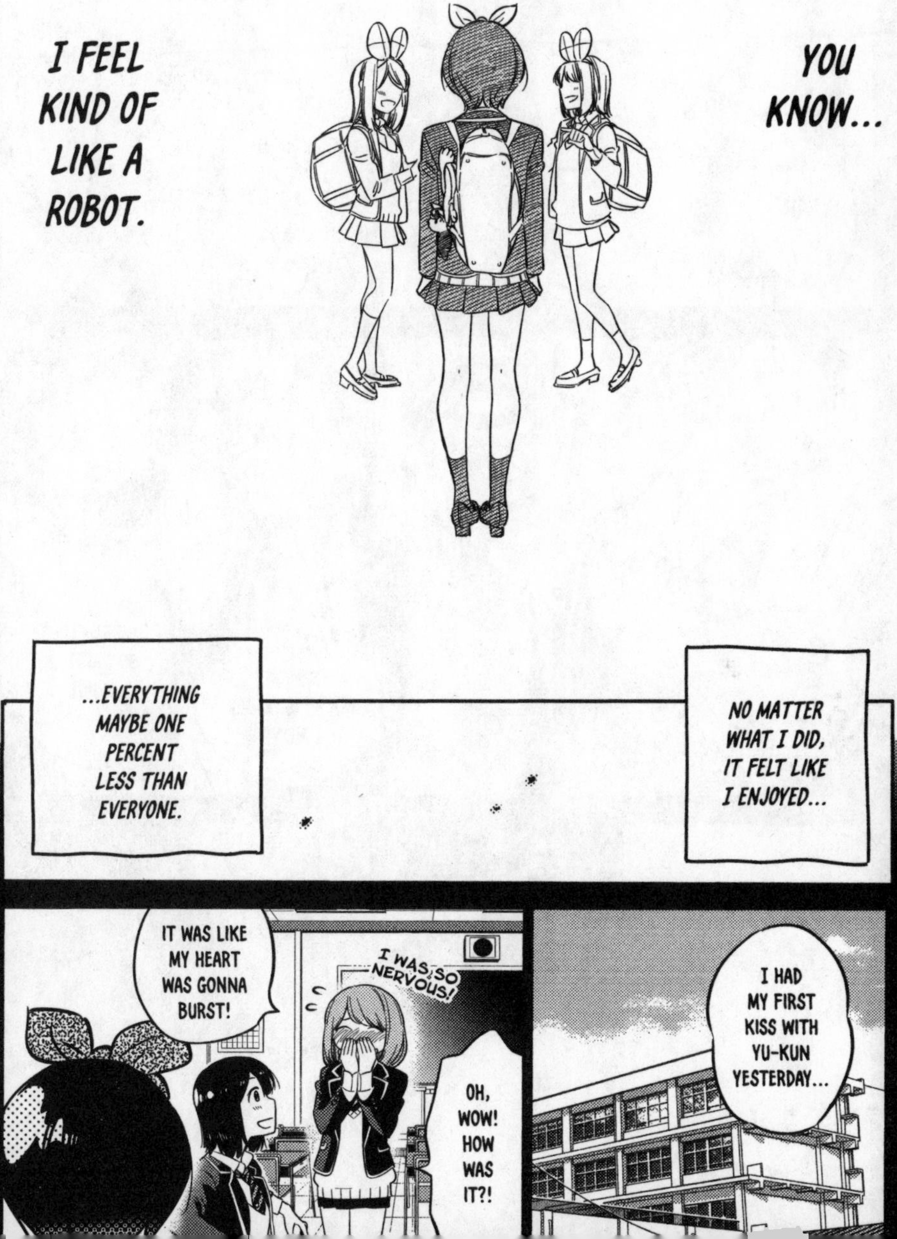
YOU KNOW...
I FEEL KIND OF LIKE A ROBOT.
NO MATTER WHAT I DID, IT FELT LIKE I ENJOYED...
...EVERYTHING MAYBE ONE PERCENT LESS THAN EVERYONE.
I HAD MY FIRST KISS WITH YU-KUN YESTERDAY...
OH, WOW! HOW WAS IT?!
I WAS SO NERVOUS!
IT WAS LIKE MY HEART WAS GONNA BURST!

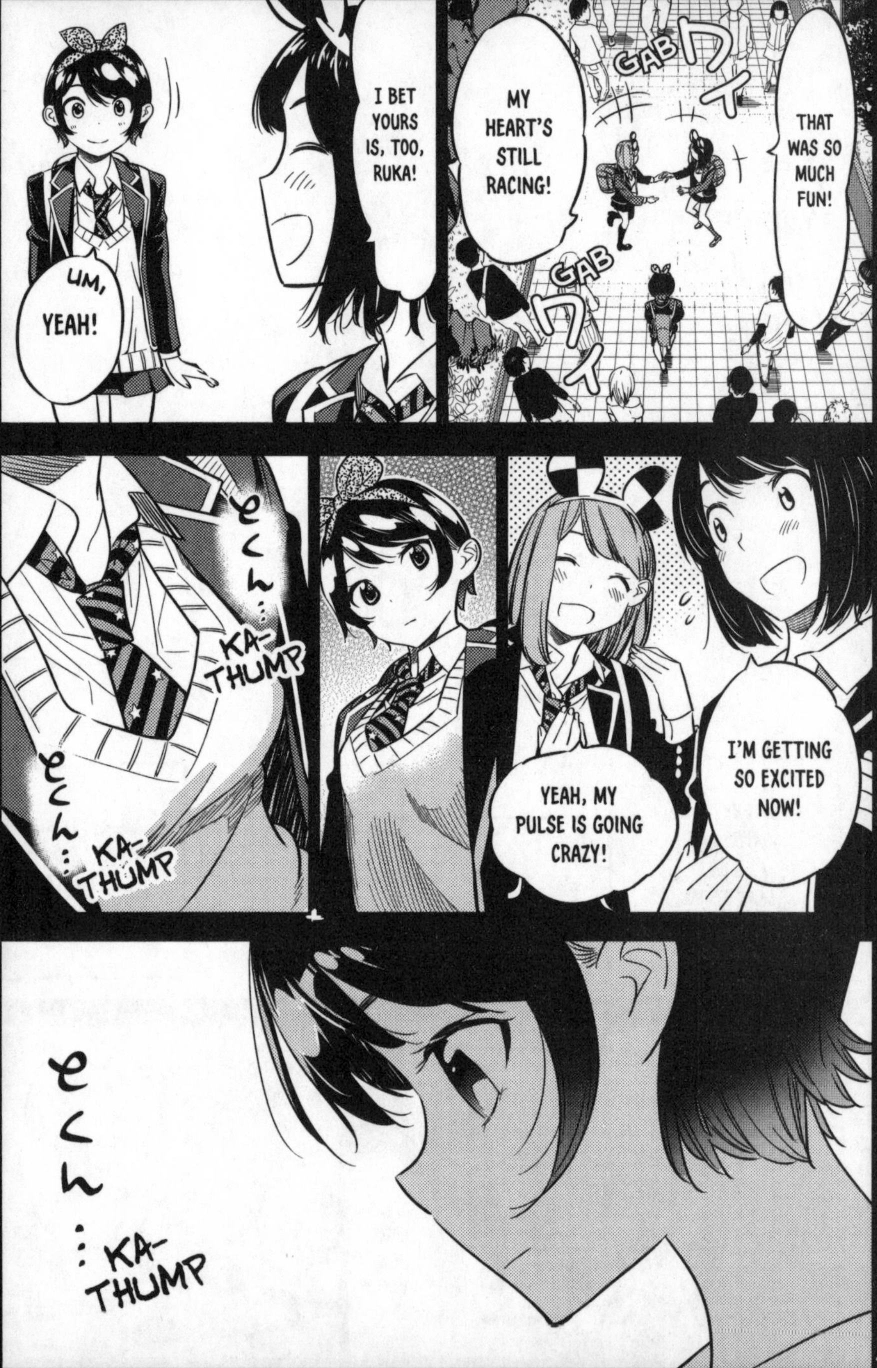
GAB ワイ
THAT WAS SO MUCH FUN!
MY HEART'S STILL RACING!
GAB ワイ
I BET YOURS IS, TOO, RUKA!
UM, YEAH!
I'M GETTING SO EXCITED NOW!
YEAH, MY PULSE IS GOING CRAZY!
とくん… KA-THUMP
とくん… KA-THUMP
とくん… KA-THUMP

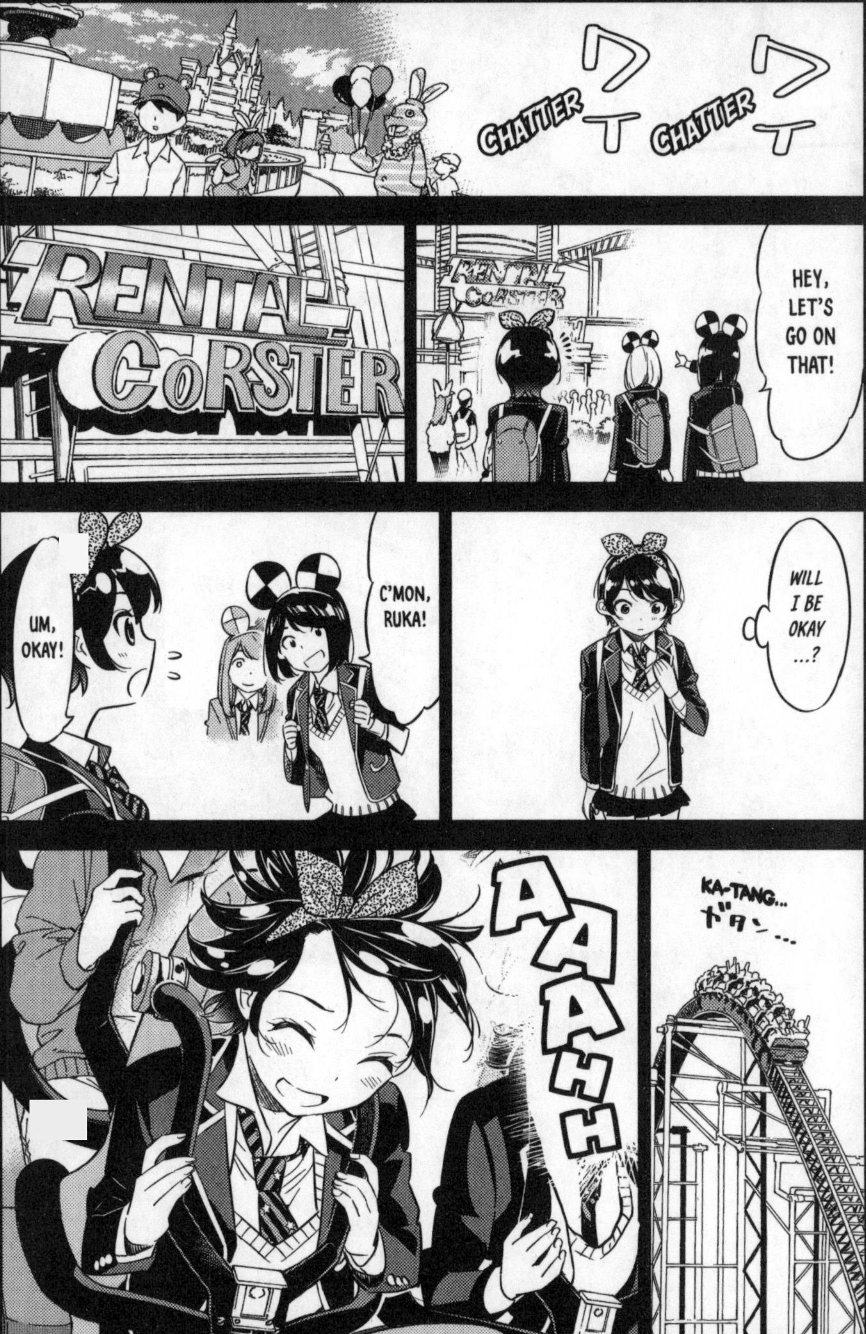
CHATTER ワイ
CHATTER ワイ
HEY, LET'S GO ON THAT!
RENTAL CORSTER
RENTAL CoRSTER
WILL I BE OKAY ...?
C'MON, RUKA!
UM, OKAY!
KA-TANG... ガタン…
AAAHH

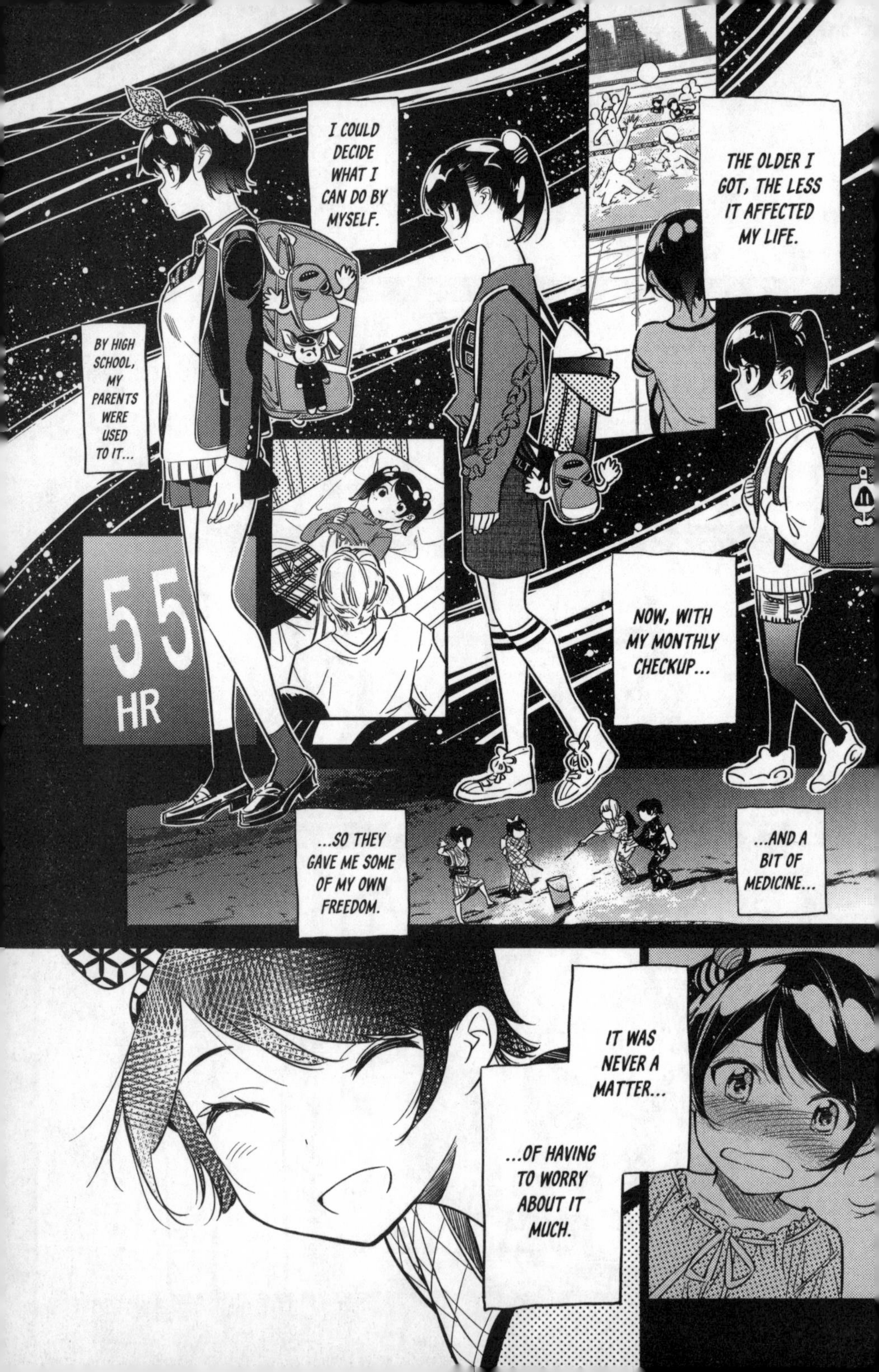
NOW, WITH MY MONTHLY CHECKUP...
...AND A BIT OF MEDICINE...
THE OLDER I GOT, THE LESS IT AFFECTED MY LIFE.
BY HIGH SCHOOL, MY PARENTS WERE USED TO IT...
...SO THEY GAVE ME SOME OF MY OWN FREEDOM.
I COULD DECIDE WHAT I CAN DO BY MYSELF.
55 HR
IT WAS NEVER A MATTER...
...OF HAVING TO WORRY ABOUT IT MUCH.

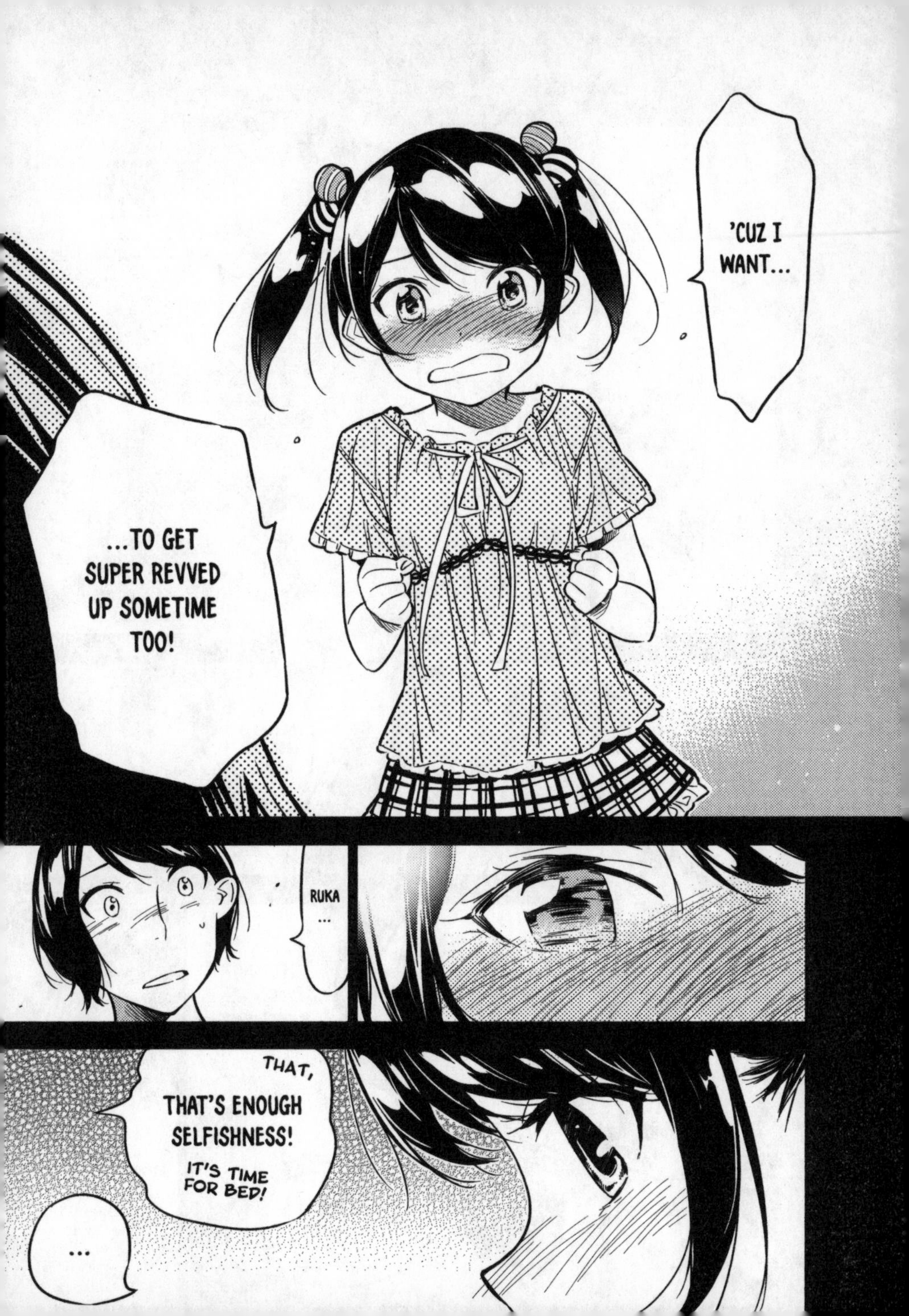
'CUZ I WANT...
...TO GET SUPER REVVED UP SOMETIME TOO!
RUKA ...
THAT, THAT'S ENOUGH SELFISHNESS! IT'S TIME FOR BED!
...

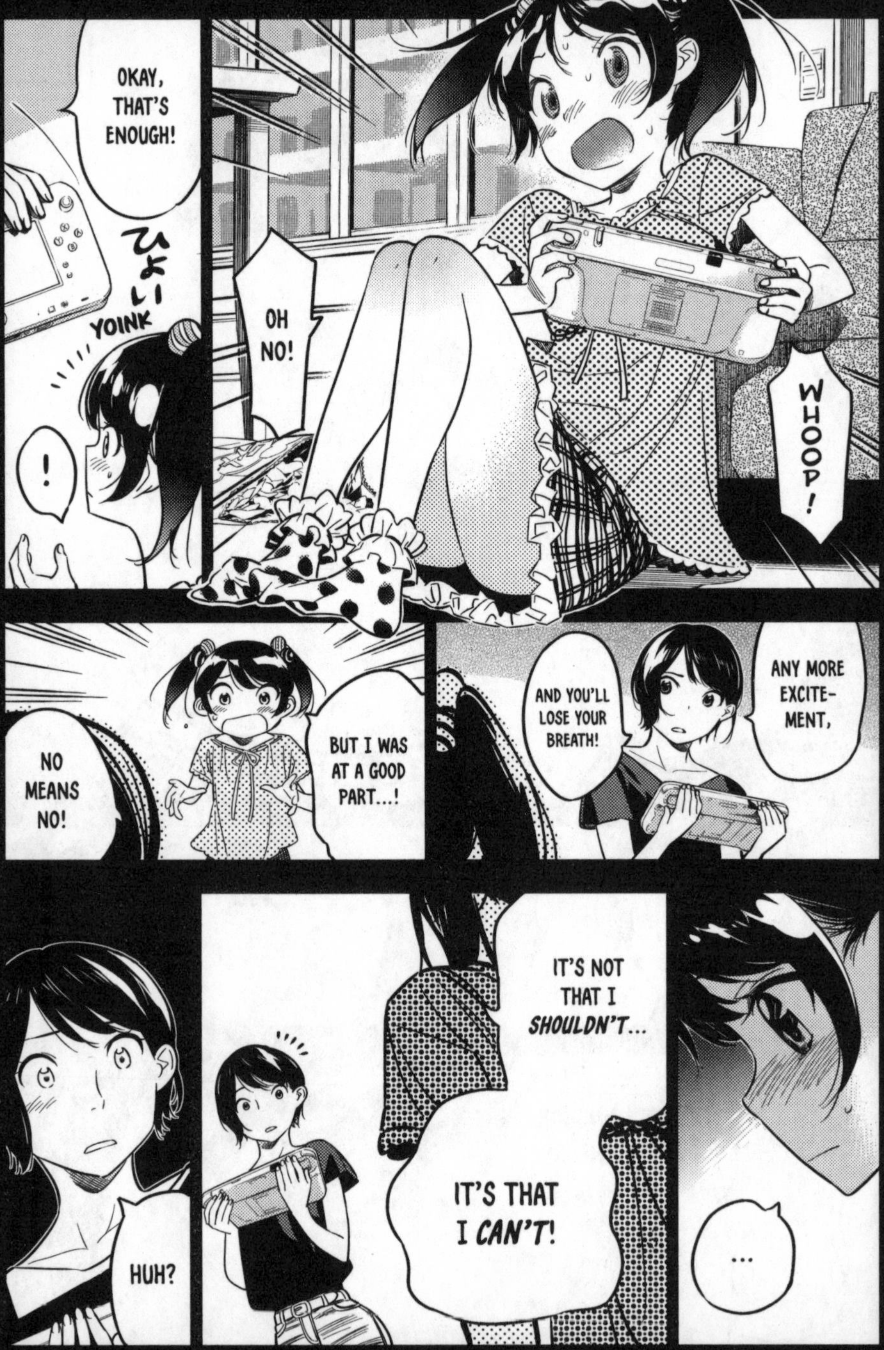
WHOOP!
OH NO!
OKAY, THAT'S ENOUGH!
ひょい
YOINK
!
ANY MORE EXCITE- MENT,
AND YOU'LL LOSE YOUR BREATH!
BUT I WAS AT A GOOD PART...!
NO MEANS NO!
...
IT'S NOT THAT I SHOULDN'T...
IT'S THAT I CAN'T!
HUH?

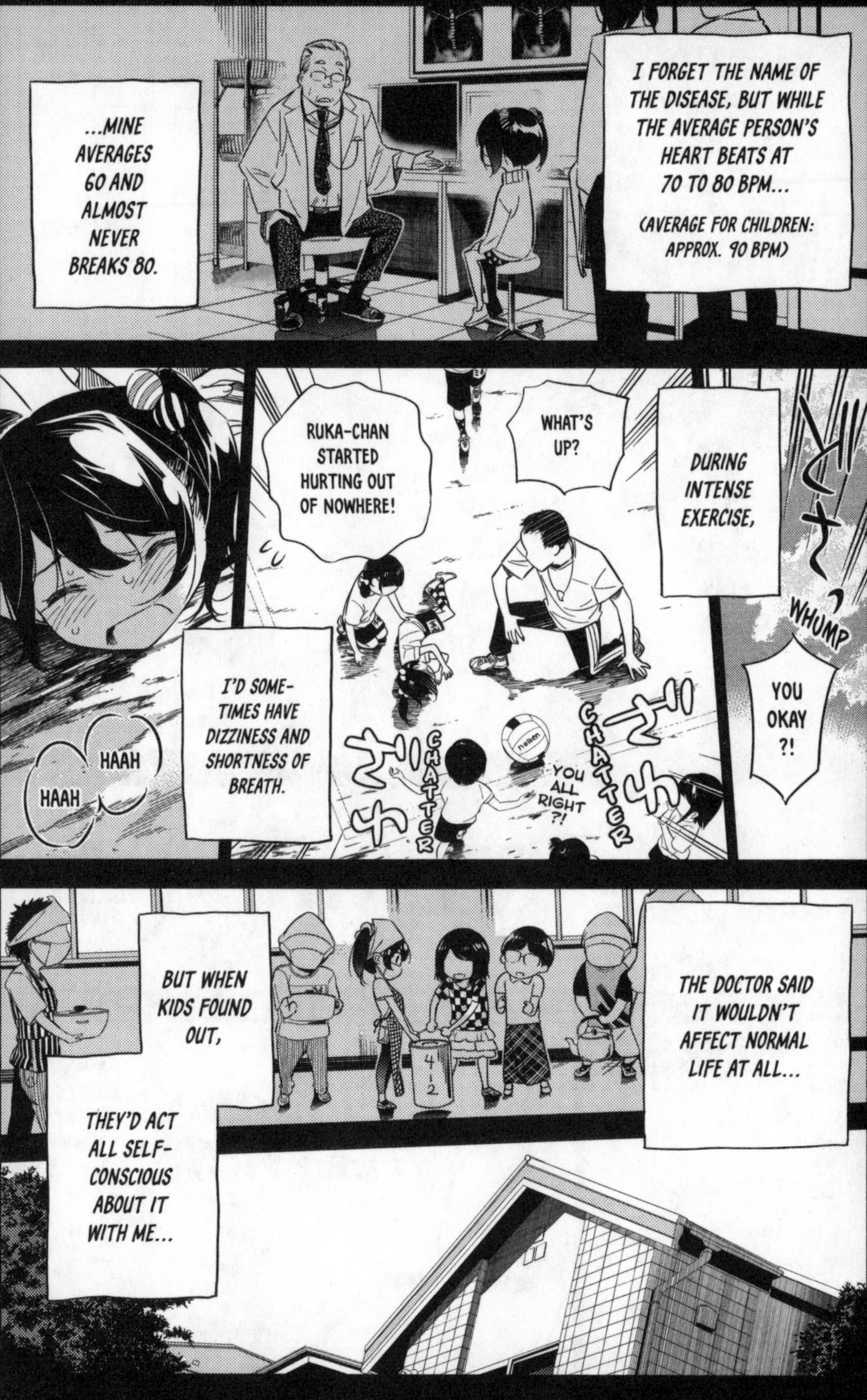
I FORGET THE NAME OF THE DISEASE, BUT WHILE THE AVERAGE PERSON'S HEART BEATS AT 70 TO 80 BPM...
(AVERAGE FOR CHILDREN: APPROX. 90 BPM)
...MINE AVERAGES 60 AND ALMOST NEVER BREAKS 80.
WHUMP
YOU OKAY?!
DURING INTENSE EXERCISE,
WHAT'S UP?
RUKA-CHAN STARTED HURTING OUT OF NOWHERE!
CHATTER
YOU ALL RIGHT?!
CHATTER
I'D SOME-TIMES HAVE DIZZINESS AND SHORTNESS OF BREATH.
HAAH
HAAH
THE DOCTOR SAID IT WOULDN'T AFFECT NORMAL LIFE AT ALL...
BUT WHEN KIDS FOUND OUT,
THEY'D ACT ALL SELF-CONSCIOUS ABOUT IT WITH ME...

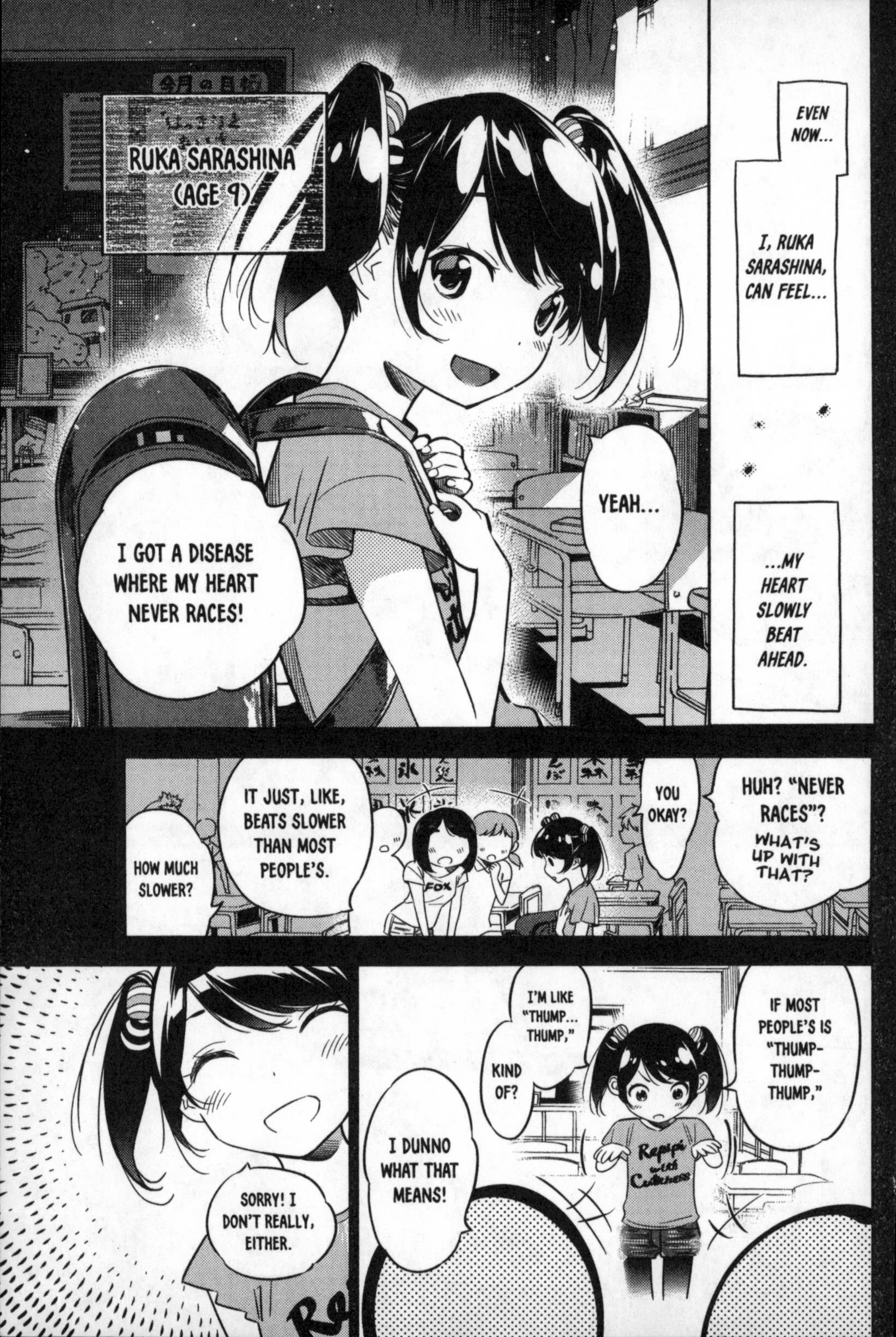
EVEN NOW...
I, RUKA SARASHINA, CAN FEEL...
...MY HEART SLOWLY BEAT AHEAD.
RUKA SARASHINA (AGE 9)
YEAH...
I GOT A DISEASE WHERE MY HEART NEVER RACES!
HUH? "NEVER RACES"? WHAT'S UP WITH THAT?
YOU OKAY?
IT JUST, LIKE, BEATS SLOWER THAN MOST PEOPLE'S.
HOW MUCH SLOWER?
IF MOST PEOPLE'S IS "THUMP-THUMP-THUMP,"
I'M LIKE "THUMP... THUMP,"
KIND OF?
I DUNNO WHAT THAT MEANS!
SORRY! I DON'T REALLY, EITHER.

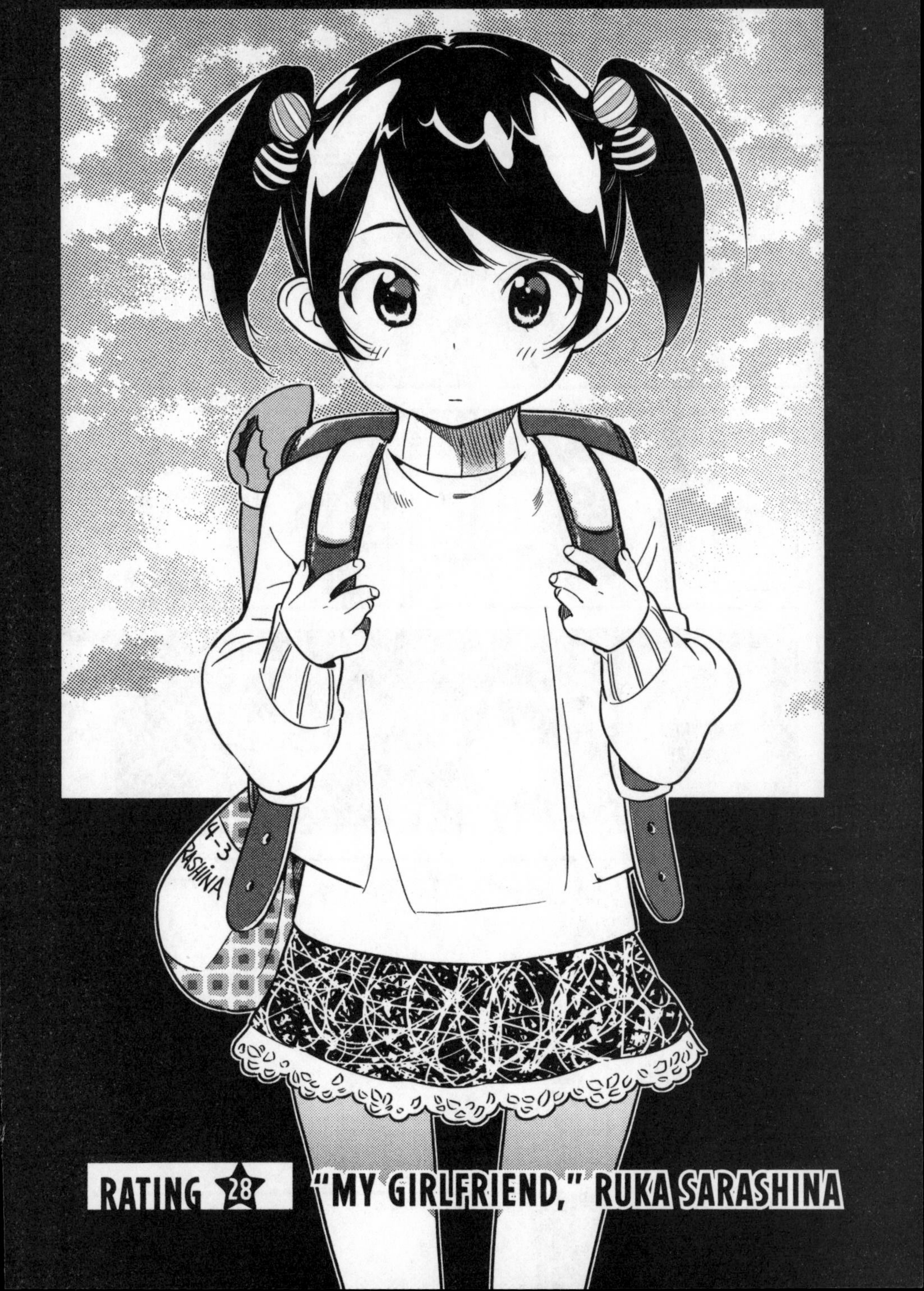
4-3
RASHINA
RATING 28 "MY GIRLFRIEND," RUKA SARASHINA

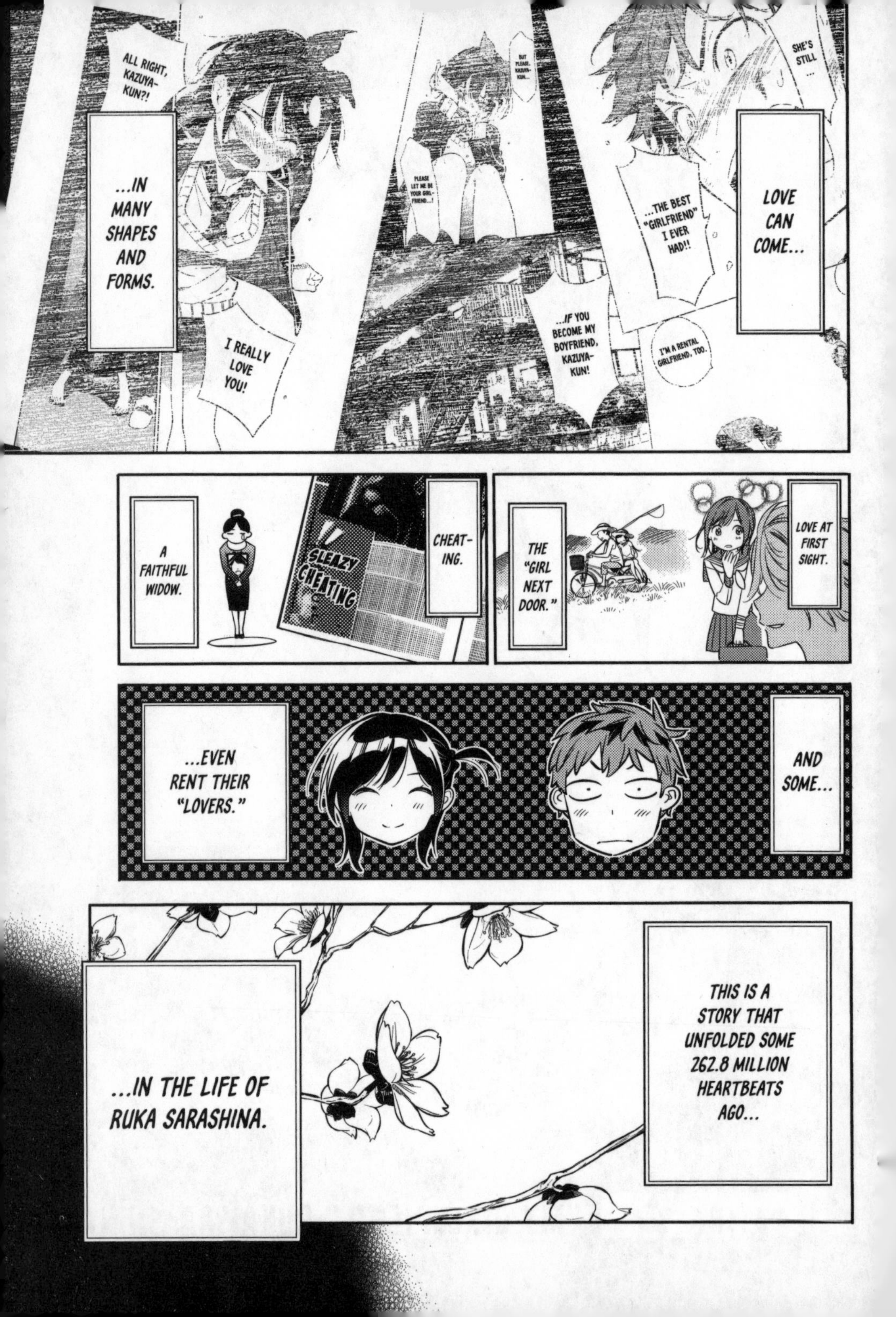
SHE'S STILL ...
LOVE CAN COME...
...THE BEST "GIRLFRIEND" I EVER HAD!!
I'M A RENTAL GIRLFRIEND, TOO.
BUT PLEASE, KAZUYA-KUN...
PLEASE LET ME BE YOUR GIRLFRIEND...!
...IF YOU BECOME MY BOYFRIEND, KAZUYA-KUN!
ALL RIGHT, KAZUYA-KUN?!
...IN MANY SHAPES AND FORMS.
I REALLY LOVE YOU!
LOVE AT FIRST SIGHT.
THE "GIRL NEXT DOOR."
CHEATING.
SLEAZY CHEATING
A FAITHFUL WIDOW.
AND SOME...
...EVEN RENT THEIR "LOVERS."
THIS IS A STORY THAT UNFOLDED SOME 262.8 MILLION HEARTBEATS AGO...
...IN THE LIFE OF RUKA SARASHINA.

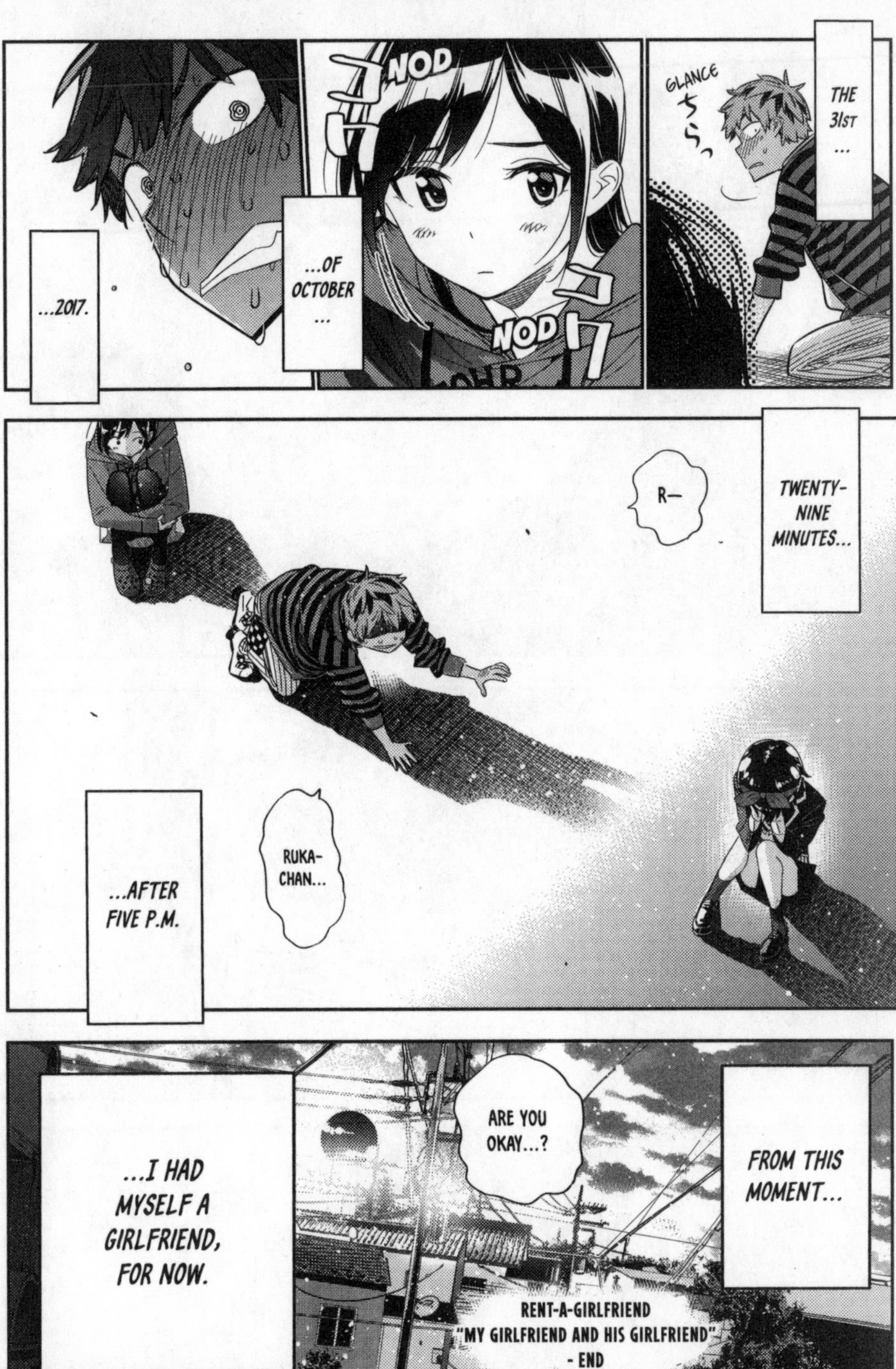
THE 31ST ...
GLANCE
ちらっ
NOD
NOD
...OF OCTOBER ...
...2017.
TWENTY-NINE MINUTES...
R—
RUKA-CHAN...
...AFTER FIVE P.M.
FROM THIS MOMENT...
ARE YOU OKAY...?
...I HAD MYSELF A GIRLFRIEND, FOR NOW.
RENT-A-GIRLFRIEND
"MY GIRLFRIEND AND HIS GIRLFRIEND"
- END

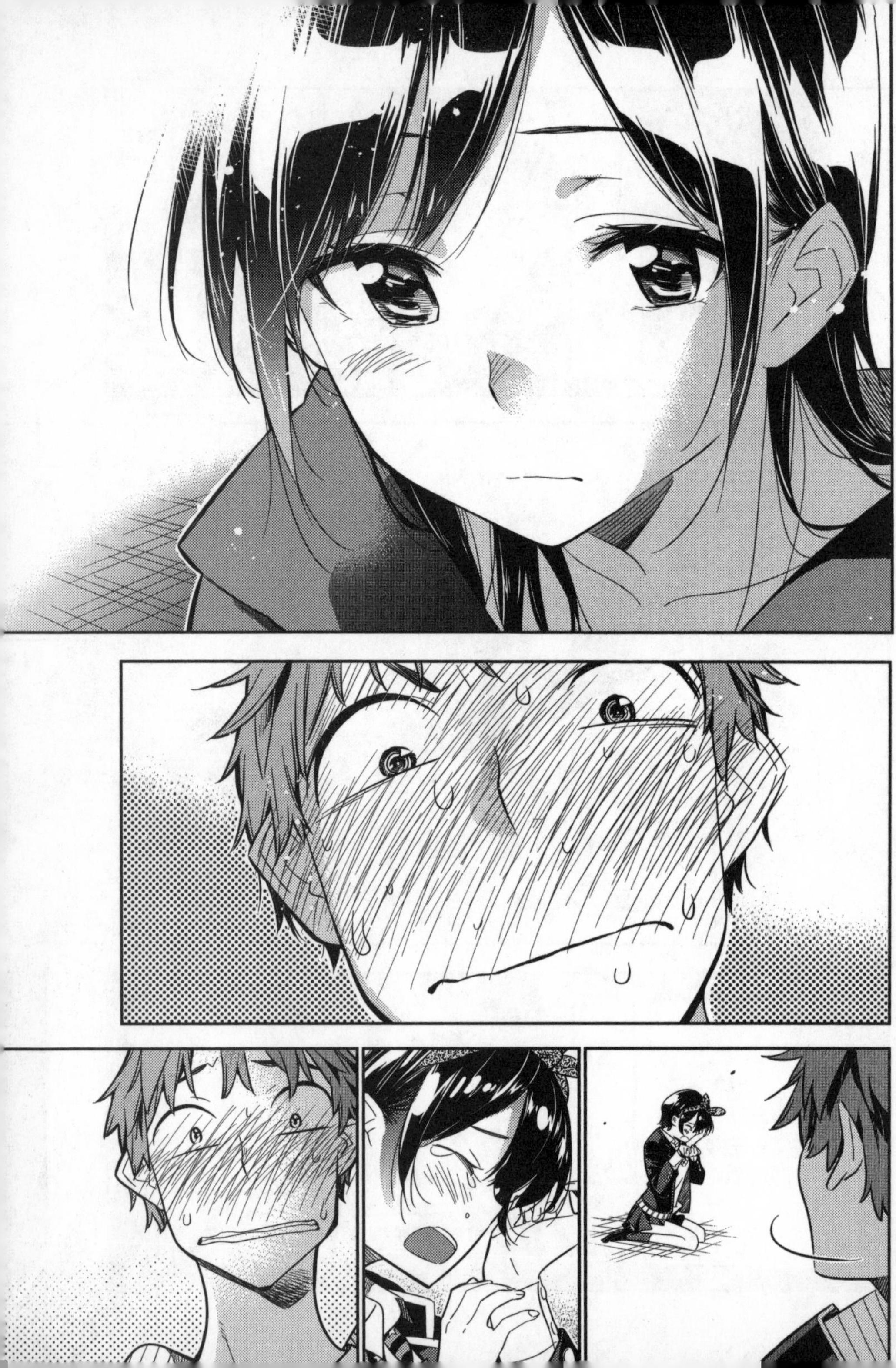

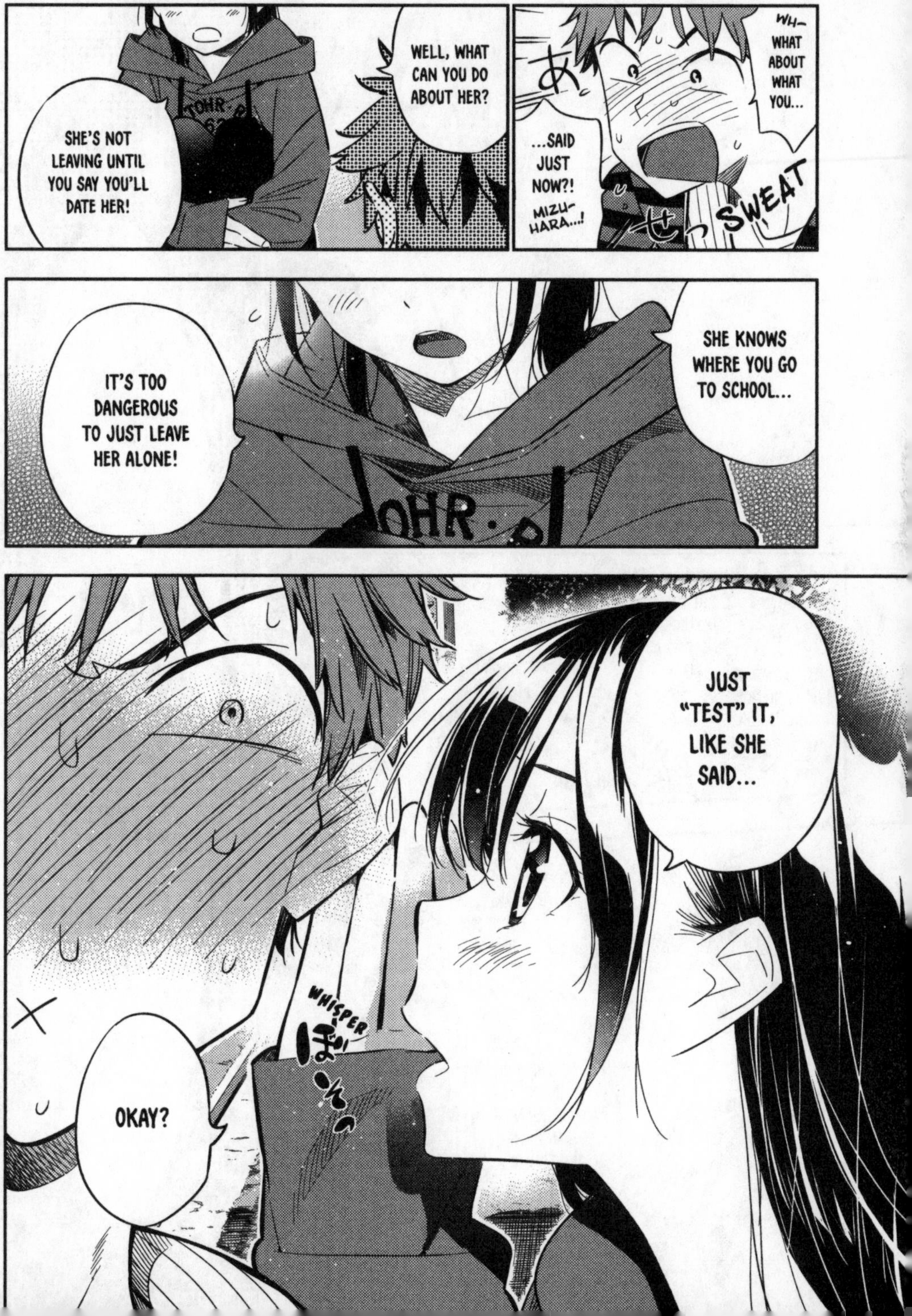
WH– WHAT ABOUT WHAT YOU...
あ
...SAID JUST NOW?!
MIZUHARA...!
せっ SWEAT
WELL, WHAT CAN YOU DO ABOUT HER?
SHE'S NOT LEAVING UNTIL YOU SAY YOU'LL DATE HER!
SHE KNOWS WHERE YOU GO TO SCHOOL...
IT'S TOO DANGEROUS TO JUST LEAVE HER ALONE!
JUST "TEST" IT, LIKE SHE SAID...
WHISPER
OKAY?

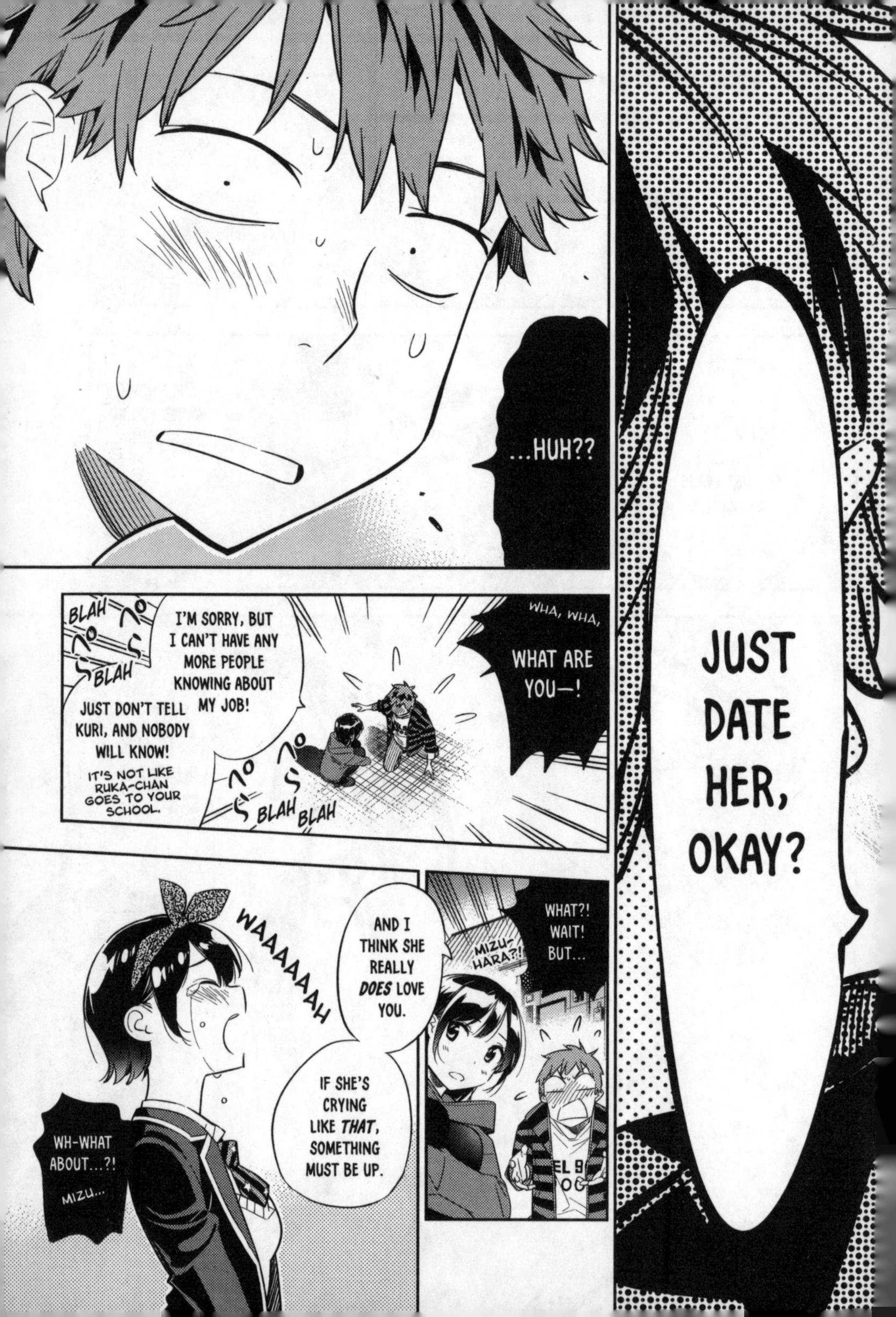
JUST DATE HER, OKAY?
...HUH??
WHA, WHA,
WHAT ARE YOU—!
I'M SORRY, BUT I CAN'T HAVE ANY MORE PEOPLE KNOWING ABOUT MY JOB!
JUST DON'T TELL KURI, AND NOBODY WILL KNOW!
IT'S NOT LIKE RUKA-CHAN GOES TO YOUR SCHOOL.
BLAH BLAH
BLAH BLAH
WHAT?! WAIT! BUT...
MIZU-HARA?!
AND I THINK SHE REALLY DOES LOVE YOU.
IF SHE'S CRYING LIKE THAT, SOMETHING MUST BE UP.
WAAAAAAAH
WH-WHAT ABOUT...?!
MIZU...

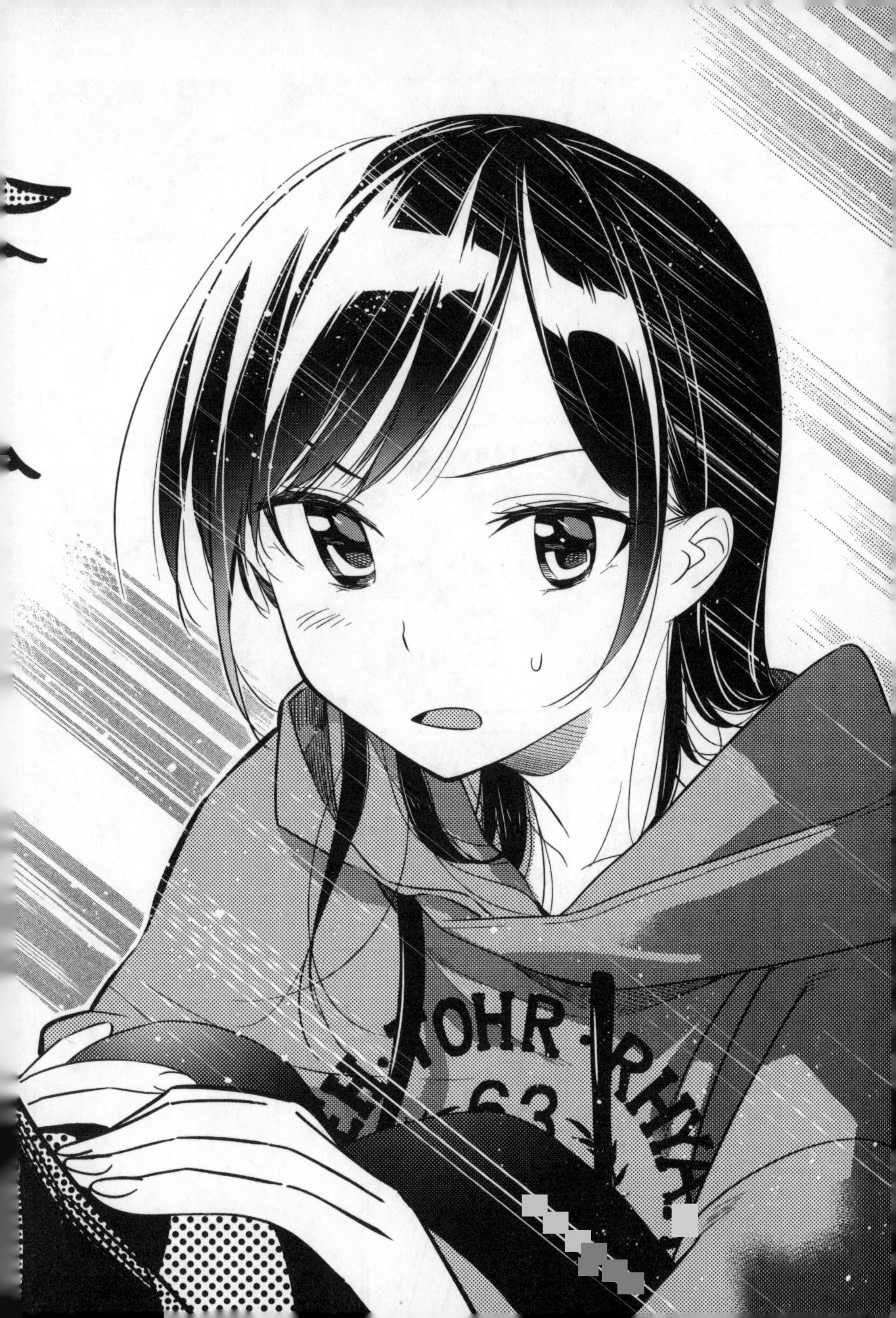

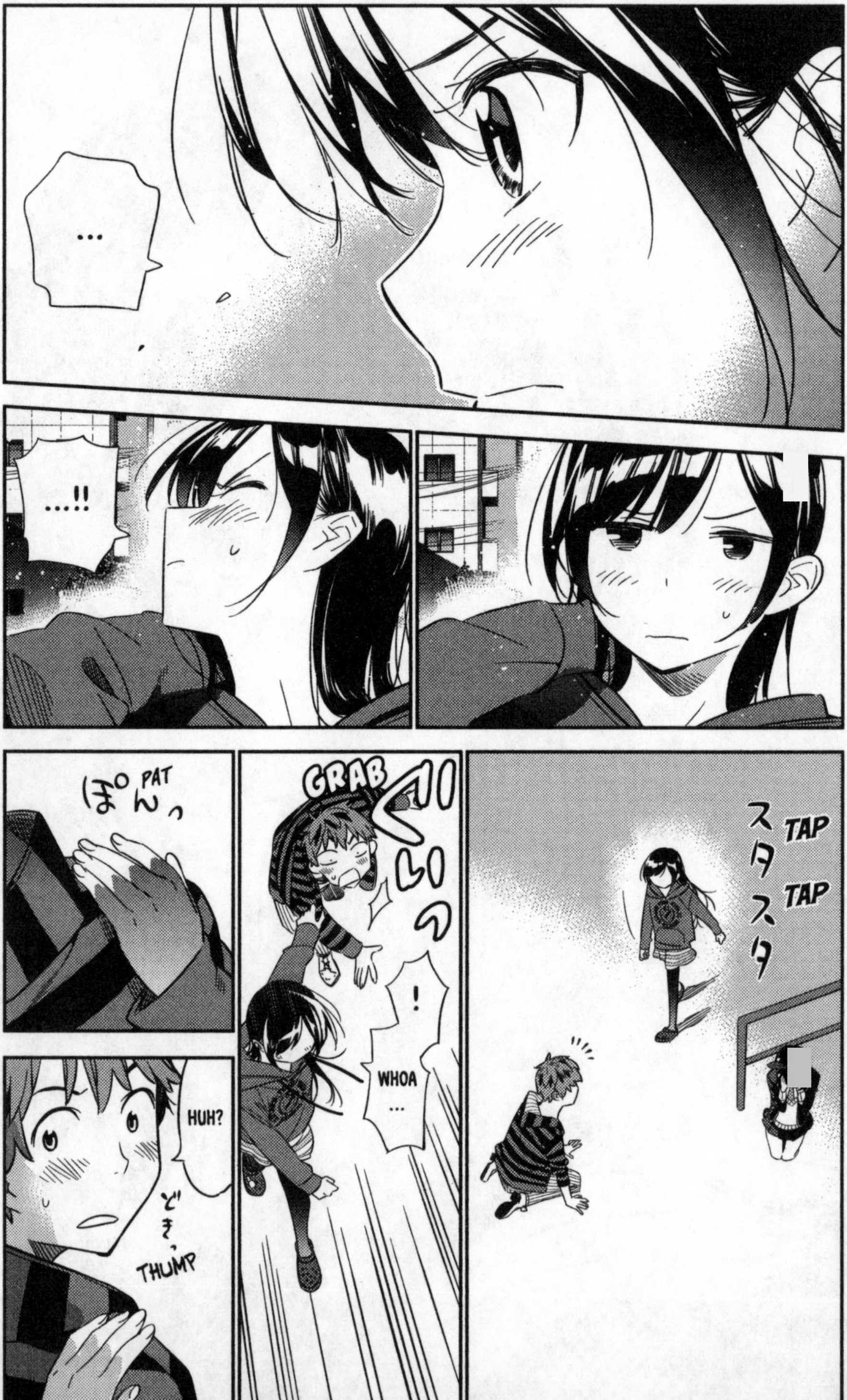
...
...!!
スタスタ
TAP TAP
ぐいっ
GRAB
!
WHOA ...
ぽんっ
PAT
HUH?
どきっ
THUMP

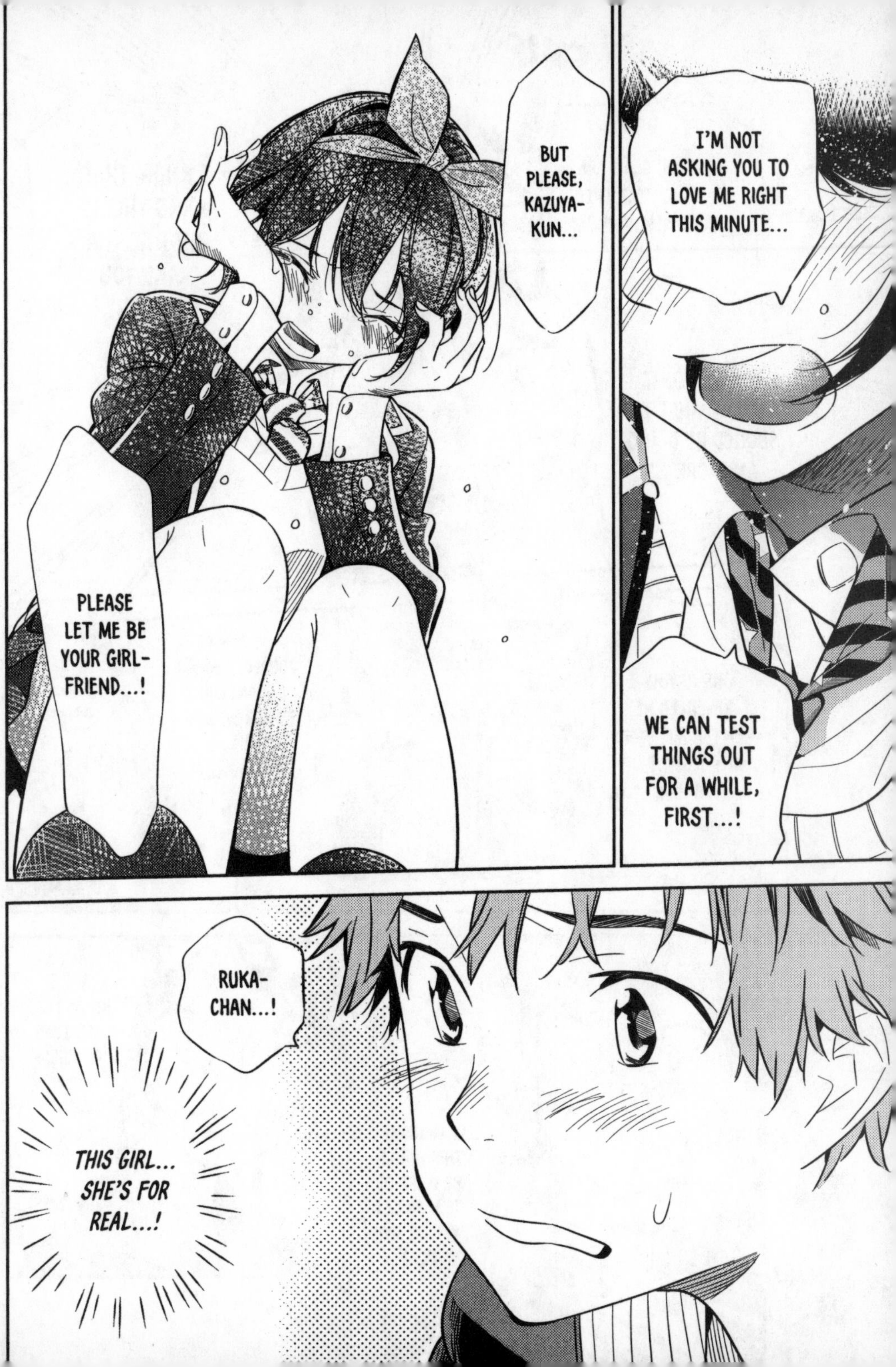
I'M NOT ASKING YOU TO LOVE ME RIGHT THIS MINUTE...
WE CAN TEST THINGS OUT FOR A WHILE, FIRST...!
BUT PLEASE, KAZUYA-KUN...
PLEASE LET ME BE YOUR GIRL-FRIEND...!
RUKA-CHAN...!
THIS GIRL... SHE'S FOR REAL...!

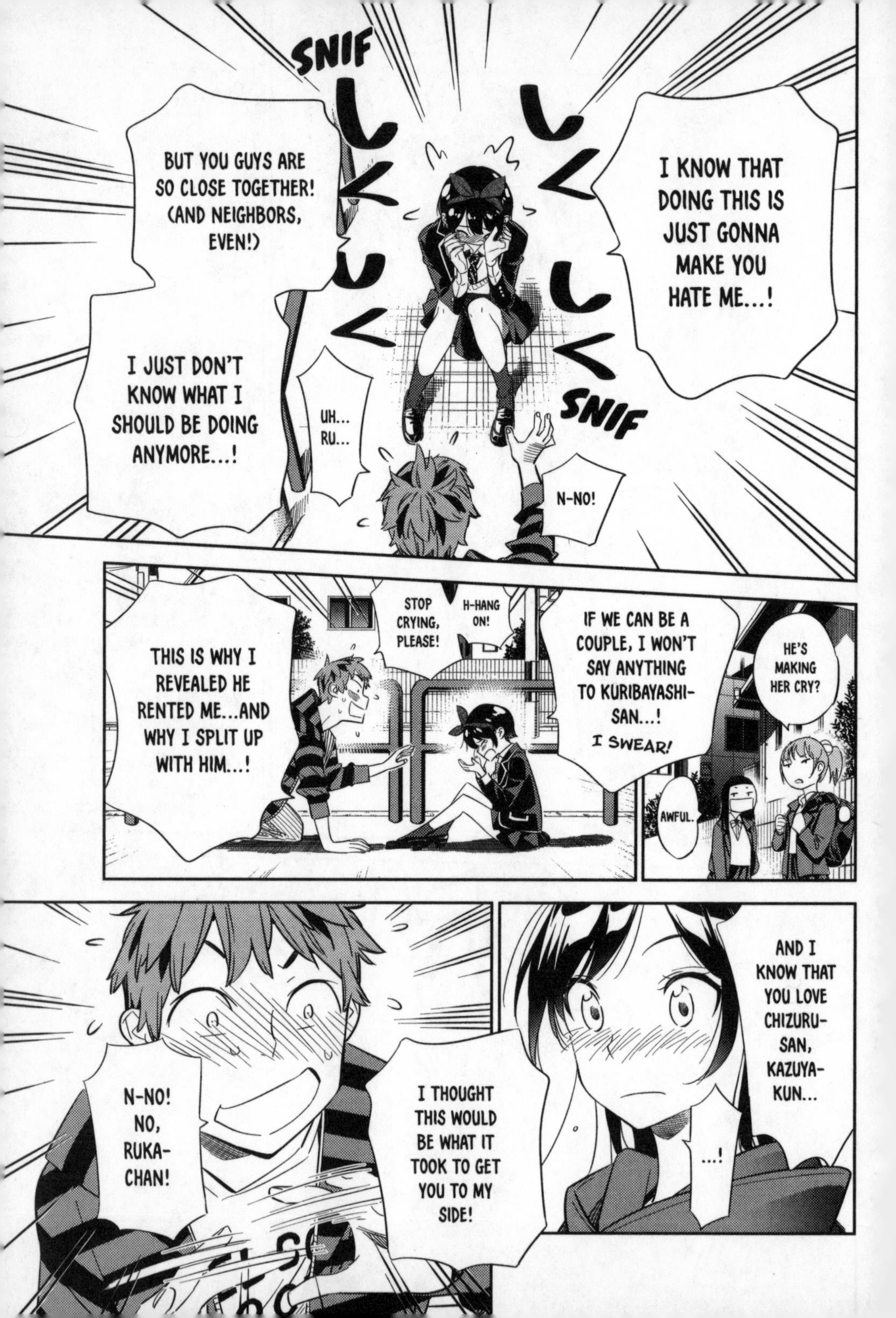
SNIF
I KNOW THAT DOING THIS IS JUST GONNA MAKE YOU HATE ME...!
BUT YOU GUYS ARE SO CLOSE TOGETHER! (AND NEIGHBORS, EVEN!)
SNIF
N-NO!
UH... RU...
I JUST DON'T KNOW WHAT I SHOULD BE DOING ANYMORE...!
HE'S MAKING HER CRY?
AWFUL.
IF WE CAN BE A COUPLE, I WON'T SAY ANYTHING TO KURIBAYASHI-SAN...!
I SWEAR!
H-HANG ON!
STOP CRYING, PLEASE!
THIS IS WHY I REVEALED HE RENTED ME...AND WHY I SPLIT UP WITH HIM...!
AND I KNOW THAT YOU LOVE CHIZURU-SAN, KAZUYA-KUN...
...!
I THOUGHT THIS WOULD BE WHAT IT TOOK TO GET YOU TO MY SIDE!
N-NO! NO, RUKA-CHAN!

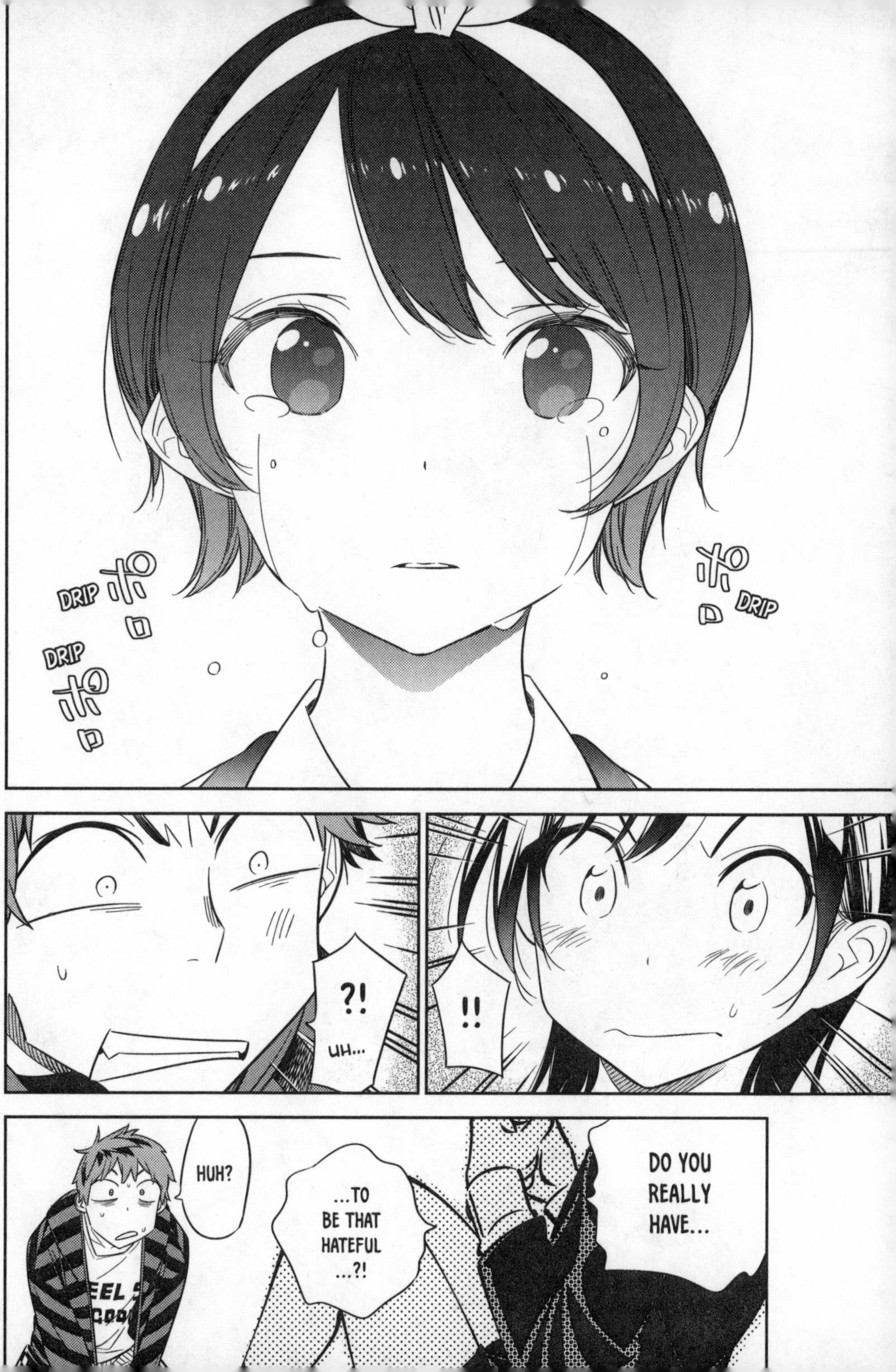
ポロ
DRIP
DRIP
ポロ
DRIP
ポロポロ
!!
?!
UH...
DO YOU REALLY HAVE...
...TO BE THAT HATEFUL ...?!
HUH?

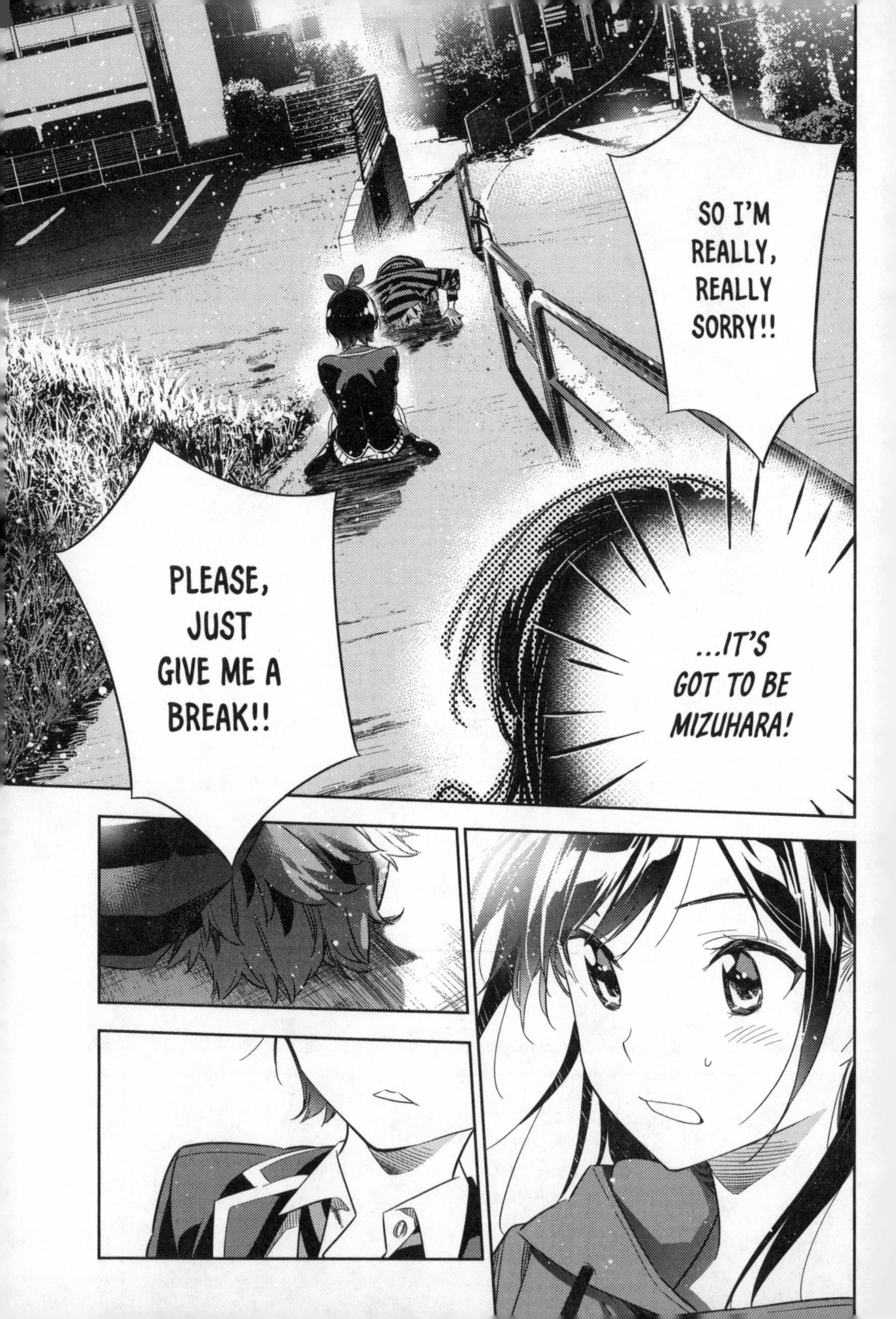
SO I'M REALLY, REALLY SORRY!!
...IT'S GOT TO BE MIZUHARA!
PLEASE, JUST GIVE ME A BREAK!!

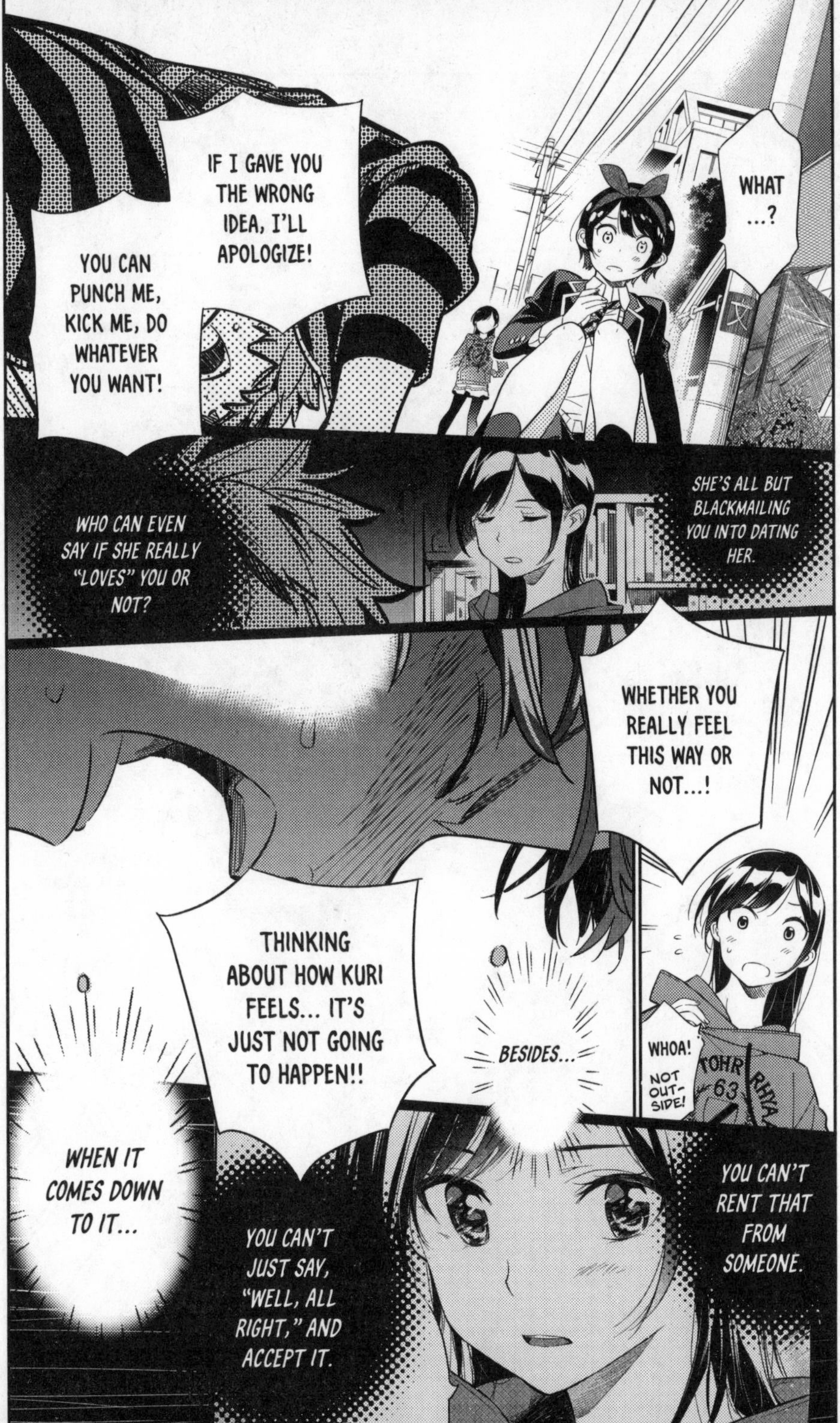
WHAT ...?
IF I GAVE YOU THE WRONG IDEA, I'LL APOLOGIZE!
YOU CAN PUNCH ME, KICK ME, DO WHATEVER YOU WANT!
SHE'S ALL BUT BLACKMAILING YOU INTO DATING HER.
WHO CAN EVEN SAY IF SHE REALLY "LOVES" YOU OR NOT?
WHETHER YOU REALLY FEEL THIS WAY OR NOT...!
WHOA!
NOT OUT-SIDE!
THINKING ABOUT HOW KURI FEELS... IT'S JUST NOT GOING TO HAPPEN!!
BESIDES...
YOU CAN'T RENT THAT FROM SOMEONE.
WHEN IT COMES DOWN TO IT...
YOU CAN'T JUST SAY, "WELL, ALL RIGHT," AND ACCEPT IT.

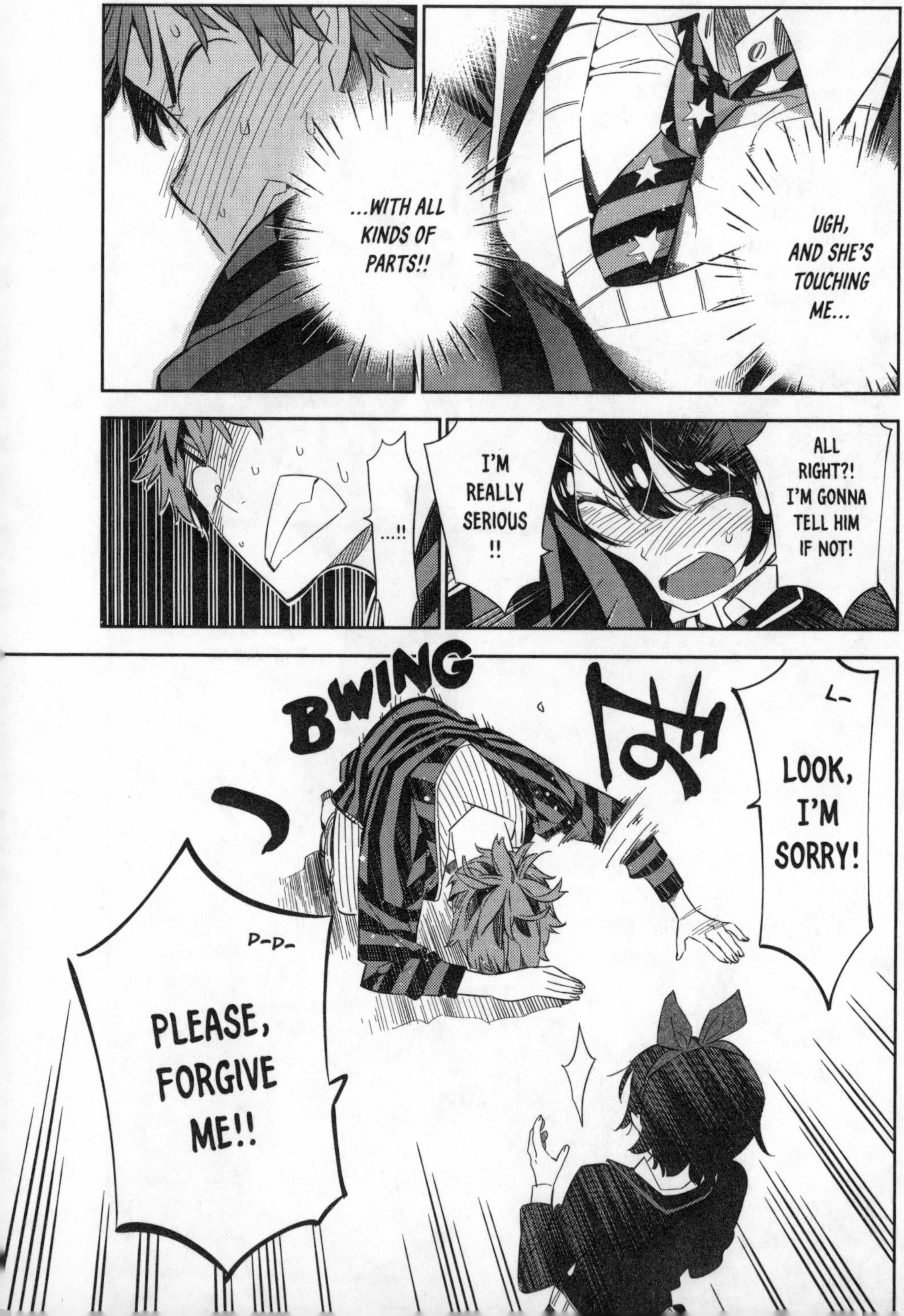
UGH, AND SHE'S TOUCHING ME...
...WITH ALL KINDS OF PARTS!!
ALL RIGHT?! I'M GONNA TELL HIM IF NOT!
I'M REALLY SERIOUS !!
...!!
L-
LOOK, I'M SORRY!
BWING
D-D-
PLEASE, FORGIVE ME!!

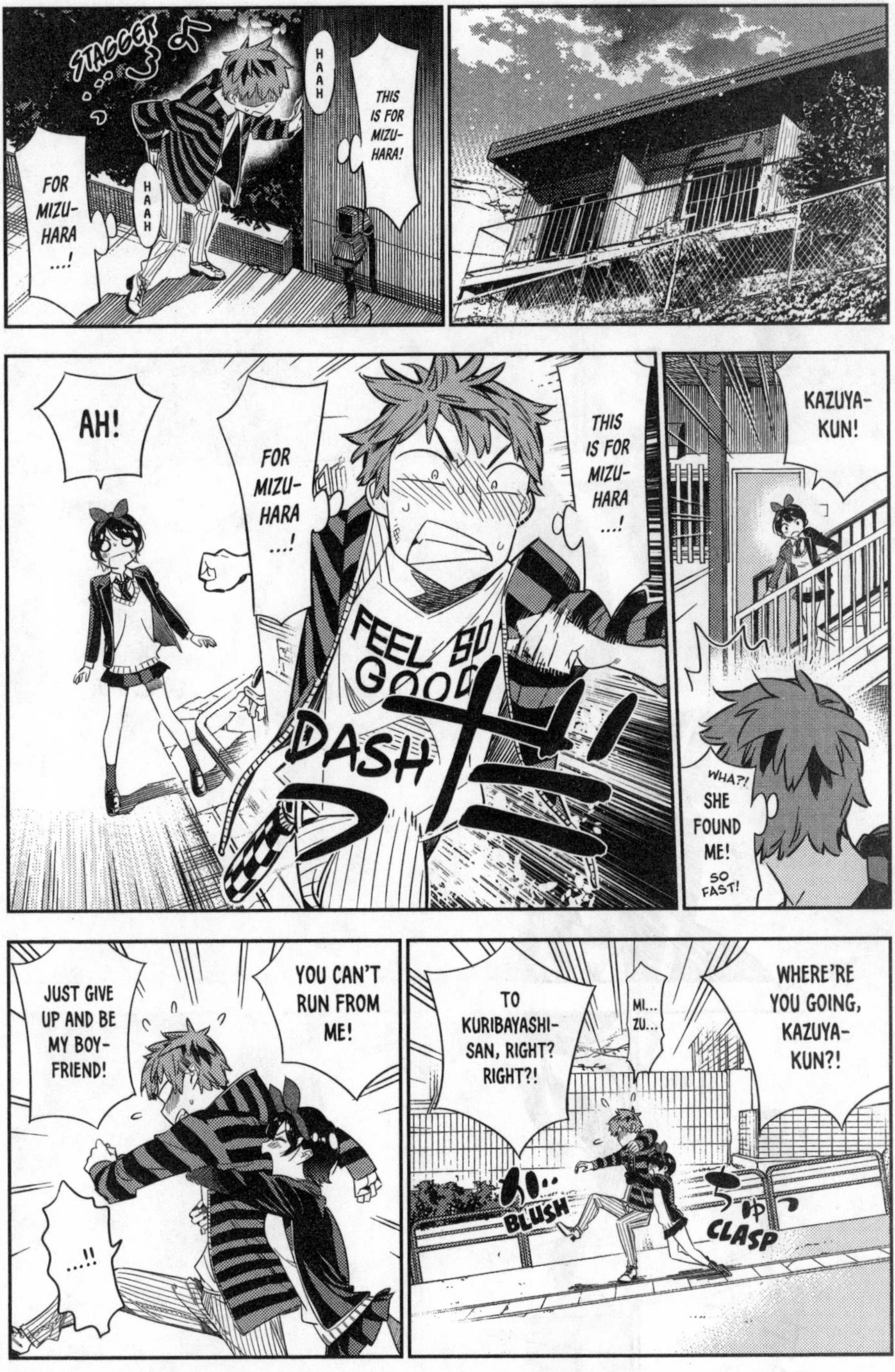
HAAH
THIS IS FOR MIZU-HARA!
STAGGER
HAAH
FOR MIZU-HARA ...!
KAZUYA-KUN!
WHA?! SHE FOUND ME! SO FAST!
THIS IS FOR MIZU-HARA ...!
FOR MIZU-HARA ...!
AH!
FEEL SO GOOD
DASH
WHERE'RE YOU GOING, KAZUYA-KUN?!
MI... ZU...
TO KURIBAYASHI-SAN, RIGHT? RIGHT?!
CLASP
BLUSH
YOU CAN'T RUN FROM ME!
JUST GIVE UP AND BE MY BOY-FRIEND!
...!!

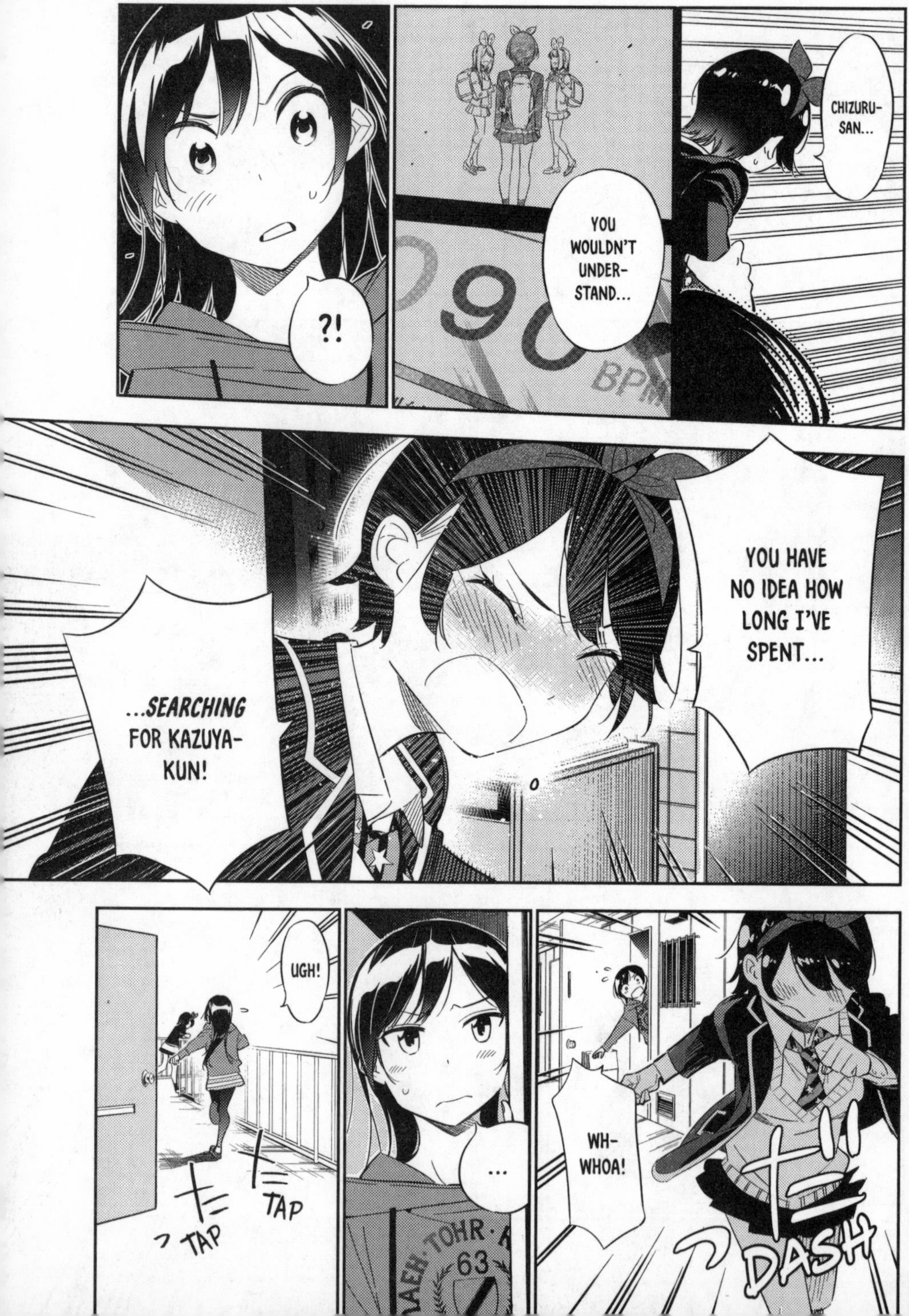
CHIZURU-SAN...
YOU WOULDN'T UNDERSTAND...
?!
YOU HAVE NO IDEA HOW LONG I'VE SPENT...
...SEARCHING FOR KAZUYA-KUN!
DASH
WH-WHOA!
...
UGH!
TAP
TAP

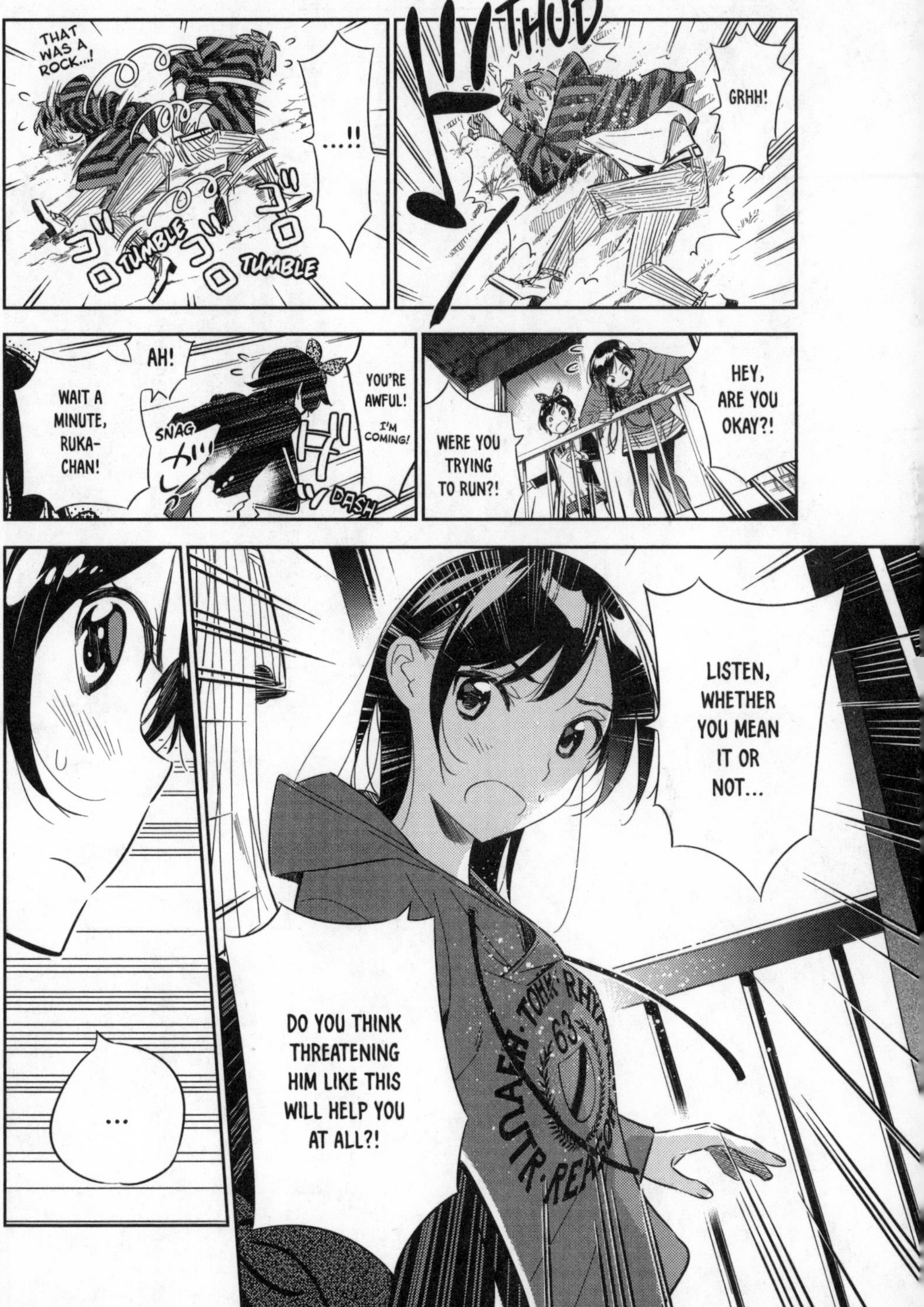
THUD
GRHH!
THAT WAS A ROCK...!
...!!
TUMBLE
TUMBLE
HEY, ARE YOU OKAY?!
WERE YOU TRYING TO RUN?!
YOU'RE AWFUL!
I'M COMING!
AH!
WAIT A MINUTE, RUKA-CHAN!
SNAG
DASH
LISTEN, WHETHER YOU MEAN IT OR NOT...
DO YOU THINK THREATENING HIM LIKE THIS WILL HELP YOU AT ALL?!
...

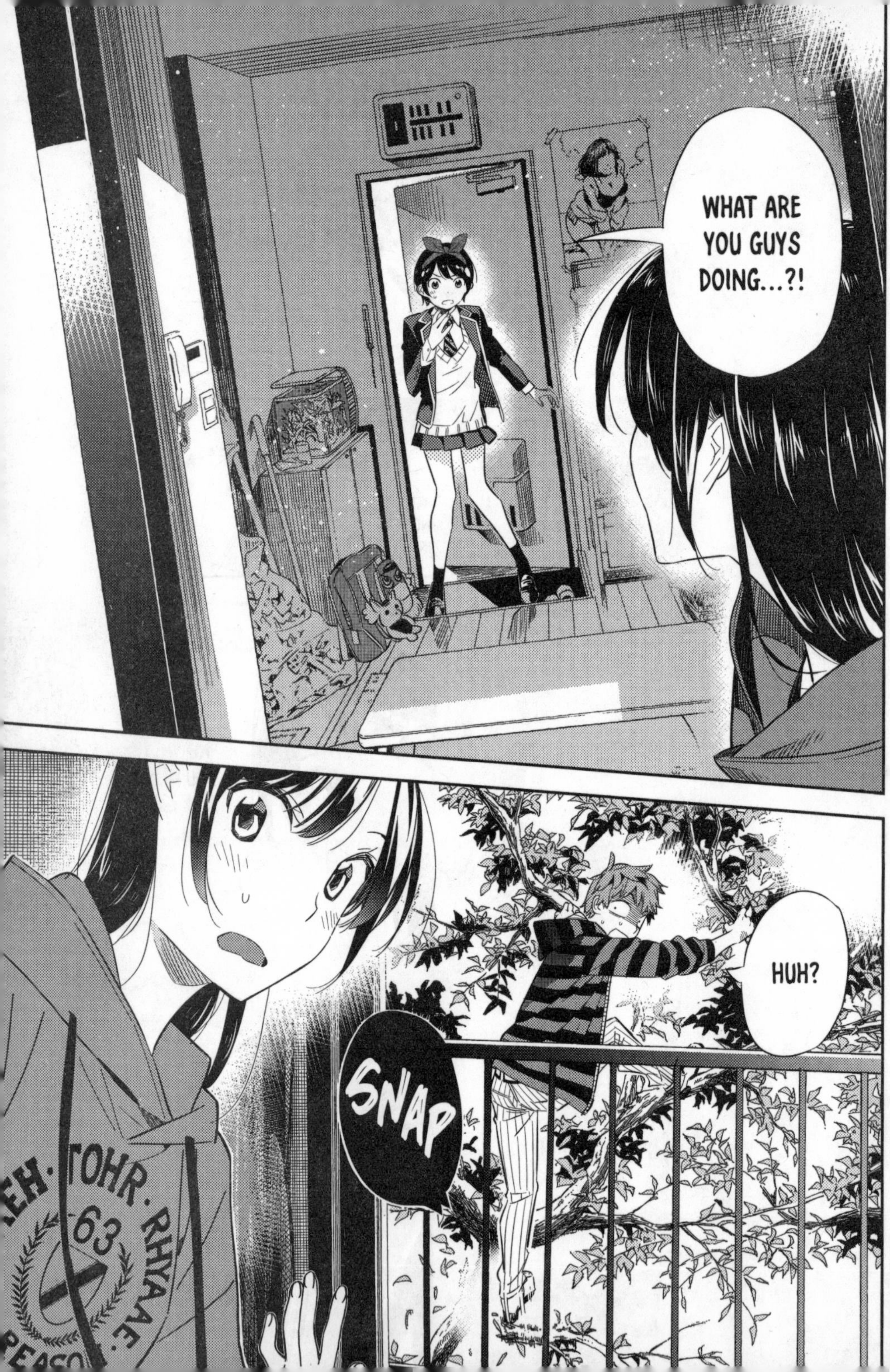
WHAT ARE YOU GUYS DOING...?!
HUH?
SNAP

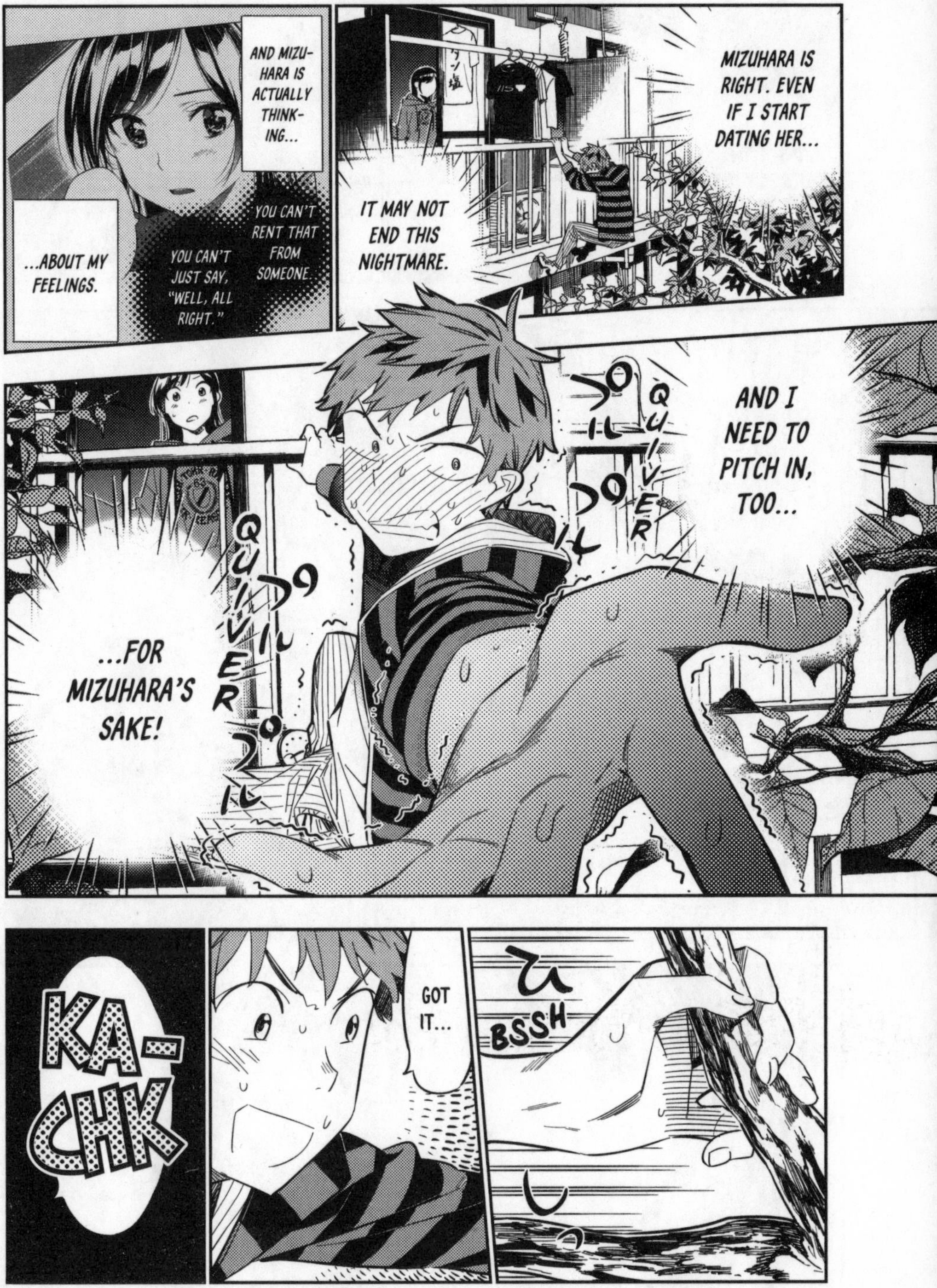
MIZUHARA IS RIGHT. EVEN IF I START DATING HER...
IT MAY NOT END THIS NIGHTMARE.
AND MIZUHARA IS ACTUALLY THINKING...
YOU CAN'T RENT THAT FROM SOMEONE.
YOU CAN'T JUST SAY, "WELL, ALL RIGHT."
...ABOUT MY FEELINGS.
AND I NEED TO PITCH IN, TOO...
QUIVER
QUIVER
...FOR MIZUHARA'S SAKE!
BSSH
GOT IT...
KA-CHK

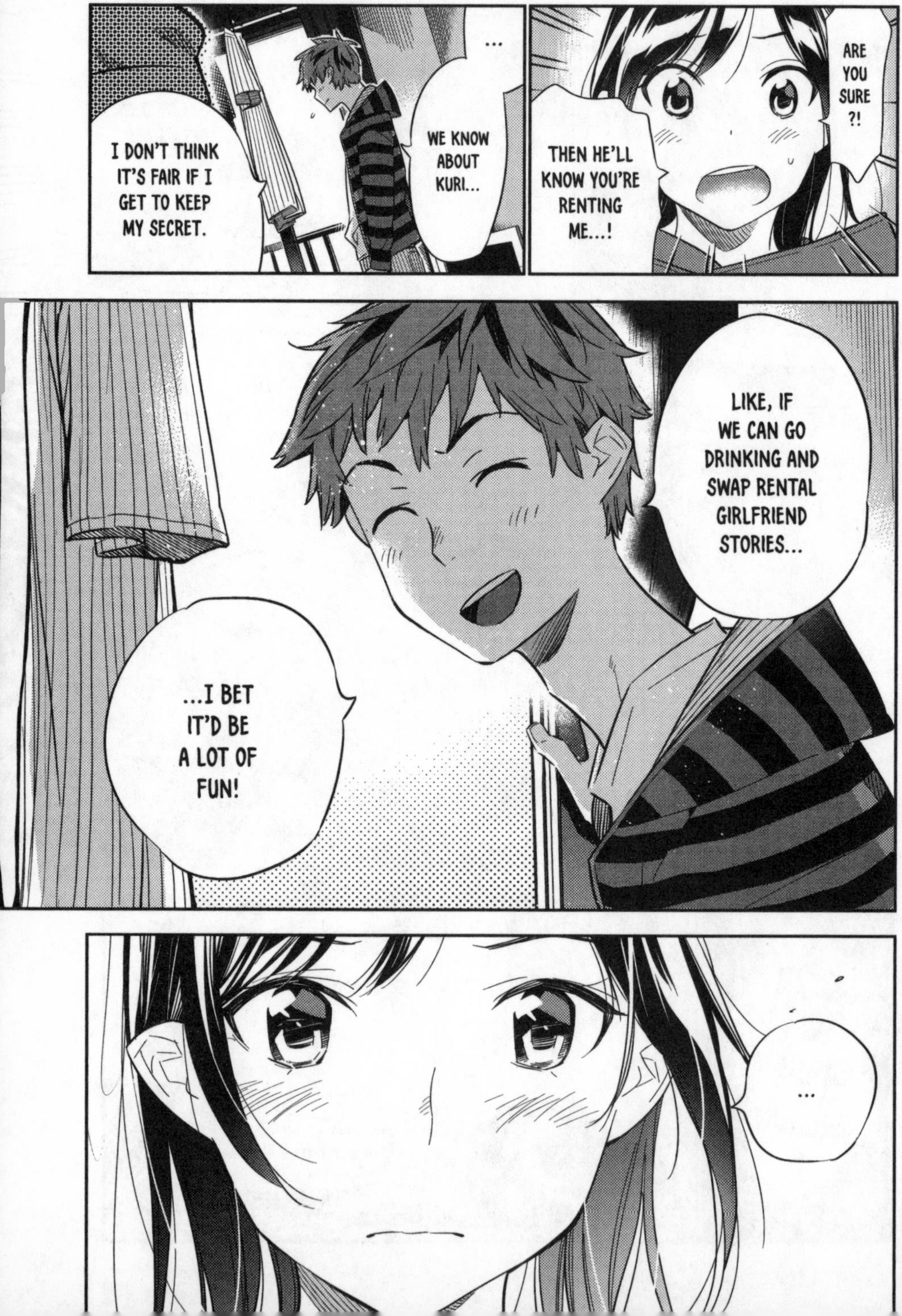
ARE YOU SURE ?!
THEN HE'LL KNOW YOU'RE RENTING ME...!
...
WE KNOW ABOUT KURI...
I DON'T THINK IT'S FAIR IF I GET TO KEEP MY SECRET.
LIKE, IF WE CAN GO DRINKING AND SWAP RENTAL GIRLFRIEND STORIES...
...I BET IT'D BE A LOT OF FUN!
...

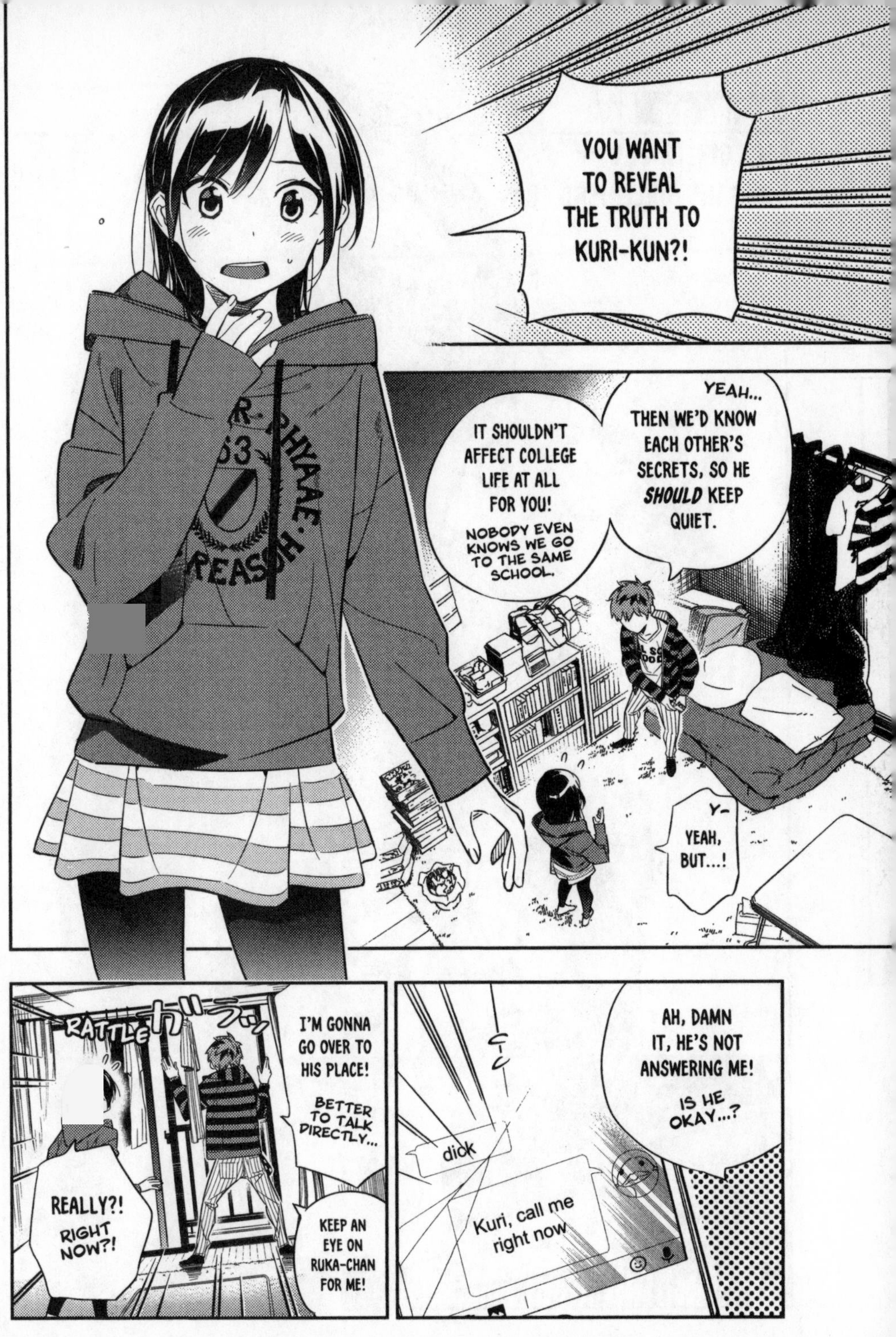
YOU WANT TO REVEAL THE TRUTH TO KURI-KUN?!
YEAH... THEN WE'D KNOW EACH OTHER'S SECRETS, SO HE *SHOULD* KEEP QUIET.
IT SHOULDN'T AFFECT COLLEGE LIFE AT ALL FOR YOU!
NOBODY EVEN KNOWS WE GO TO THE SAME SCHOOL.
Y- YEAH, BUT...!
AH, DAMN IT, HE'S NOT ANSWERING ME!
IS HE OKAY...?
dick
Kuri, call me right now
RATTLE
I'M GONNA GO OVER TO HIS PLACE!
BETTER TO TALK DIRECTLY...
REALLY?! RIGHT NOW?!
KEEP AN EYE ON RUKA-CHAN FOR ME!

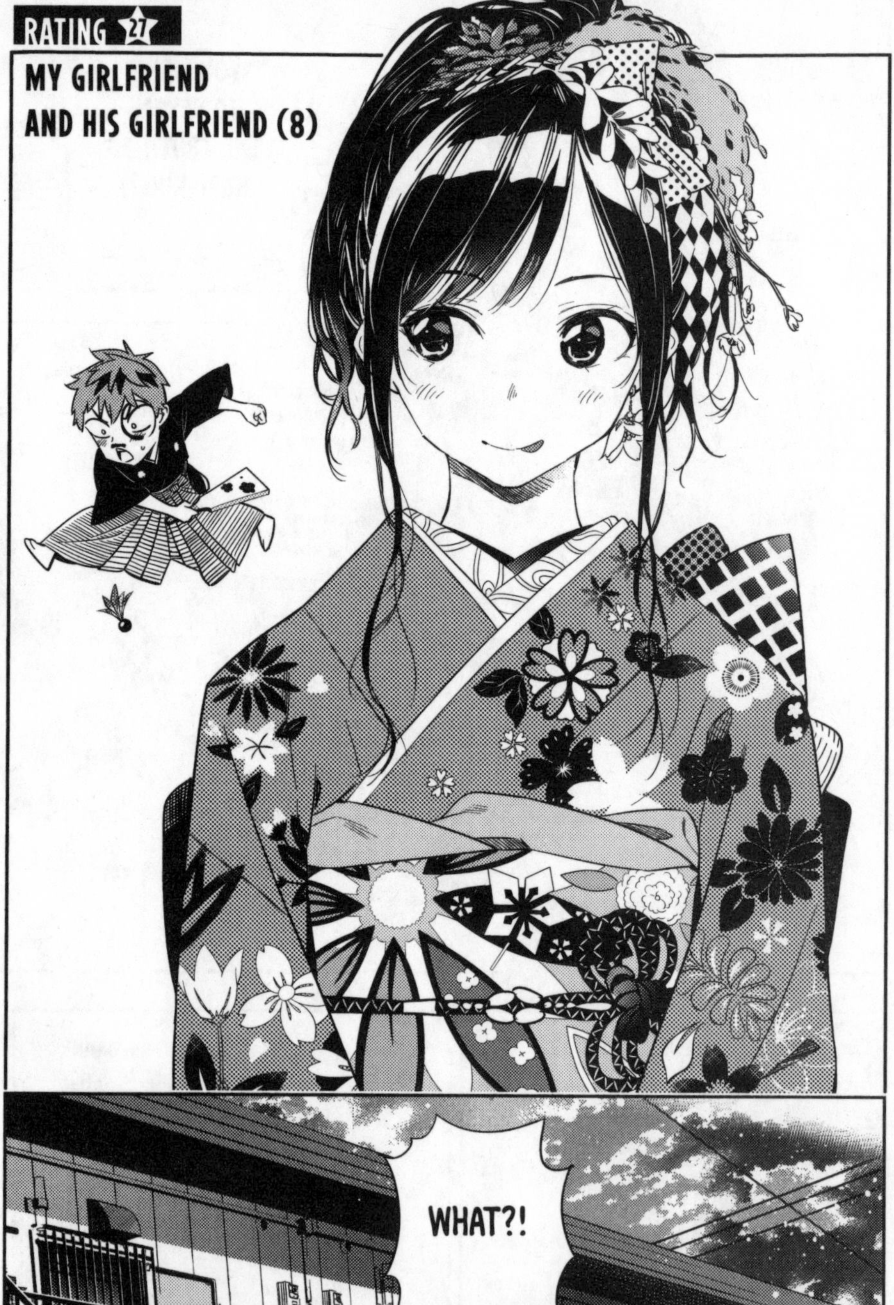
RATING 27
MY GIRLFRIEND AND HIS GIRLFRIEND (8)
WHAT?!

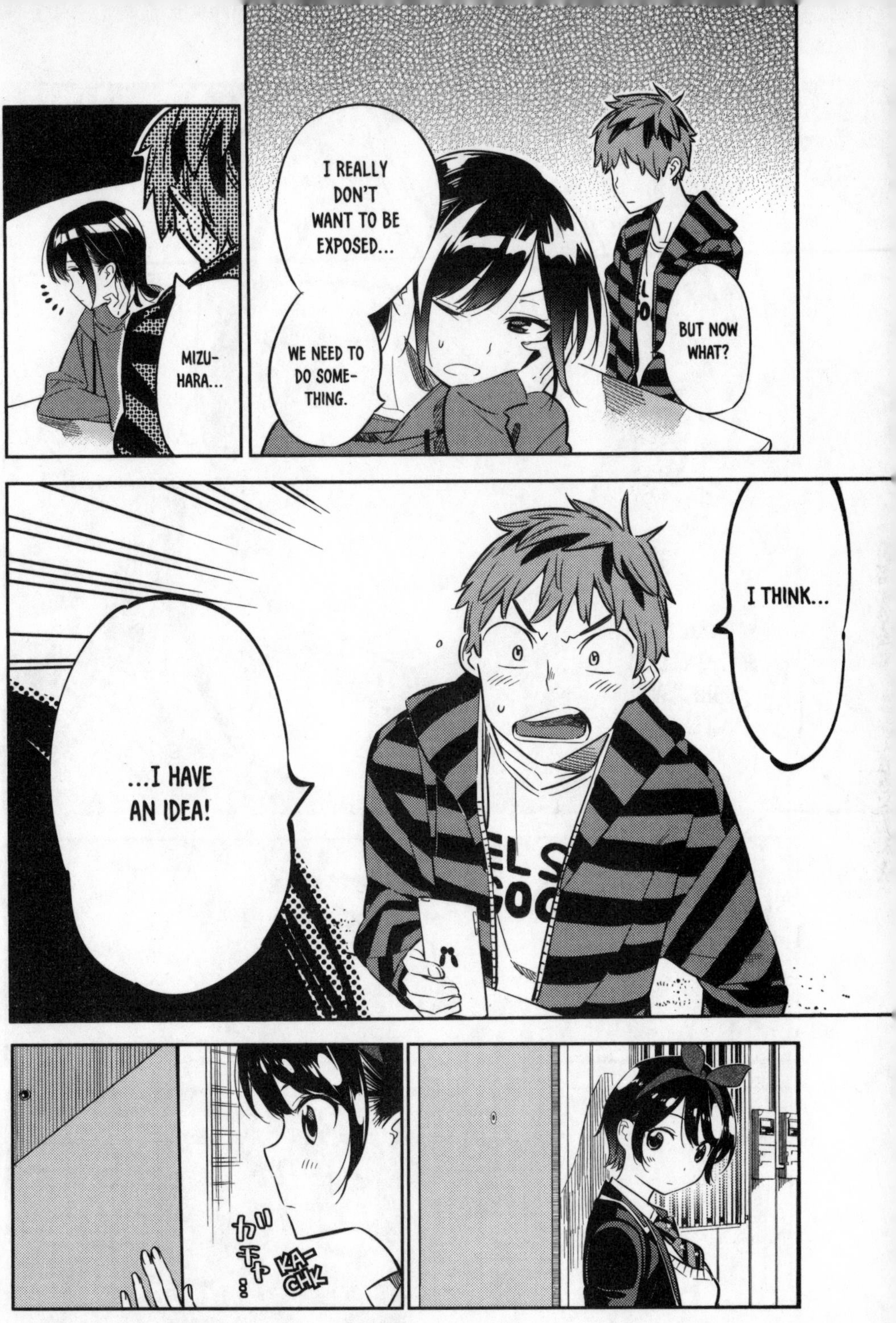
I REALLY DON'T WANT TO BE EXPOSED...
WE NEED TO DO SOME-THING.
BUT NOW WHAT?
MIZU-HARA...
I THINK...
...I HAVE AN IDEA!
ガチャ
KA-CHK

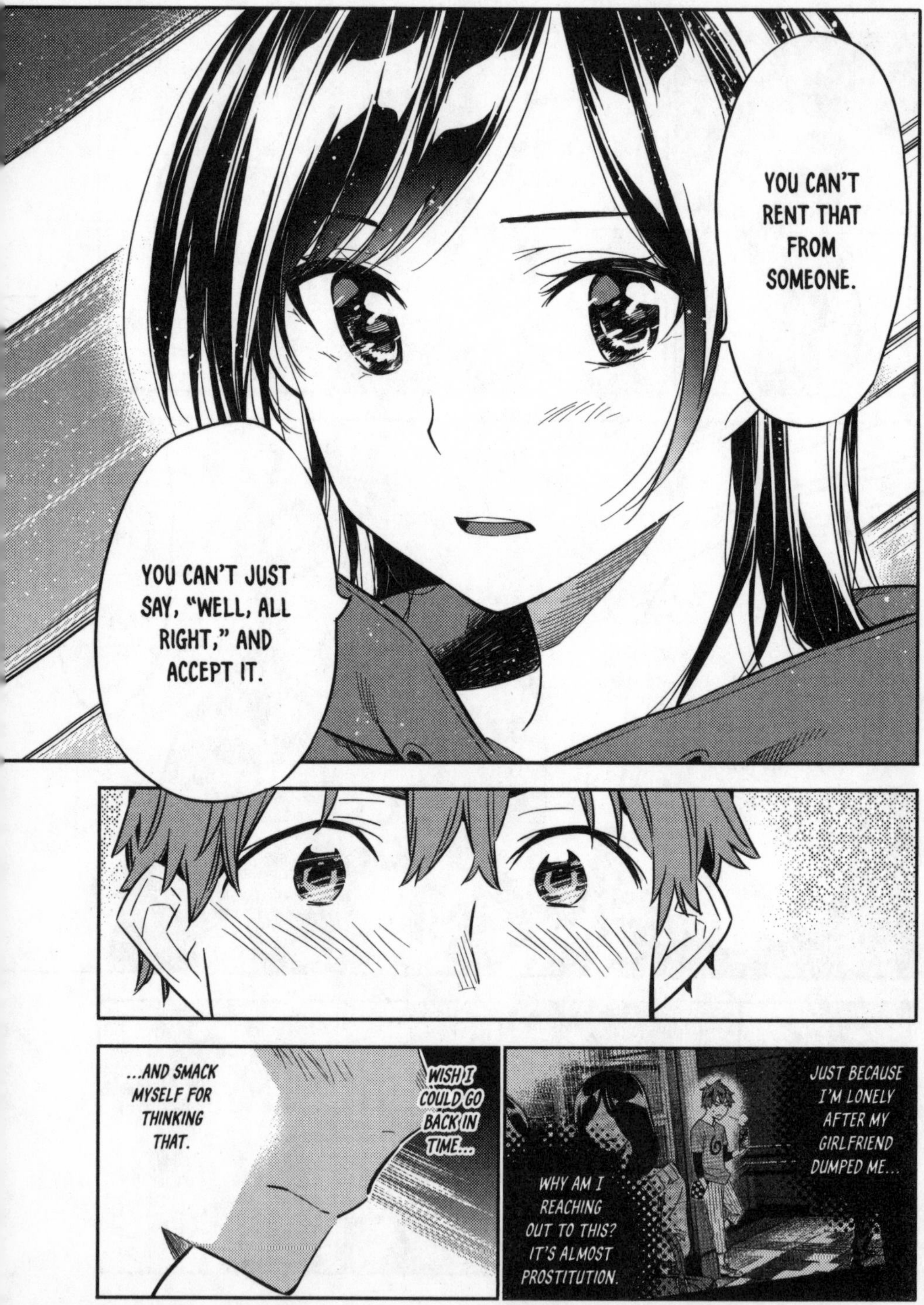
YOU CAN'T RENT THAT FROM SOMEONE.
YOU CAN'T JUST SAY, "WELL, ALL RIGHT," AND ACCEPT IT.
JUST BECAUSE I'M LONELY AFTER MY GIRLFRIEND DUMPED ME...
WHY AM I REACHING OUT TO THIS? IT'S ALMOST PROSTITUTION.
WISH I COULD GO BACK IN TIME...
...AND SMACK MYSELF FOR THINKING THAT.

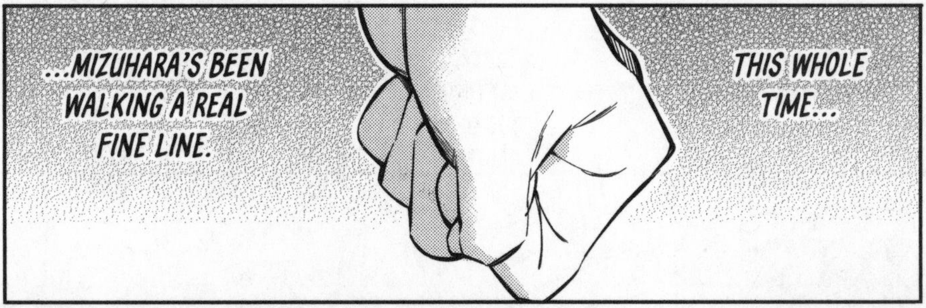
THIS WHOLE TIME...
...MIZUHARA'S BEEN WALKING A REAL FINE LINE.

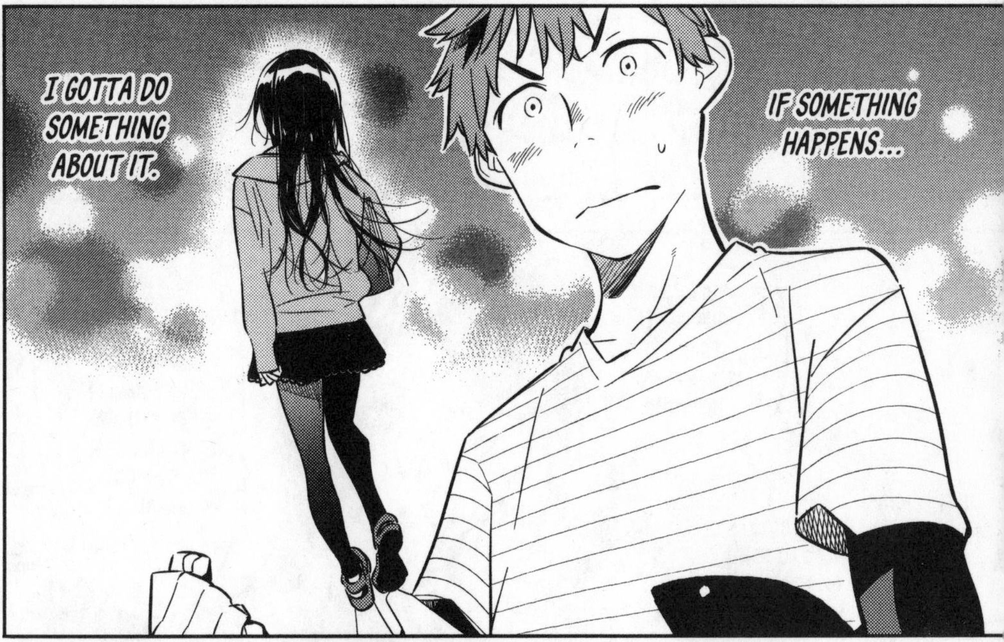
IF SOMETHING HAPPENS...
I GOTTA DO SOMETHING ABOUT IT.

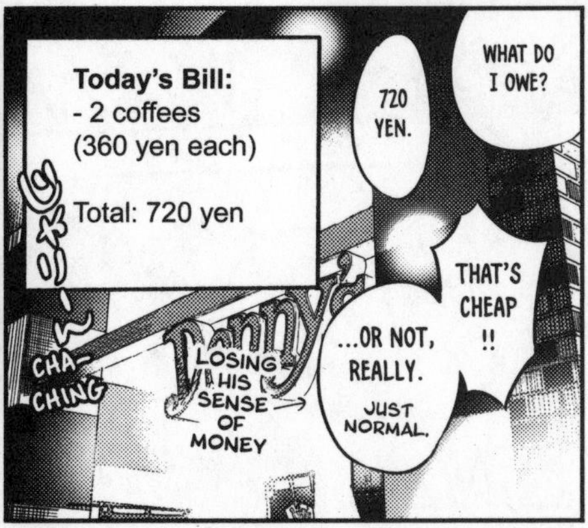
WHAT DO I OWE?
720 YEN.
THAT'S CHEAP !!
...OR NOT, REALLY.
JUST NORMAL.
Today's Bill:
- 2 coffees
(360 yen each)
Total: 720 yen
CHA-CHING
LOSING HIS SENSE OF MONEY

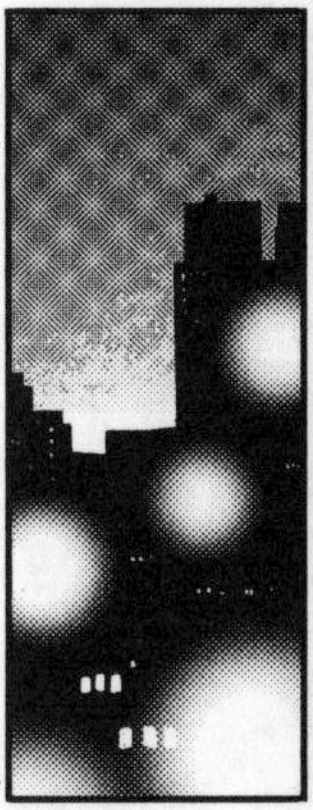

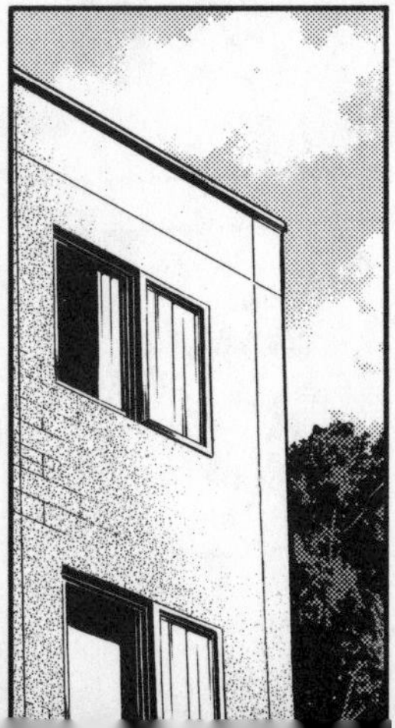

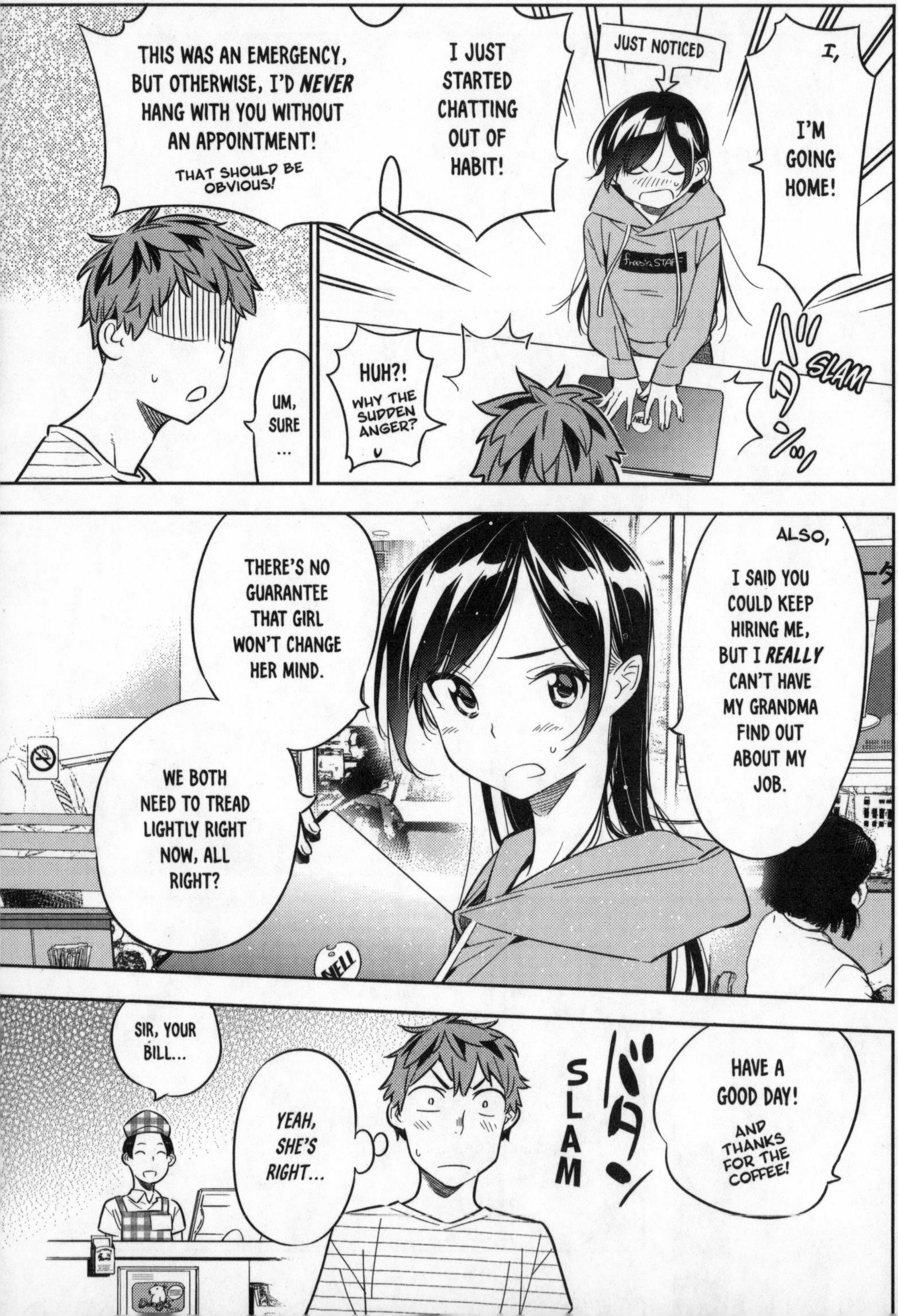
I,
I'M GOING HOME!
SLAM
JUST NOTICED
I JUST STARTED CHATTING OUT OF HABIT!
HUH?! WHY THE SUDDEN ANGER?
THIS WAS AN EMERGENCY, BUT OTHERWISE, I'D *NEVER* HANG WITH YOU WITHOUT AN APPOINTMENT!
THAT SHOULD BE OBVIOUS!
UM, SURE ...
ALSO,
I SAID YOU COULD KEEP HIRING ME, BUT I *REALLY* CAN'T HAVE MY GRANDMA FIND OUT ABOUT MY JOB.
THERE'S NO GUARANTEE THAT GIRL WON'T CHANGE HER MIND.
WE BOTH NEED TO TREAD LIGHTLY RIGHT NOW, ALL RIGHT?
HAVE A GOOD DAY!
AND THANKS FOR THE COFFEE!
SLAM
YEAH, SHE'S RIGHT...
SIR, YOUR BILL...

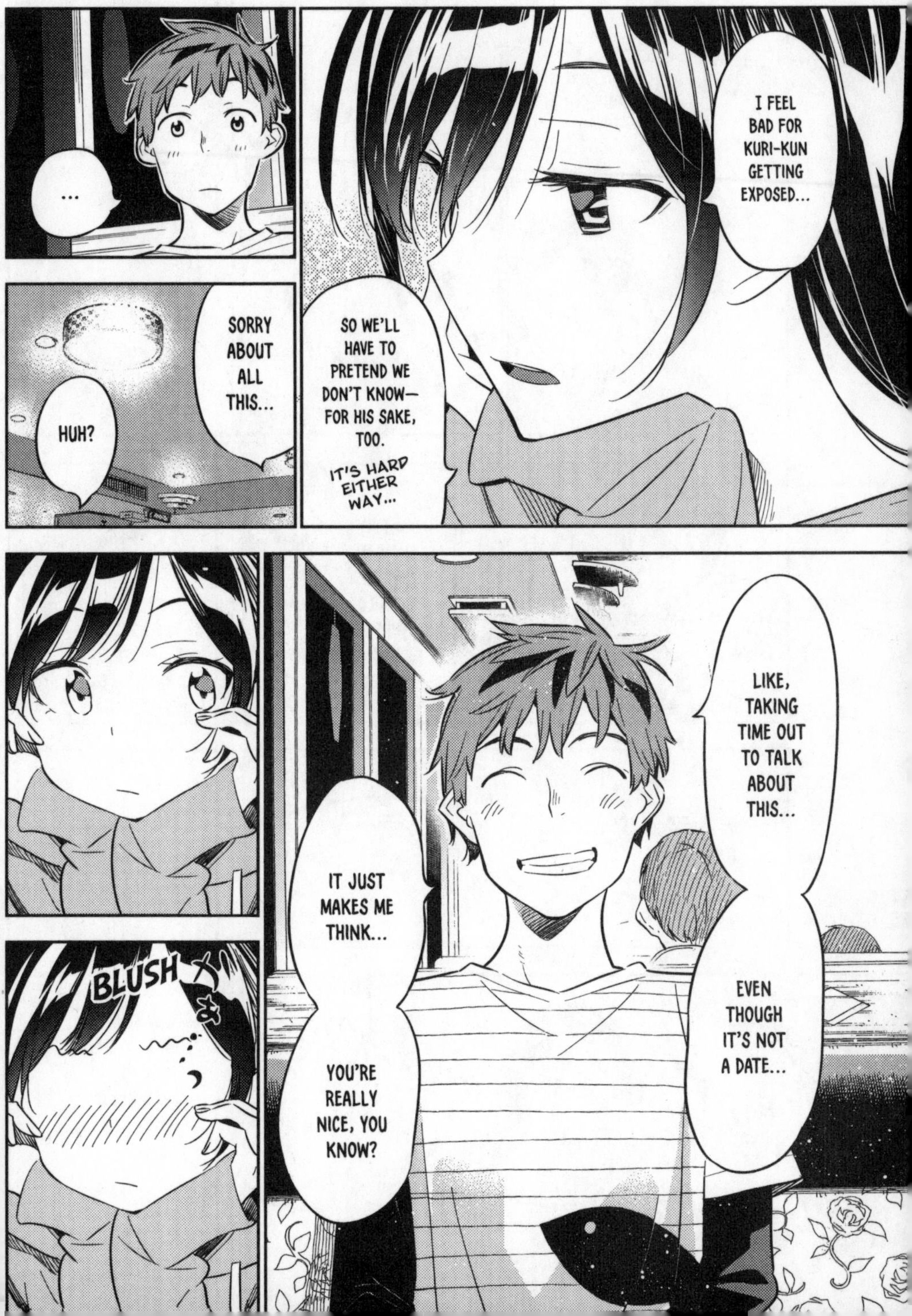
I FEEL BAD FOR KURI-KUN GETTING EXPOSED...
SO WE'LL HAVE TO PRETEND WE DON'T KNOW—FOR HIS SAKE, TOO.
IT'S HARD EITHER WAY...
...
SORRY ABOUT ALL THIS...
HUH?
LIKE, TAKING TIME OUT TO TALK ABOUT THIS...
EVEN THOUGH IT'S NOT A DATE...
IT JUST MAKES ME THINK...
YOU'RE REALLY NICE, YOU KNOW?
BLUSH

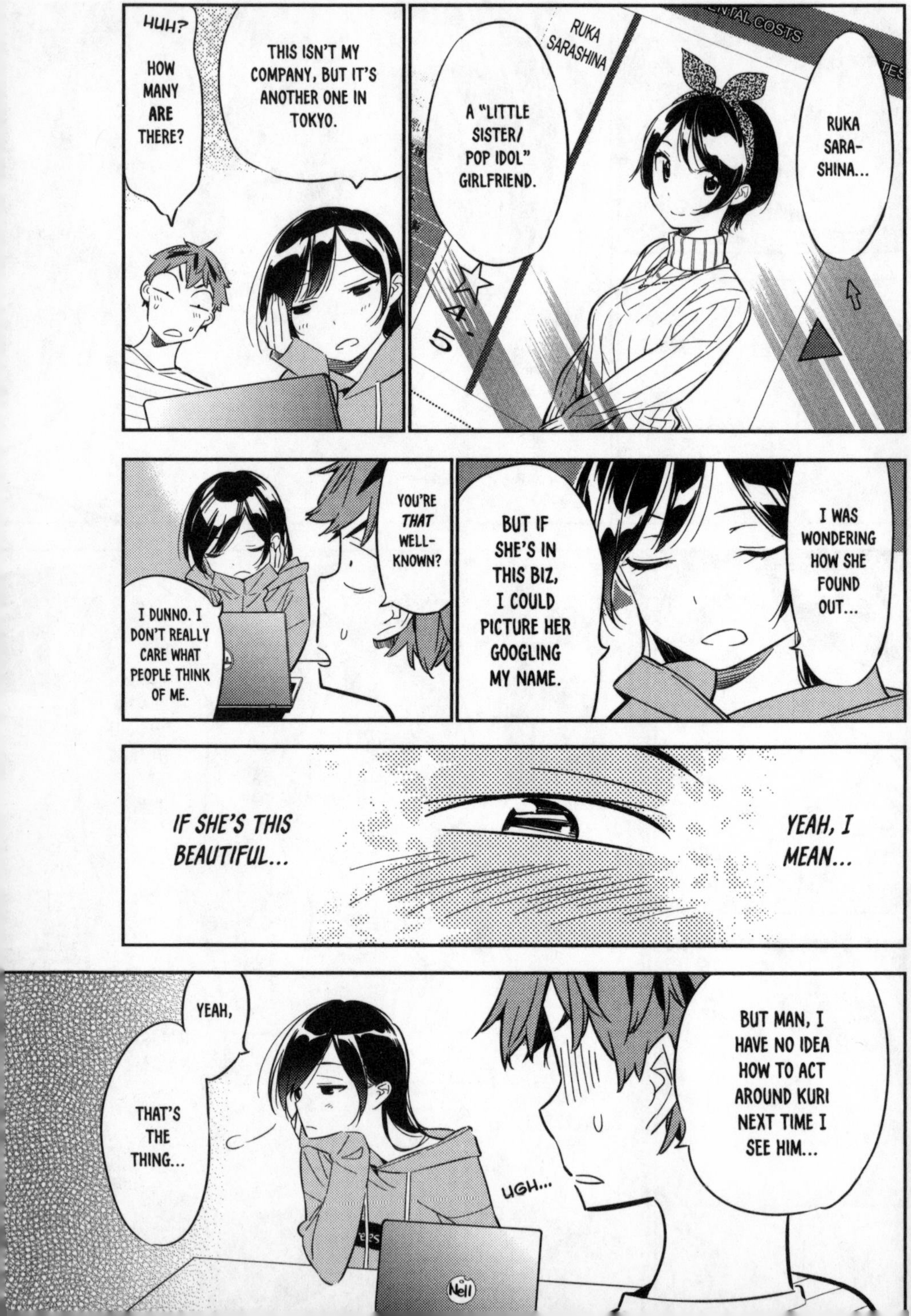
RUKA SARA-SHINA...
RUKA SARASHINA
A "LITTLE SISTER/ POP IDOL" GIRLFRIEND.
THIS ISN'T MY COMPANY, BUT IT'S ANOTHER ONE IN TOKYO.
HUH? HOW MANY ARE THERE?
I WAS WONDERING HOW SHE FOUND OUT...
BUT IF SHE'S IN THIS BIZ, I COULD PICTURE HER GOOGLING MY NAME.
YOU'RE *THAT* WELL-KNOWN?
I DUNNO. I DON'T REALLY CARE WHAT PEOPLE THINK OF ME.
YEAH, I MEAN...
IF SHE'S THIS BEAUTIFUL...
BUT MAN, I HAVE NO IDEA HOW TO ACT AROUND KURI NEXT TIME I SEE HIM...
UGH...
YEAH, THAT'S THE THING...

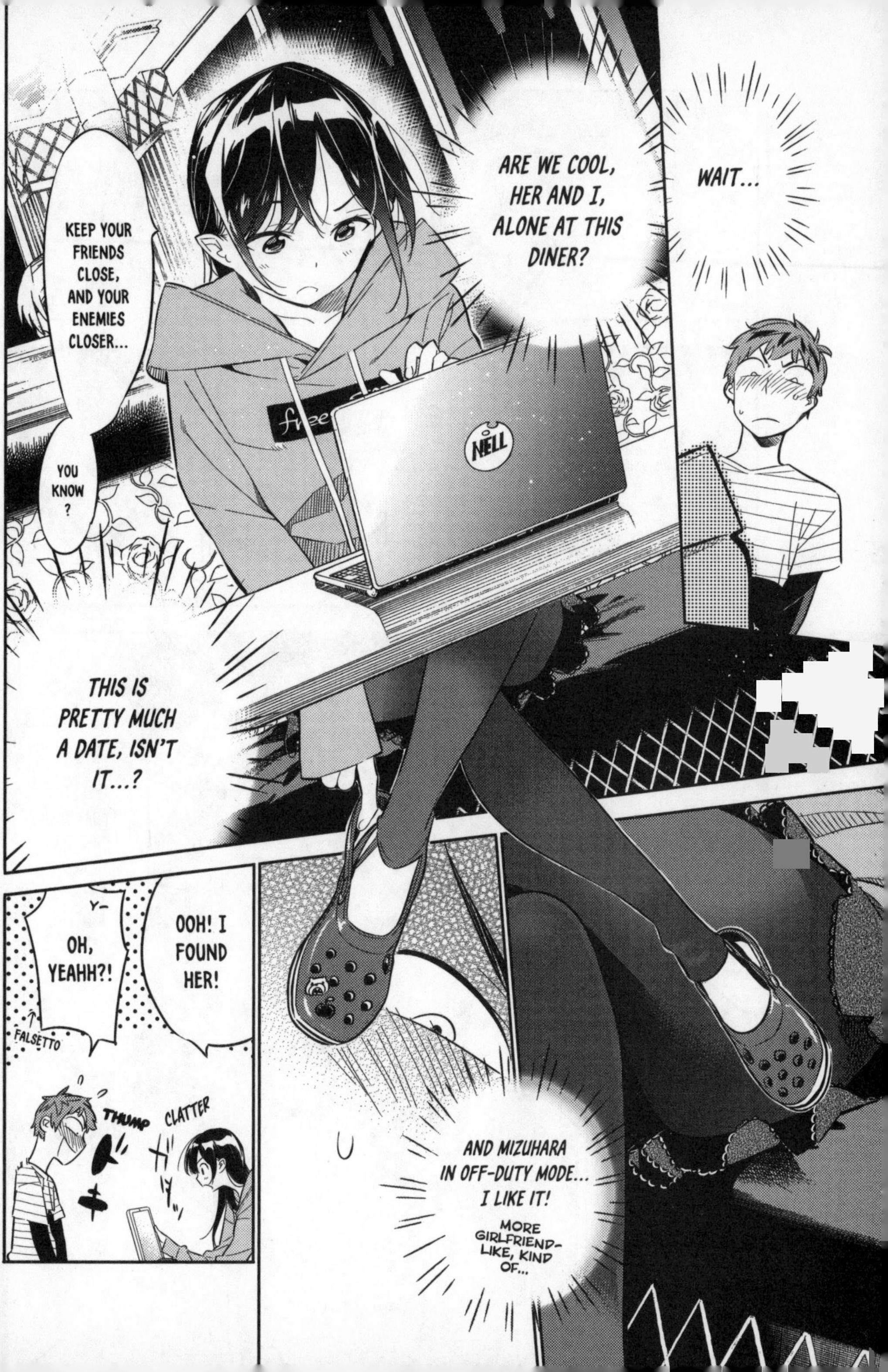
WAIT...
ARE WE COOL, HER AND I, ALONE AT THIS DINER?
KEEP YOUR FRIENDS CLOSE, AND YOUR ENEMIES CLOSER...
YOU KNOW?
free
NELL
THIS IS PRETTY MUCH A DATE, ISN'T IT...?
AND MIZUHARA IN OFF-DUTY MODE... I LIKE IT!
MORE GIRLFRIEND-LIKE, KIND OF...
OOH! I FOUND HER!
Y— OH, YEAHH?!
FALSETTO
CLATTER
THUMP

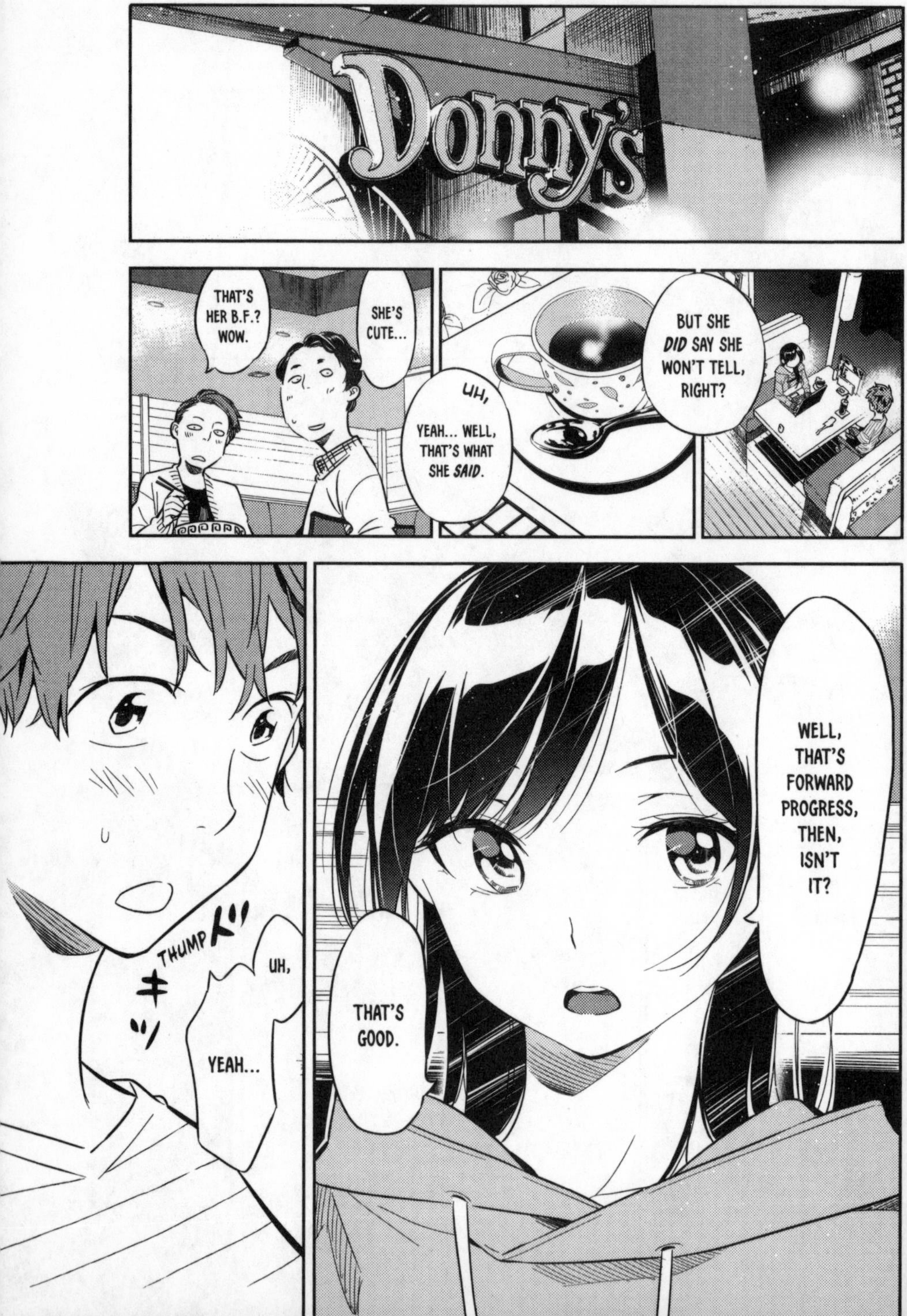
Donny's
BUT SHE DID SAY SHE WON'T TELL, RIGHT?
UH, YEAH... WELL, THAT'S WHAT SHE SAID.
SHE'S CUTE...
THAT'S HER B.F.? WOW.
WELL, THAT'S FORWARD PROGRESS, THEN, ISN'T IT?
THAT'S GOOD.
THUMP ドキッ
UH, YEAH...

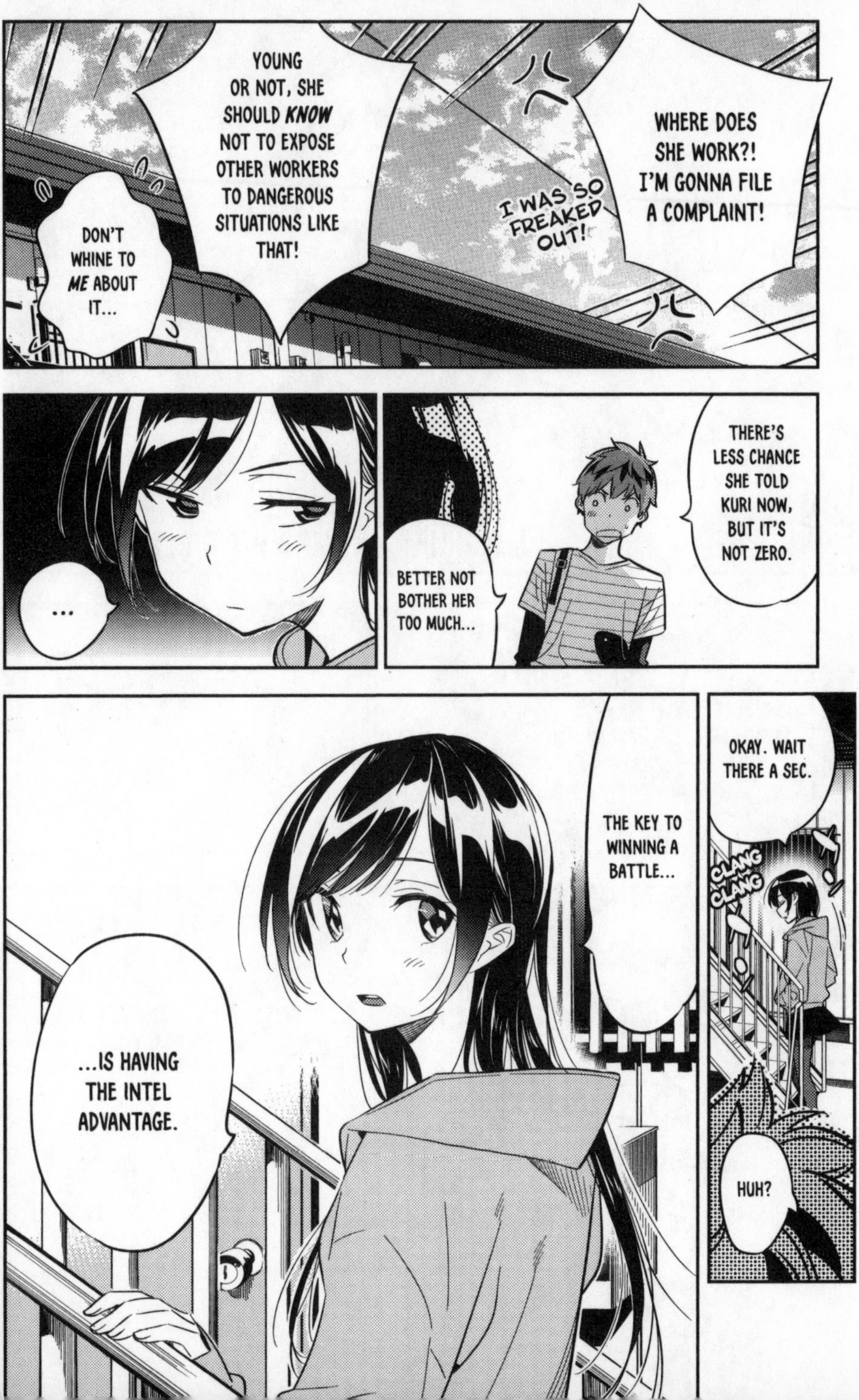
WHERE DOES SHE WORK?! I'M GONNA FILE A COMPLAINT!
I WAS SO FREAKED OUT!
YOUNG OR NOT, SHE SHOULD KNOW NOT TO EXPOSE OTHER WORKERS TO DANGEROUS SITUATIONS LIKE THAT!
DON'T WHINE TO ME ABOUT IT...
THERE'S LESS CHANCE SHE TOLD KURI NOW, BUT IT'S NOT ZERO.
BETTER NOT BOTHER HER TOO MUCH...
...
OKAY. WAIT THERE A SEC.
CLANG CLANG
HUH?
THE KEY TO WINNING A BATTLE...
...IS HAVING THE INTEL ADVANTAGE.

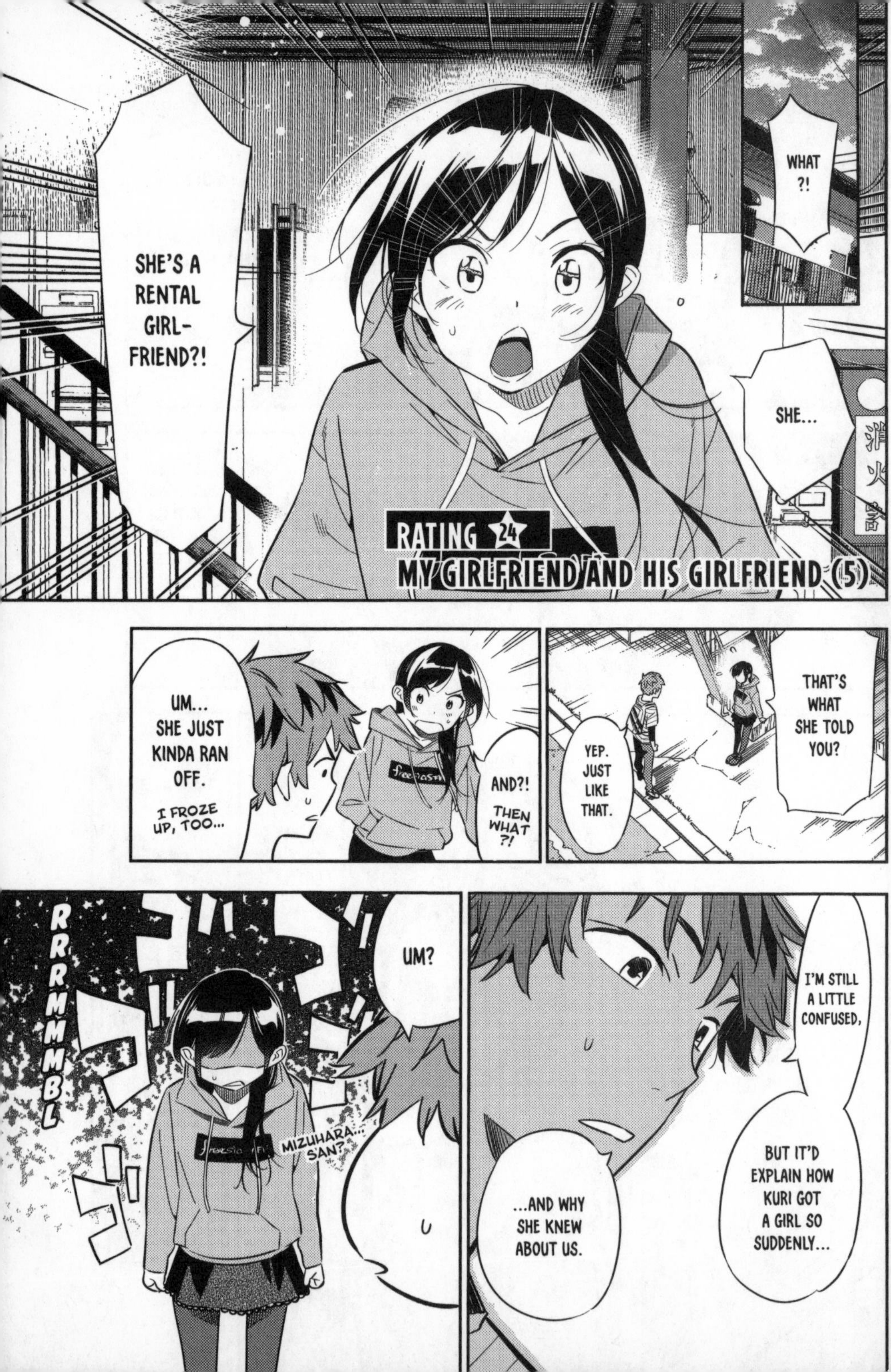
WHAT ?!
SHE...
SHE'S A RENTAL GIRL-FRIEND?!
RATING 24
MY GIRLFRIEND AND HIS GIRLFRIEND (5)
THAT'S WHAT SHE TOLD YOU?
YEP. JUST LIKE THAT.
AND?!
THEN WHAT ?!
UM... SHE JUST KINDA RAN OFF.
I FROZE UP, TOO...
I'M STILL A LITTLE CONFUSED,
BUT IT'D EXPLAIN HOW KURI GOT A GIRL SO SUDDENLY...
...AND WHY SHE KNEW ABOUT US.
UM?
MIZUHARA... SAN?
RRRMMMBL

VOLUME 4

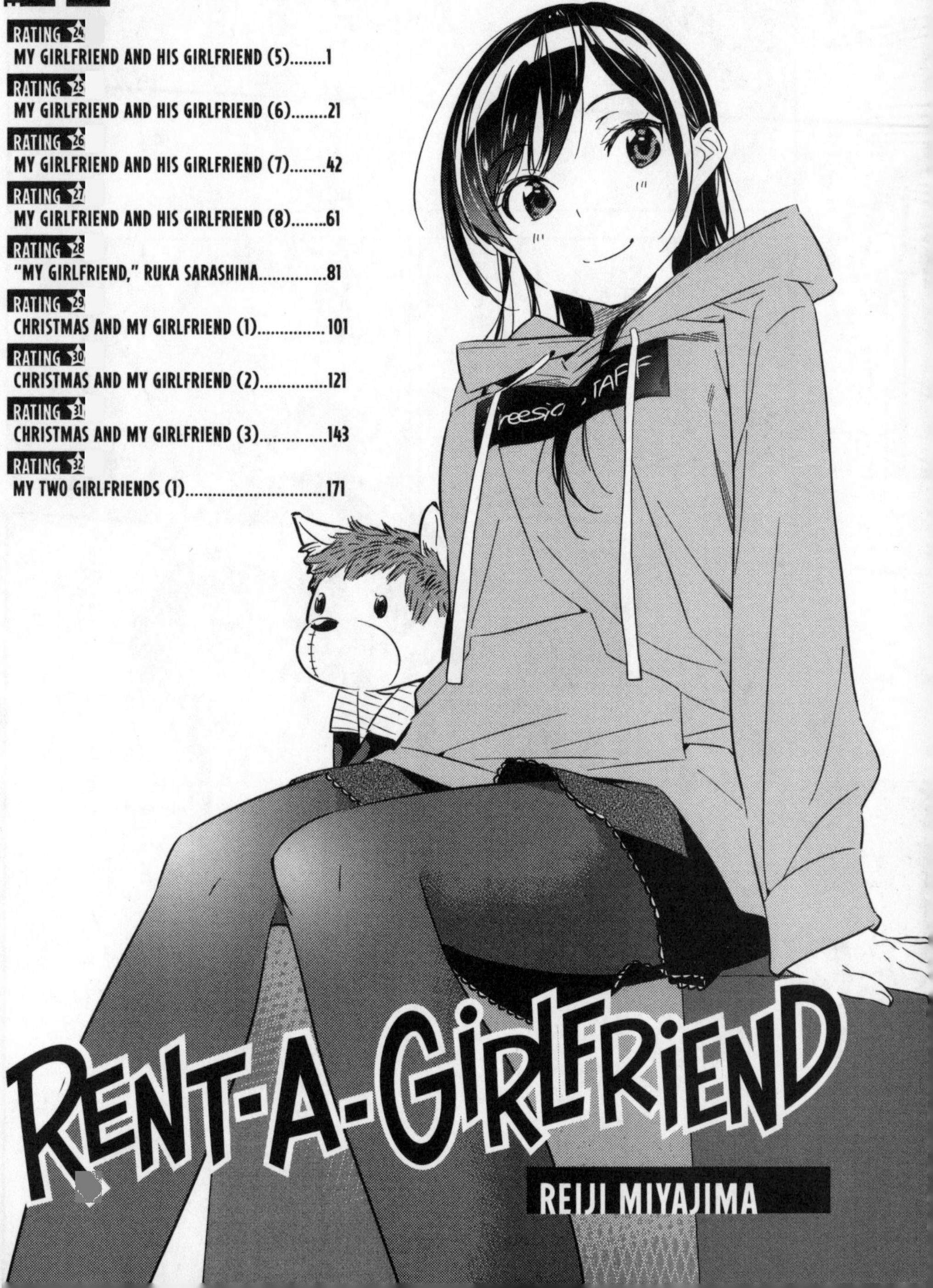

RENT-A-GIRLFRIEND

REIJI MIYAJIMA

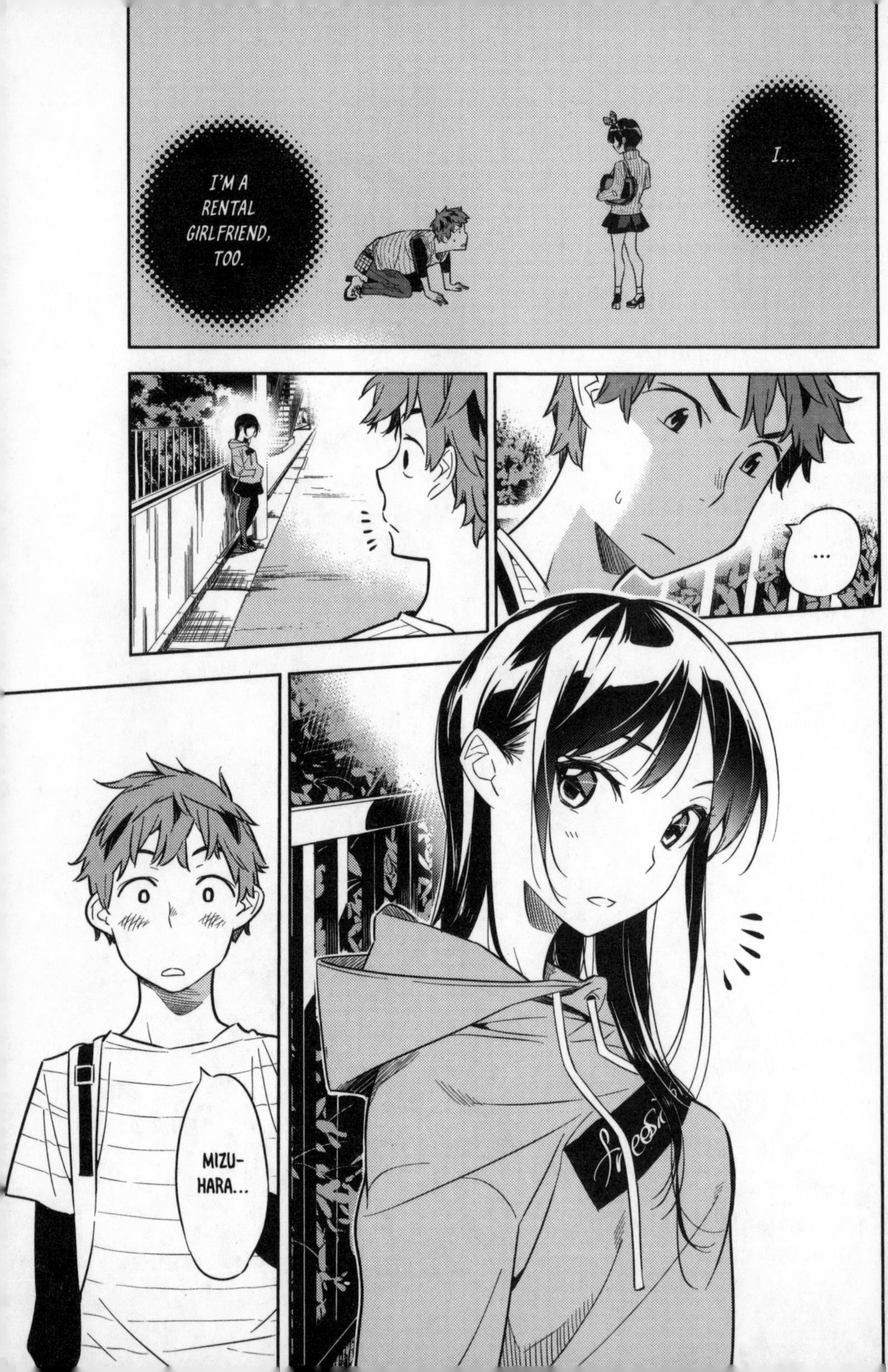
I...
I'M A RENTAL GIRLFRIEND, TOO.
...
MIZU-HARA...